English 2200

with Writing
Applications

A PROGRAMMED COURSE IN
GRAMMAR AND USAGE

Fourth College Edition

Joseph C. Blumenthal

THOMSON
—★—™
HEINLE

Australia Canada Mexico Singapore Spain United Kingdom United States

English 2200 with Writing Applications
A Programmed Course in Grammar and Usage
Fourth Edition
Joseph C. Blumenthal

Publisher: *Ted Buchholz*
Acquisitions Editor: *Stephen T. Jordan*
Project Editor: *Nancy Lombardi*
Cover Designer: *Diana Jean Parks*
Production Managers: *Kelly Donaldson; Erin Gregg*

Printed in the United States of America
  6 7 8 9 10 11   07 06 05 04 03 02
For more information contact Heinle, 25 Thomson Place, Boston, MA 02210 USA,
or you can visit our Internet site at http://www.heinle.com

ISBN: 0-1550-0859-5

Library of Congress Catalog Card Number: 92-83970

The College Series

English 2200

English 2600

English 3200

TESTS FOR ENGLISH 2200

TESTS FOR ENGLISH 2600

TESTS FOR ENGLISH 3200
Alternate Tests for English 3200

ANSWER KEY FOR EACH TEST BOOK

About the Author

Joseph C. Blumenthal received his A.B. and A.M. degrees from the University of Michigan. He also did graduate work at the University of Chicago and at Columbia University. From 1938 to 1959 he was head of the English Department at Mackenzie High School in Detroit. Among his writings are the *Common Sense English* series, the *English Workshop* series (with John F. Warriner and others), and *The English Language* series (with Louis Zahner and others).

About the Fourth Edition

This edition retains the index that is intended to make *English 2200* more useful to students and instructors by giving them ready access to the entire body of material treated in the text. Each entry is indexed by frame and page numbers to facilitate reference.

New to this edition is a writing applications section, designed to move students from mastering skills to using those skills in real writing situations.

The Test Booklet

The 60-page test booklet designed for use with *English 2200* consists of a Pre-Test, two parallel tests for each of the eleven units, two Halfway Tests, and a Final Test.

PREFACE

English 2200, English 2600, and *English 3200* are the original programmed courses in grammar, usage, sentence-building, capitalization, and punctuation. Since the introduction of the series in colleges in 1963, it has proved effective in teaching the elements of English to more than a million students of all abilities in a wide range of institutions: state and private universities, community, junior, and four-year colleges, vocational and technical institutes, and business colleges.

The Self-Teaching Method

Like their predecessors, the 1994 College Editions of the series are self-pacing, self-correcting, thorough, and flexible. They are programmed to make the learning of grammar and usage a positive, success-oriented experience. Each lesson in *English 2200, English 2600,* and *English 3200* contains twenty to forty sequential learning "frames." Each frame has three elements: an easy-to-understand explanation of a small but significant step in the mastery of the lesson topic; a question or statement about the topic to which the student must respond; and the answer to the preceding frame's question. Students perform and correct their work individually, at their own pace. Correct responses are immediately reinforced and incorrect responses are corrected at once. This step-by-step format, based on decades of in-class testing and refinement, provides the immediate positive reinforcement and encouragement students need to maximize learning.

Three Parallel, Graduated Programs

English 2200, English 2600, and *English 3200* are parallel in approach and design and may therefore be used cumulatively. As their titles indicate, they vary in length according to the number of frames, and they vary in emphasis. *English 2200* and *English 2600* focus on the parts of speech and how they are combined into correctly punctuated sentences. In *English 2200,* students are introduced to words that make up and enrich sentences. In *English 2600,* they expand on this knowledge by studying the function of verbs, subjects, and modifiers, as well as the patterns of simple sentences. *English 3200* guides students directly from one unit on the simple sentence to six units on more sophisticated ways of handling sentences. It treats compound and complex sentences, devices of subordination, and techniques for writing sentences with variety and smoothness.

Pedagogical Flexibility

College instructors have found that the cumulative programmed format of the series offers an extraordinary degree of pedagogical flexibility. They have used the same book as a basic text for an entire class, as an independent course of study for individuals, as a review for groups outside the classroom, and as a remedial text for individuals or groups. These last two uses have made the series especially attractive to writing laboratories and learning centers. Further, because the three programs in the series cover the same principles of grammar and usage, they may be used sequentially in three graduated courses or even together in a single class. For example, using the results of the diagnostic Pre-Test for *English 2600,* instructors may assign students either *English 2200, English 2600,* or *English 3200.* Instead of spending many class hours on details of grammar and usage, instructors assigning these self-teaching programs are free to devote more time to the teaching or writing, vocabulary, spelling, and other skills.

The Writing Applications

The writing applications in the second part of this book correspond to the units on grammar, sentence-building, usage, and punctuation in the first part. They are designed to complement the programmed instruction so that students can use the information already learned in their writing. The writing applications give students the opportunity to apply directly the principles of grammar and usage mastered in the first part of the book.

Each writing application asks the student to write about a topic, using a six-stage process, called the *writing process.* Learning to use the writing process will enable the student to plan, compose, and revise more quickly, easily, and accurately.

Indexes

A detailed index, useful to both instructors and students, follows each programmed course. Every entry in the index is followed by the frame number and the page, in parentheses, on which the frame appears. The frames indexed are those containing key concepts, definitions, or illustrations. For example, under the entry "fragment" in the index to *English 3200* are eleven subentries; these entries direct students to various kinds of fragments, as well as to methods for correcting them. Students may turn to particular entries to answer their own questions about specific points of grammar and usage. Besides offering a handy reference, however, the index is a useful aid for planning remedial and review exercises. When students reveal that they have not yet mastered a particular concept, the instructor, by consulting the index, can guide them to review the appropriate frames. Students who require help in correcting specific errors when revising a composition may be alerted to frames that show them how to identify and remedy those errors.

Test Booklets and Answer Keys

A 60- or 64-page test booklet for each volume in the series is provided free to college instructors in class quantities, one booklet for each textbook ordered. Additional copies of the test booklets are sold separately and may be ordered from the publisher. An alternate test booklet, parallel in form and content to the original, is available for *English 3200*. When placing orders for *English 3200*, instructors should indicate whether they wish the original or the alternate test booklets. In addition, an Answer Key for each of the test booklets is available to instructors.

Each test booklet contains a diagnostic Pre-Test, two parallel Mastery Tests (labeled A and B) for each unit in the textbook, two parallel Halfway Tests, and a Final Test.

This testing apparatus considerably enhances the flexibility of the series. Whether a test is given to individual students or to an entire class at the same time depends on how the textbook itself is used. If students proceed at their own rate until they complete the entire book, individual testing will be necessary. If the class waits until all students complete a given unit before proceeding to the next unit, the class may be tested simultaneously. The Pre-Test enables instructors to determine a student's overall grasp of fundamentals, to identify his or her strengths and weaknesses, and to plan an individualized program while avoiding material the student has already mastered.

The inclusion of parallel Mastery Tests offers flexibility in meeting the needs of a specific class in providing for various classroom situations. For example:

1. Test A may be used as a pre-test for every unit and Test B as a final test.

2. Test A may serve as a practice test and Test B as the official test.

3. Test A or B may be used as a makeup test for students who did not achieve satisfactory scores on their first test.

4. Tests A and B may be used with different classes or with alternate rows in the same classroom.

No matter how the tests are used, one idea, basic to the method of programmed learning, should be kept in mind: a response should have an immediate reinforcement.

To the Student

English 2200 is a programmed course in grammar, sentence-building, correct usage, and punctuation. A feature of this edition is an index that can help you locate a particular topic quickly when you need it for reference or review.

If this is your first experience with a programmed textbook, you may be puzzled by its appearance. As you leaf through its pages, you may wonder why it looks so different from other books you have studied.

Why the zebra-like pages with alternating bands of gray and white?

Why is the material divided into small bits, or *frames*?

Why don't you read the pages from top to bottom as you do other books?

Why are the answers printed in the marginal strips where they can be so easily seen?

English 2200 looks so different because it is built upon some modern learning principles. For many years, the problems of learning have been studied scientifically in colleges and universities all over the country. As a result, new discoveries have been made that can make learning faster, surer, more thorough (and, we hope, more fun). *English 2200* is based on some of the most important of these discoveries.

1. In a programmed course, often called simply a *program*, the material is broken down into very small and carefully arranged steps—approximately 2,200 in this book—through which you reason your way, one step at a time. There is no separation between explanation and exercise, as in other language textbooks; the two are tightly interwoven. Every step, or *frame*, calls for a written response, which requires both *thinking* and *concentration*. The advantages of "reasoning your own way" instead of "being told" have been known to good teachers ever since the days of Socrates. By thinking your way through the program, you are likely to understand better and to remember longer.

2. Programs are constructed to prevent mistakes before they happen. The psychologists call this "errorless learning" and have proved its importance by scientific experiment. The steps are so small and their arrangement is so orderly that you are not likely to make many errors. When an error occurs, you catch it immediately by turning the page for the answer. You are corrected before a wrong habit can become established. You spend your time *learning*—not *unlearning*. Using a programmed textbook is like having a private tutor who watches you as you work and who sets you back on the track the moment you wander off.

3. A very important factor in this method is what the psychologists call *reinforcement*. Its importance in learning cannot be stated too strongly.

With the usual textbook, you first study the lesson, (which you may or may not understand completely). Then you apply what you have studied to an exercise. Unfortunately, you do not find out until some time later (often the next day) whether you did the exercise correctly. With *English 2200* you discover immediately whether your answer is right or wrong. At this point something very interesting and mysterious happens. The instant you find out you are right, the idea "takes root," so to speak, in your brain. This does not happen as successfully when time (even a moment or two) is allowed to elapse before you discover that you are right.

Finding out immediately that you are right is called *reinforcement*, and the quicker and more often this happens, the better you learn and remember. A reinforcement is something like a reward; and if you have ever taught a dog tricks, you know from experience how the biscuits speed up learning.

4. With programmed instruction you can advance at your own speed. Since you work by yourself, no one needs to wait for you, and you don't need to wait for anyone else. Many students complete an entire course of study in a fraction of the time usually required by the traditional textbook method. The time you save by this method can be used profitably in other language activities.

How to Use *English 2200*

Each step, or frame, requires that you perform some operation. For example, in many of the frames you will do one of two things:

1.   If there is a blank line, write in the missing word or letter.

     Example: Jones is the name of a _person_.

2.   If there are two or more words or letters in parentheses, underline the correct answer.

     Example: Jones is the name of a (_person_, _place_).

(Note: Your instructor will tell you whether to write your answers in this book, in a notebook, or on sheets of paper.)

The first work frame is Frame 2 (on page 3). After you complete Frame 2, turn to Frame 3, *in the same position* on the next *right-hand* page (page 5). In the column to the left of Frame 3, you will find the correct answer to Frame 2. If your answer is not correct, turn back and correct it before doing Frame 3. You will always find the answer to a frame in the column to the left of the frame that you are to do next. Thus you find the answer to Frame 3 to the left of Frame 4, the answer to Frame 4 to the left of Frame 5, and so on.

Go completely through the book, taking only the top gray frame on each *right-hand* page (3, 5, 7, 9, 11, and so on) until you reach the end. When you reach the end of the book, turn back to page 1 and follow the second band—a white one—through the book, still working only on the *right-hand* pages. Then proceed to the third horizontal band, which is gray, going through all the *right-hand* pages. Continue in this way through the fourth, fifth, and sixth bands. When you come to the last white band on the last *right-hand* page (Frame 1128), turn back to page 2 and start reading the gray bands at the top of the *left-hand* pages. Continue through the book, following each horizontal band through the *left-hand* pages. The last frame is 2249 on page 372.

The alternating bands of white and gray will make it easy for you to stay on the same horizontal band as you advance through the book. Since both frame and answer are numbered (each in the lower right corner), you will always know where you are and where to go next.

The Writing Applications

The writing applications in the second part of this book correspond to the units on grammar, sentence-building, usage, and punctuation in the first part. They are designed to complement the programmed instruction so that you can use the information you have already learned in your writing. The writing applications give you the opportunity to apply directly the principles of grammar and usage you mastered in the first part of the book.

Each writing application asks you to write about a topic, using a six-stage process, called the *writing process*. Learning to use the writing process will enable you to plan, compose, and revise more quickly, easily, and accurately.

How to Use the Writing Applications

Preceding the writing applications is a basic introduction to the writing process. Read this information carefully before you complete your first writing application. Then use this section for reference whenever you want to review the basic concepts and stages of the writing process.

Following the introduction to the writing process are the writing applications. There are three writing applications for each unit. Your teacher will tell you exactly which writing applications to complete and when.

Each writing application follows a specific order that will enable you to practice using the stages of the writing process. Each application begins with an introductory paragraph and examples of a particular writing skill that you will be asked to demonstrate. Following this information is a writing assignment, which gives you the opportunity to plan and write your first draft.

Since evaluation is an important stage in the writing process, each writing assignment is followed by an evaluation checklist. The checklist will enable you to analyze your writing for weaknesses. Thus you always have the opportunity to revise your writing before you prepare a final version. The writing applications and the programmed instruction, although different in several ways, are alike in that they have you follow a step-by-step process that enables you to evaluate your own progress.

Each application concludes with steps for revising, proofreading, and writing a final version.

Getting the Most from *English 2200*

1. Whenever you are unsure about the correct answer to a frame, read the frame again very carefully, looking for clues. You will generally find a clue that guides you to the right answer. As the lesson advances, fewer and fewer clues will be given; so if you make a mistake, you will need to go back a few frames to try to correct your thinking. If you still don't understand where your mistake lies, ask your instructor for help.

2. Take as much time as you need in figuring out your answer. But once you write your answer, turn immediately to the next frame to check its correctness. Scientific experiment has proved that the more quickly you check your answer, the better you learn. *Even the delay of a few seconds makes a big difference.*

3. Don't cheat yourself out of the valuable experience of thinking. Don't look at the answer in the next frame until *after* you have figured it out for yourself. Thinking things through takes effort, but it is this kind of effort that results in the most effective kind of learning. You are not working for grades on these lessons because the lessons will not be scored. In fact, you will always end with a perfect score because you are expected to correct each error immediately (and you will probably make very few). However, your instructor may want to evaluate your work by administering and scoring the tests that accompany *English 2200*. "Peeking ahead" for the answer will not give you the reasoning ability you will need to pass the tests.

If you use *English 2200* in the mature way in which it is designed to be used, you may discover that, working at your own pace, you have achieved a better command of the fundamentals of your language—and in a much shorter time. You may also find that you have developed your ability to think and concentrate in ways that will help you in your other studies. You will have profited from letting science help you with its most recent and exciting discoveries about how people learn.

Contents

LESSON NUMBER	FRAME NUMBERS	BEGINS ON PAGE

UNIT 7: **WORD GROUPS THAT BUILD UP SENTENCES**

UNIT 8: **AVOIDING SENTENCE FRAGMENTS AND RUN-ONS**

UNIT 9: **LEARNING TO PUNCTUATE**

LESSON NUMBER	FRAME NUMBERS	BEGINS ON PAGE

Lesson **1** We Must Have Nouns

[Frames 2-25]

---

some

188

Underline the one pronoun:

The *dog* with the black *spots* is *mine.*

189

---

relationship

376

Lesson **13** Prepositions Make Useful Phrases

[Frames 378-403]

---

given, gave

564

Write the correct past forms of **give:**

Tina _____ away all the stamps that her friend *had* _____ **her.**

565

---

taken, run

752

Mr. Wong (*gave, give***) us some unusual roses that he had (***grown, grew***) in his backyard.**

753

There's

940

There (*were, was***) several planes circling the airport.**

941

page 1

No
 	
1128
	The object forms of pronouns are used for the direct objects of verbs.
	They are also used for the objects of prepositions.
	
	    a. **The class voted for** *her*.
	    b. **The class elected** *her*.
	
	In which sentence is *her* the object of a preposition?____
	1129

If . . . afternoon 1315	**The dog chewed up the letter before Dad had read it.** The adverb clause starts with the clause signal _____ and ends with the word _____. 1316
Yes 1502	Can a clause stand by itself as a sentence? (*Yes, No*) 1503
cabin. Uncle 1689	**As we were working very hard at chopping down weeds on Saturday afternoon Uncle John drove up.** _____ 1690

Yes
 	
1876
	We often put an address right after a name, with no preposition such as **at, in, on,** or **of** to tie it in. Then we surround even a one-part address with commas.
	
	    a. **Write to the Royal Hotel in** *Miami* **for reservations.**
	    b. **Write to the Royal Hotel** *Miami* **for reservations.**
	
	In which sentence should two commas be used? _____
	1877

"Has the dog been fed?" asked Mother. 2063	Here is the same quotation at the *end* of the sentence: **Mother asked, "Has the dog been fed?"** This entire sentence is not a question. It merely contains a question. To show that the quotation is a question. we put the question mark (*inside, outside*) the quotation marks. 2064

In grammar, we study different kinds of words. We learn how these words are fitted together to mean something. The study of words and the way they are put together is called *gr*_____.

Note to student:
Do not write in your book without your teacher's permission.

2

---

mine

189

To be a sentence, a group of words generally needs to have both a *subject* and a _____.

190

In the previous lesson, you saw that every preposition is followed by a noun or pronoun.

The name *of* the colt was Smoky.

The preposition *of* is followed by the noun _____.

378

---

gave, given

565

PRESENT	SIMPLE PAST	PAST WITH HELPER
pull	pulled	(have) pulled
paint	painted	(have) painted
see	saw	(have) seen

All the above verbs are regular except the verb _____.

566

---

gave, grown

753

I had (*wrote, written*) a letter but had (*threw, thrown*) it out.

754

---

were

941

(*Where are, Where's*) the books for our class?

942

a 1129	a. **The dog followed** *him*. b. **The dog walked behind** *him*. In which sentence is *him* the object of a preposition? ____ 1130
before ... it 1316	Lesson **45** Putting Adverb Clauses to Work [Frames 1318-1346]
No 1503	An adverb clause does the job of an _____. 1504
afternoon, Uncle 1690	**He went through the cabin** **then he began to laugh.** _____ 1691
b 1877	Punctuate this sentence: **The Filmcraft Shop 88 Main Street repairs cameras.** 1878
inside 2064	Punctuate this sentence: **Mother asked** **Has the dog been fed** 2065

grammar	To talk or write to other people, we need many different kinds of words. For example, we need names for all the things we see around us.
	Underline two words that are the names of things in this room:
	wall tree chair moon
2	3

verb	**The people voted for Barbara Jordan.**
	The verb in this sentence is _____.
190	191

colt	The noun or pronoun that follows a preposition is called the **object of the preposition**.
	The name *of* the colt was Smoky.
	The object of the preposition *of* is the noun _____.
378	379

see	Lesson **19** Seven Irregular Verbs
566	[Frames 568-604]

written, thrown	**Philip (*run, ran*) to the phone and reported what he had (*seen, saw*).**
754	755

Where are	**How much (*was, were*) the rides at the carnival?**
942	943

b 1130	a. **The police blamed ....** b. **... won three games.** Which sentence would require the subject form of the missing pronoun? ____ 1131
	In one way, a sentence and a clause are alike. Both have a subject and a verb. However, there is one big difference between them. A clause (*can, cannot*) stand by itself. 1318
adverb 1504	An adjective clause does the job of an _____. 1505
cabin. Then 1691	**His amusement puzzled us did he think that we had done a poor job?** ——————————————— 1692

Shop, Street,
 	
1878
	Dates, just like addresses, can also have more than one part.
	    a. **On** *Monday, June 27,* **we start for Seattle.**
	    b. **On** *Monday* **we start for Seattle.**
	In which sentence does the date have more than one part? ____
	
	1879

Mother asked, "Has the dog been fed?" 2065	Punctuate this sentence. Notice that the quotation is a question: **How is the fishing Lisa asked** 2066

wall, chair 3	Underline two words that are the names of foods: **cloud** **bread** **lettuce** **cement** 4
voted 191	When we change a sentence from present to past time, or from past to present time, the word that usually changes is the _____. 192
colt 379	**The store** *around* **the corner sells school supplies.** In this sentence, the object of the preposition *around* is the noun _____. 380
	Look at the simple past forms of the seven verbs we shall study in this lesson: SIMPLE PAST: **drove** **spoke** **took** **fell** **broke** **wrote** **ate** Do any of these simple past forms end in *–ed*? (*Yes, No*) 568
ran, seen 755	**The bell** (*rang, rung*) **before we had** (*sang, sung*) **our school song.** 756
were 943	(*Where are, Where's*) **the bag of apples?** 944

b

a. John met ... at school.
b. ... met John at school.

Which sentence would require the object form of the missing pronoun? ____

1131

1132

---

cannot

a. **our <u>town</u> is small**
b. *although* **our <u>town</u> is small**

Which one of these word groups should start with a capital letter and end with a period because it is a complete sentence? ____

1318

1319

---

adjective

a. **when, while, because, if, although, unless**
b. **who (whom, whose), which, that**

Which group of clause signals are used to start adverb clauses? ____

1505

1506

---

us. Did

He finally controlled his laughter   then he gave Dad and me the shock of our lives.

_____

1692

1693

---

a

We punctuate dates just as we do addresses. After you write the first part of a date, put a comma both *before* and *after* each additional part.

Punctuate this sentence:

On Friday August 3 1492 Columbus set forth on his historic voyage.

1879

1880

"How is the fishing?" Lisa asked.

Now punctuate this same sentence turned around:

Lisa asked   How is the fishing

2066

2067

bread, lettuce 4	Underline two words that are the names of living things: **man stone window horse** 5
verb 192	PRESENT: **Phyllis often writes me letters.** If you changed this sentence to past time, you would need to change the word _____ to _____. 193
corner 380	a. **The seat** *behind* **Juan was vacant.** b. **The seat** *behind* **him was vacant.** In which sentence is the object of the preposition *behind* a pronoun? ____ 381
No 568	SIMPLE PAST: **drove spoke took fell broke wrote ate** The past forms of these verbs do not end in –*ed*, as most verbs do. They are therefore (*regular, irregular*) verbs. 569
rang, sung 756	**After we had** (*ate, eaten*) **our lunch, we** (*set, sat*) **and talked for a while.** 757
Where's 944	(*Was, Were*) **these pictures taken at school?** Note to student: You are now ready for Unit Test 4. 945

page 9

a 1132	**Dave lives with *them*.** We use the object form of the pronoun because it is the object of the preposition _____. 1133
a 1319	a. **Our town is small.** b. *although our town is small* When we add the clause signal *although* to sentence *a*, the sentence becomes a _____. 1320
a 1506	a. **I read a book** *which my friend recommended.* b. **I read a book** *because my friend recommended it.* Which sentence contains an adverb clause? ____ 1507
laughter. Then 1693	**This wasn't Uncle John's cabin it belonged to the Fosters.** _____ 1694
Friday, 3, 1492, 1880	Punctuate this sentence: **I was born on Saturday December 8 1951 in Cleveland.** 1881
Lisa asked, "How is the fishing?" 2067	Compare a quotation that is an exclamation with one that is a question: a. **"How is the fishing?" Lisa asked.** b. **"What an enormous fish!" Lisa exclaimed.** There is only one difference: Where sentence *a* has a question mark, sentence *b* has an _____ point. 2068

man, horse 5	Underline two words that are the names of persons: **pencil Frank desk Judy** 6
writes, wrote 193	**My friend very seldom sees his grandparents.** The verb in this sentence is _____. 194
b 381	A group of words that begins with a preposition and ends with its object is called a **prepositional phrase.** A prepositional phrase would need to have at least _____ words. (How many?) 382
irregular 569	Now let's look at the helper forms of these same verbs: **(have) driven (have) spoken (have) taken (have) fallen** **(have) broken (have) written (have) eaten** Each of these helper forms ends with the two letters _____. 570
eaten, sat 757	**We had (*gone, went*) to the office and had (*spoken, spoke*) to the manager of the store.** 758
were 945	UNIT 5: **USING THE RIGHT MODIFIER** Lesson **32** **Choosing Between Adjectives and Adverbs** *page 11* [Frames 947-973]

with	The words that generally change their form when they are moved from the subject to the direct object position are (*nouns, pronouns*).
1133	1134
clause	**The stores were closed.** Underline the clause signal that could turn the above sentence into an adverb clause: **all because yesterday**
1320	1321
b	A clause that modifies a noun or a pronoun is called an _____ clause.
1507	1508
cabin. It	**During the past winter, one cabin had been torn down therefore Uncle John's cabin was now the third from the road.** _____
1694	1695
Saturday, 8, 1951,	In this and the following frames, add commas for addresses and dates wherever they are needed. If no commas are needed, make no changes. **We shall stop at Topeka Kansas for one day.**
1881	1882
exclamation	a. **"What an enormous fish!" Lisa exclaimed.** b. **Lisa exclaimed, "What an enormous fish!"** By putting the exclamation point inside the quotation marks, we show that the (*quotation, sentence*) is an exclamation.
2068	2069

Frank, Judy 6	Underline two words that are the names of places: **sugar** **airport** **London** **coat** 7
sees 194	Can a verb consist of more than one word? (*Yes, No*) 195
two 382	Between the preposition and its object, you will often find words that modify the object. **We sent a plant** *with many large pink flowers.* How many words stand between the preposition and its object? _____ 383
–en 570	Here are the three basic forms of the verb **drive**. PRESENT SIMPLE PAST PAST WITH HELPER **drive** **drove** **(have) driven** We say, "Dad *drove* us to school," but we say, "Dad *had* _____ us to school." 571
gone, spoken 758	**I had** (*ran, run*) **into some barbed wire and had** (*tore, torn*) **my best shirt.** 759
	Do you remember that adjectives modify nouns and pronouns? **Bill Cosby is comical.** The word **comical** is an adjective because it modifies the noun _____. 947

pronouns 1134	Two pronouns do not change their form when they are moved from the subject to direct object position. These two pronouns are (*she, you, it, they*). 1135
because 1321	*because my brother plays the piano* This is an adverb clause. It could be changed to a sentence by dropping the clause signal _____. 1322
adjective 1508	ADJECTIVE CLAUSE SIGNALS: **who (whom, whose), which, that** All these adjective clause signals are pronouns. When the pronoun is the subject of the verb in the adjective clause, use the subject form (*who, whom*). 1509
down. Therefore 1695	**We then moved over to Uncle John's cabin which we found in very bad condition.** _____ Note to student: You are now ready for Unit Test 8. 1696
Topeka, Kansas, 1882	**We shall stop at Topeka for one day.** 1883
quotation 2069	Now we are ready to turn to another problem. Here is a quotation that continues for several sentences without interruption: **"The score was tied. We had two outs. There was a player on third," explained Ricky.** Is each sentence surrounded by quotation marks? (*Yes, No*) 2070

airport, London 7	Can you talk about anything that doesn't have a name? (*Yes, No*) 8
Yes 195	Underline two helping verbs in this sentence: **It has been raining all morning.** 196
three 383	**My grandmother taught in a very small country school.** How many words stand between the preposition and its object? _____ 384
driven 571	Write the two past forms of **drive:** **Art** _____ **as though he** *had* _____ **all** **his life.** 572
run, torn 759	**We** (*seen, saw*) **several uniforms that had been** (*worn,* *wore*) **in the Battle of Gettysburg.** 760
Bill Cosby 947	Adjectives can modify only nouns and pronouns. They cannot modify verbs. **Bill Cosby replied comically.** In the above sentence, **comically** tells *how* about the verb _____ . 948

you, it 1135	a. **I, he, she, we, they** b. **me, him, her, us, them** In which group are the object forms of the pronouns? ____ 1136
because 1322	if while **because** although If you put one of these words at the beginning of a sentence, would it still be a sentence? (*Yes, No*) 1323
who 1509	ADJECTIVE CLAUSE SIGNALS: **who (whom, whose), which, that** When the verb in the adjective clause already has another word as its subject, use the object form (*who, whom*). 1510
cabin, which 1696	UNIT 9: **LEARNING TO PUNCTUATE** Lesson **59** **End Marks of the Sentence** [Frames 1698-1721]
No commas 1883	**We selected Friday June 17 as the date for our party.** 1884
No 2070	**"The score was tied. We had two outs. There was a player on third," explained Ricky.** Only one set of quotation marks ("—") is needed although this quotation continues for _____ sentences. (How many?) 2071

No 8	You can't talk about anything unless it has a _____. 9
has been 196	Underline two helping verbs in this sentence: **Someone must have taken my coat.** 197

four 384	When you hear or read a preposition, you are not satisfied until its object comes along to complete its meaning.
	
	    a. **in a** c. **in a very few**
	    b. **in a very** d. **in a very few minutes**
	
	Which is a completed prepositional phrase? ___ 385

drove, driven 572	Underline the correct form of the verb: **We** *have* (*drove, driven*) **to Chicago many times.** 573
saw, worn 760	**It** (*began, begun*) **to rain after we had** (*driven, drove*) **only a few blocks.** 761
replied 948	**Bill Cosby replied comically.** The word **comically** doesn't modify a noun or pronoun. It modifies the verb **replied.** Is **comically** an adjective? (*Yes, No*) 949

b

1136

Write the subject form of each of these pronouns:

me _____

him _____

1137

No

1323

I remembered the answer ... *I had turned in my paper.*

Underline the clause signal that would make the best sense in the above sentence:

because   so that   after   where

1324

---

whom

1510

Underline the correct pronoun:
The woman (*who, whom*) **won the Nobel Prize was Dr. Yalow.**

1511

Every sentence needs a mark of punctuation to show that it has ended. The three end marks are a period (.), a question mark (?), and an exclamation point (!).

Is a comma one of the end marks that can show the end of a sentence? (*Yes, No*)

1698

Friday, 17,

1884

We selected June 17 as the date for our party.

1885

---

three

2071

One set of quotation marks ("—") will take care of any number of sentences as long as the quotation is not interrupted.

Add the missing quotation marks:

The bus swerved. It missed the dog. The passengers praised the driver for her skill, said Leslie.

2072

name 9	In grammar, we have a special name for any word that is used to name a *person, place,* or *thing.* We call such a word a **noun.** A noun is a word used to _____ a person, place, or thing. 10
must have 197	Underline two helping verbs in this sentence: **The plane should be arriving soon.** 198
d 385	a. **for an entire** c. **for a long, tiresome** b. **for my mother** d. **for a very young** Which is a completed prepositional phrase? ____ 386
driven 573	a. **My mom . . . the same car for eight years.** b. **My mom** *has* **. . . the same car for eight years.** In which sentence would *drove* be the correct verb?____ 574
began, driven 761	**Del must have** (*knew, known*) **that the price was soon going to** (*rise, raise*). 762
No 949	Besides adjectives, we also have adverbs. Do you remember that many adverbs are used to tell *how* about the action of the verb? **Bill Cosby replied comically.** The word that tells us how Cosby **replied** is the adverb _____. 950

I
he
 	
1137
	Write the subject form of each of these pronouns:
	
	      her _____
	
	      us _____
	
	      them _____
	
	1138

after 1324	... *Lincoln had little formal schooling,* **he was highly educated.** Underline the clause signal that would make the best sense in the above sentence: **Until Although If Unless** 1325
who 1511	Underline the correct pronoun: **One girl** (*who, whom*) *we invited* **couldn't come.** 1512

No
 	
1698
	Put a period (.) after a sentence that states a fact. This is what most sentences do.
	
	    a. **The rain flooded the streets**
	    b. **Did the rain flood the streets**
	
	One sentence states a fact; the other asks a question.
	
	Which sentence should end with a period? ____
	
	1699

No commas 1885	**Richard Hatcher became mayor of Gary Indiana on November 7 1967.** 1886

"The bus ...
skill,"
 	
2072
	When you write conversation, start a new paragraph each time the speaker changes.
	        "Why are you stopping?" I asked.
	        "The light just turned red," replied Joe.
	        "That's a very good reason," I laughed.
	This conversation requires _____ paragraphs. (How many?)
	
	2073

name 10	A word that is used to name a person, place, or thing is called a _____. 11
should be 198	a. I *did* **solve the problem.** b. I *did* **the problem easily.** In which sentence is *did* used as a helping verb? ____ 199

b
 	
386
	To find where a prepositional phrase begins, always look for a preposition.
	
	    a. **to, from, by, in, with, of, near**
	    b. **was, this, our, there, top, all**
	
	The words that can start prepositional phrases are those in group ____.
	
	387

a 574	PRESENT SIMPLE PAST PAST WITH HELPER **break** **broke** **(have) broken** We say, "I *broke* my pencil," but we say, "I *have* _____ my pencil." 575
known, rise 762	**Our neighbors** (*did, done*) **nothing about the branches that had** (*fell, fallen*) **into our yard.** 763
comically 950	Here are only a few of many, many adverbs that tell *how* about the action of a verb: **cleverly** **cheerfully** **proudly** **bravely** **timidly** All the above adverbs end with the two letters ____. 951

she we they 1138	Write the object form of each of these pronouns: he _____ they _____ 1139
Although 1325	**We lived ...** *there were very few stores.* Underline the clause signal that would make the best sense in the above sentence: **although as where while** 1326
whom 1512	The *two* adjective clause signals that can be used to refer to persons are (*who, which, that*). 1513
a 1699	Also put a period after a sentence that gives a command or makes a request. a. **Shut off the motor.** b. **Please open the door for me.** Which sentence makes a request? ____ 1700
Gary, Indiana, 7, 1886	**We drove on November 24 from El Paso to Phoenix.** 1887
three 2073	"Look at that cloud," said Anna. "It looks just like a big fish," said Paul. "To me it looks just like one more cloud," said Jack. "You have very little imagination," commented Paul. How many paragraphs does this conversation require? _____ 2074

noun 11	Underline two nouns in this sentence: **The girl became an artist.** 12
a 199	**is, am, are — was, were, been** These six words are all forms of the verb (*be, do, have*). 200
a 387	Underline the prepositional phrase: **Pam's answer to the question was correct.** 388
broken 575	Write the two past forms of **break:** **Jerry _____ his record after I** *had* _____ **mine.** 576
did, fallen 763	**Our neighbor (***came, come***) over and (***brung, brought***) us** **some vegetables from his garden.** 764
–ly 951	There are many words that have both an adjective and an adverb form: ADJECTIVES: **clever cheerful proud brave** ADVERBS: **cleverly cheerfully proudly bravely** The words that end in *–ly* are _____. 952

him them 1139	Write the object form of each of these pronouns: I _____ we _____ she _____ 1140
where 1326	**I wrote a note to myself** ... *I would remember my appointment.* Underline the clause signal that would make the best sense in the above sentence: **so that until since because** 1327
who, that 1513	Underline the correct pronoun: **The teacher** (*who, which*) **directs our band can play every instrument.** 1514
b 1700	a. **Sign your name here** b. **Did you sign your name** Which sentence should end with a period because it gives a command? ____ 1701
No commas 1887	**Helen Cummings 3417 Ashton Road was a witness to the accident.** 1888
four 2074	Beginning with this frame, each sentence contains a *direct* quotation. Copy each sentence, adding the necessary punctuation and capitalization. (Use an exclamation point only when the frame directs you to do so.) **The clerk replied we don't accept checks** 2075

girl, artist 12	**The girl became an artist.** Both underlined nouns in this sentence are the names of (*persons, places, things*). 13
be 200	A word that receives the action of the verb or shows the result of this action is called a *direct* _____. 201
to the question 388	Underline the prepositional phrase: **My cousins live in another city.** 389
broke, broken 576	Underline the correct form of the verb: **Mr. Thomas** *had* (*broken, broke*) **his glasses.** 577
came, brought 764	**I had** (*swam, swum*) **the length of the pool ten times and had** (*begun, began*) **to feel tired and hungry.** 765
adverbs 952	Adjectives can modify only nouns and pronouns. Adjectives cannot modify verbs. Should you ever use an adjective to tell *how* about the action of a verb? (*Yes, No*) 953

Lesson **39** The Trick of
"Splitting the Doubles"

[Frames 1142-1170]

---

so that

1327

... *you do something about your spelling,* **you can't expect it to improve.**

Underline the clause signal that would make the best sense in the above sentence:

Because   When   As if   Unless

1328

---

who

1514

The *two* adjective clause signals that can be used to refer to things and animals are (*who, which, that*).

1515

---

a

1701

a. **Irma signed the letter**
b. **Sign the letter**
c. **Did you sign your name**
d. **Please sign this letter**

Every one of these sentences should end with a period except sentence ____.

1702

Cummings, Road,

1888

On May 1 1884 the first skyscraper was started in Chicago Illinois.

1889

The clerk replied,
"We don't accept
checks."

2075

We are flying over Houston   announced the pilot

_____

_____

page 26

2076

persons 13	Underline two nouns in this sentence: **Chicago has many parks.** 14
object 201	Is every action verb followed by a direct object? (*Yes, No*) 202
in another city 389	Underline the prepositional phrase: **The new article about Joe Louis is good.** 390
broken 577	a. **The hot water** *has* . . . **the glass.** b. **The hot water** . . . **the glass.** In which sentence would *broke* be the correct verb? ____ 578
swum, begun 765	**They** (*throwed, threw*) **out all the records that had been** (*broke, broken*) **by the children.** 766
No 953	a. **clever** **cheerful** **proud** **brave** **timid** b. **cleverly** **cheerfully** **proudly** **bravely** **timidly** To tell *how* about the action of a verb, use the words in group ____. 954

a. I, he, she, we, they
b. me, him, her, us, them

In which group are the pronouns in the subject form? ____

1142

Unless

1328

The coach spoke ... *he expected to win.*

Underline the clause signal that would make the best sense in the above sentence:

until   as though   so that   after

1329

---

which, that

1515

Underline the correct pronoun:

The farmer showed us a calf (*who, that*) **was only a week old.**

1516

---

c

1702

If a sentence states a fact, gives a command, or makes a request, end it with a _____.

1703

1, 1884, Chicago,

1889

Lana recently took a job with the Pacific Oil Company of San Diego.

1890

"We are flying over Houston," announced the pilot.

2076

The librarian said   you will like this book

_____

_____

2077

Chicago, parks 14	**Chicago** has many **parks.** Both underlined nouns in this sentence are the names of (*persons, places, things*). 15
No 202	a. **The captain shouted loudly.** b. **The captain shouted her orders.** In which sentence is the action verb **shouted** followed by a direct object? ____ The direct object is _____. 203
about Joe Louis 390	Underline the prepositional phrase: **My dad came home with several large boxes.** 391
b 578	PRESENT SIMPLE PAST PAST WITH HELPER **speak** **spoke** **(have) spoken** We say, "Tom *spoke* to the principal," but we say, "Tom *has* _____ to the principal." 579
threw, broken 766	**Our cat was (*lying, laying*) in a box that we had (*sat, set*) on our back porch.** 767
b 954	a. **Bill is . . . .** b. **Bill answered . . . .** In which sentence should you use the adverb **comically?** ____ 955

a 1142	Underline the correct pronoun: (*He, Him*) **went to the game.** 1143
as though 1329	WHEN? **while, when, whenever, as, before, after, since, until** HOW? **as if, as though** **Some people break out in a rash** ... *they eat strawberries.* To start the clause in the above sentence, you would select a clause signal from the (WHEN? HOW?) group. 1330
that 1516	In this and the following frames, combine each pair of sentences. Change the italicized sentence to the kind of word group indicated in the parentheses. Make no change in the other sentence. *I turned on the hose.* **No water came out.** (adverb clause) _____ 1517

period
 	
1703
	Put a question mark (**?**) after a sentence that asks a question.
	        a. **That direction is north**
	        b. **Which direction is north**
	Which sentence should end with a question mark because it asks a question? ____
	
	1704

No commas 1890	**The first telephone call between New York and San Francisco took place on January 25 1915.** 1891
The librarian said, "You will like this book." 2077	**This corn was just picked** **said the farmer** _____ _____ 2078

places	Underline two nouns in this sentence: **The key was in the lock.**
15	16

b orders	a. **School opened on Monday.** b. **The children opened the package.** In which sentence is the action verb **opened** followed by a direct object? ____ The direct object is _____.
203	204

with several large boxes	Underline the prepositional phrase: **Our hike through the woods was exciting.**
391	392

spoken	Write the two past forms of **speak:** **Doris** _____ **to me after I** *had* _____ **to her.**
579	580

lying, set	**Dr. Cruz had** (*gave, given*) **Judy strict orders to** (*lie, lay*) **quietly in bed for several days.**
767	768

b	a. **Lavinia** <u>writes</u> **very cleverly.** b. **Lavinia** <u>is</u> **very clever.** In which sentence does the verb show action? ____
955	956

He 1143	**He went to the game.** We use **He,** the subject form of the pronoun, because it is the subject of the verb _____. 1144
WHEN? 1330	WHERE? **where, wherever** WHY? **because, since, as, so that** ... _Nancy had grown so much,_ **we could hardly recognize her.** To start the clause in the above sentence, you would select a clause signal from the (WHERE? WHY?) group. 1331
When (As, Although) I turned on the hose, no water came out. 1517	**Sue can play the piano.** _She has never taken lessons._ (adverb clause) _____ _____ 1518
b 1704	Punctuate these two sentences: **I have two sandwiches_____ Do you want one_____** 1705
'25, 1891	Lesson **66** Unit Review [Frames 1893-1913]
"This corn was just picked," said the farmer. 2078	**Mr. Grove repeated our test will be tomorrow** _____ _____ 2079

key, lock 16	**The <u>key</u> was in the <u>lock</u>.** Both underlined nouns in this sentence are the names of (*persons, places, things*). 17
b package 204	a. **The train stopped the traffic.** b. **The train stopped for a few minutes.** In which sentence is the action verb **stopped** followed by a direct object? _____ The direct object is _____. 205
through the woods 392	**This is a poem about a beautiful spring day.** In this sentence, the prepositional phrase begins with the preposition _____ and ends with its object _____. 393
spoke, spoken 580	Underline the correct form of the verb: **The Turners** *have* (*spoke, spoken*) **about going to Mexico.** 581
given, lie 768	**Grandmother had** (*drunk, drank*) **her tea and had** (*lain, laid*) **down to rest.** 769
a 956	Underline the correct modifier: **Lavinia writes very** (*clever, cleverly*). 957

went 1144	Underline the correct pronoun: (*I, Me*) **went to the game.** 1145

WHY?
 	
1331
	WHEN? **while, when, whenever, as, before, after, since,
	        until**
	WHERE? **where, wherever**
	   Mother hid the candy ... *none of us could find it.*
	
	To start the clause in the above sentence, you would select
	a clause signal from the (WHEN? WHERE?) group. 1332

Sue can play the piano although (though) she has never taken lessons. 1518	*I was reading a magazine.* **I rode past my stop.** (adverb clause) _____ _____ 1519

sandwiches.
one?
 	
1705
	To be polite, we often put a request in the form of a ques-
	tion rather than a command. Since we are not asking a
	question that requires an answer, we could use a period.
	
	    a. **Does this window open?**
	    b. **Will you please repeat the question?**
	
	We could use a period after sentence _____. 1706

	In this review lesson, you will find the story of Fritzie, a very sensitive dog. Add the commas that are needed, ac- cording to the rules you studied in this unit. Several sen- tences do not require commas. Also put an end mark— a period, a question mark, or an exclamation point—at the end of each sentence. (*Turn to the next frame.*) 1893
Mr. Grove repeated, "Our test will be tomorrow." 2079	**You owe me a quarter** **Kip reminded me** _____ _____ 2080

things 17	You can see or touch most of the things that nouns name but not all of them. Underline *one* word that names something you *cannot* see or touch: door desk **freedom** 18
a traffic 205	Underline the direct object: **Gwendolyn Brooks signed her name in my copy of her new book.** 206
about, day 393	**I stepped over the sleeping dog very carefully.** In this sentence, the prepositional phrase begins with the preposition _____ and ends with its object _____. 394
spoken 581	a. **Judy** *had* **... about her hobbies.** b. **Judy ... about her hobbies.** In which sentence would *spoke* be the correct verb? ____ 582
drunk, lain 769	**Dad (***laid, lay***) some newspapers on the grass and (***laid, lay***) down to relax.** 770
cleverly 957	**Lavinia writes very cleverly.** We use the adverb **cleverly** because it tells *how* about the action of the verb _____. 958

I
1145

I **went** to the game.

We use **I**, the subject form of the pronoun, because it is

the subject of the verb _____.

1146

WHERE?
1332

ON WHAT CONDITION? **if, unless, although, though**
HOW? **as if, as though**

... *you will read the poem again,* **you will like it better.**

To start the clause in the above sentence, you would select
a clause signal from the (ON WHAT CONDITION? HOW?)
group.

1333

Because (While,
As) I was reading
a magazine, I
rode past my
stop.
1519

We found a store. *It was having a sale.* (adjective clause)

_____

_____

1520

---

b
1706

a. **Will you please shut off the water?**
b. **Will the store refund your money?**

After which sentence could we use a period because it is

really a request rather than a question? ____

1707

**The Hunters have lived at 32 Calvert Avenue Glendale Cali-
fornia for many years**

1894

"You owe me a
quarter," Kip
reminded me.

2080

Are you going to play   asked Flora

_____

_____

2081

freedom 18	**freedom courage imagination** These nouns are not the names of persons, places, or things. They are the *names of ideas* we have in our minds. Can we talk about these ideas just as we can talk about *teachers, schools,* or *books*? (*Yes, No*) 19
name 206	Underline the direct object: **I took my camera to school yesterday.** 207
over, dog 394	**The weather on my last birthday was rainy.** The prepositional phrase begins with the preposition _____ and ends with its object _____. 395
b 582	PRESENT SIMPLE PAST PAST WITH HELPER **write** **wrote** **(have) written** We say, "Stan *wrote* for a sample," but we say, "Stan *has* _____ for a sample." 583
laid, lay 770	**I** (*lay, laid*) **aside my books and** (*lay, laid*) **down on the sofa.** 771
writes 958	You have seen that many modifiers have two forms: one without *-ly* and another with *-ly*. To describe the action of the verb, you would use the form (*with, without*) *-ly*. 959

went 1146	**He** **went** to the game. **I** **went** to the game. Now let's put these two sentences together by using a compound subject: _____ and ____ went to the game. 1147
ON WHAT CONDITION? 1333	WHERE? **where, wherever** HOW? **as if, as though** **Dick played ...** *he were very tired.* To start the clause in the above sentence, you would select a clause signal from the (WHERE? HOW?) group. 1334
We found a store which (that) was having a sale. 1520	**A woman sat next to me.** *She was holding a baby.* (adjective clause) _____ _____ (Are you changing the italicized sentences?) 1521
a 1707	a. **Will this train leave on time?** b. **Will you kindly let me know if you can go?** After which sentence could we use a period? ____ 1708
Avenue, Glendale, California, years. 1894	**On Tuesday July 17 two police officers came to their door** 1895
"Are you going to play?" asked Flora. 2081	**Just look at your room exclaimed Father** (Use an exclamation point.) _____ _____ 2082

Yes 19	**freedom courage imagination** Because these words are the names of ideas in our mind, they are called _____. 20
camera 207	Underline the direct object: **Many explorers have lost their lives in the Arctic.** Note to student: You are now ready for Unit Test 1. 208
on, birthday 395	**I kept my collection in a large wooden box.** The prepositional phrase begins with the preposition ____ and ends with its object _____. 396
written 583	Write the two past forms of **write:** **Paul** _____ **to his uncle after he** *had* _____ **to his parents.** 584
laid, lay 771	**Don had** (*laid, lain*) **his skates where someone might have** (*fallen, fell*) **over them.** 772
with 959	a. **Dena spoke** *proudly* **of her team's success.** b. **Dena was** *proud* **of her team's success.** In which sentence does the verb show action? ____ 960

He, I 1147	**He** <u>went</u> to the game.　　<u>I</u> <u>went</u> to the game. **He** and **I** <u>went</u> to the game. When we combine these two sentences, do we use the same forms of the pronouns? (*Yes, No*) 1148
HOW? 1334	Adverb clauses are useful for combining sentences. The clause signal shows how the facts or ideas are related. a. **The field was muddy. We decided to play.** b. *Although the field was muddy,* **we decided to play.** Which arrangement shows more clearly how the two facts are related? ____ 1335
A woman who (that) was holding a baby sat next to me. 1521	**We followed our friends.** *We hoped to overtake them.* (*-ing* word group) _____ _____ . 1522
b 1708	Put an exclamation point (**!**) after a sentence that expresses sudden or strong feeling, such as *fear, surprise, anger, disgust,* or *delight.* a. **The storm was terrible**　　b. **It rained slightly today** Which sentence would you end with an exclamation point to show your strong feeling about the weather? ____ 1709
Tuesday, 17, door. 1895	**A neighbor it seems had reported them to the police for mistreating their dog** 1896
"Just look at your room!" exclaimed Father. 2082	**What took so much time　　asked Betty** _____ _____ 2083

nouns	Underline *one* noun that is the name of an idea:
	Sylvia equality gym elevator
20	21

lives	UNIT 2: **WORDS THAT ENRICH THE SENTENCE**
	Lesson **8** Adjectives Make Pictures
208	[Frames 210-240]

in, box	Some words can be used as either prepositions or adverbs. If the word has an object, it is a preposition. Otherwise, it is an adverb that modifies the verb.
	The crowd traveled on.
	Is the word *on* followed by an object? (*Yes, No*)
396	397

wrote, written	Underline the correct past form of the verb:
	Sonia *has* (*written, wrote*) **a very good story.**
584	585

laid, fallen	**Dr. Bunche had** (*rose, risen*) **early and had** (*flew, flown*) **to Washington.**
	Note to student: You are now ready for Unit Test 3.
772	773

a	Underline the correct modifier:
	Dena spoke (*proud, proudly*) **of her team's success.**
960	961

Yes 1148	We seldom hear anyone except small children say, "*Him* went to the game" or "*Me* went to the game." However, we do sometimes hear grown-ups say, "*Him* and *me* went to the game." Is this the same mistake? (*Yes, No*) 1149
b 1335	a. **Ted played the radio** *while I was trying to study.* b. **Ted played the radio. I was trying to study.** Which arrangement shows more clearly how the two facts are related? ____ 1336
We followed our friends, hoping to overtake them. 1522	*I looked at his face.* **I wondered if he was serious.** (*–ing* word group) _____ _____ 1523
a 1709	a. **We missed the bus.** b. **We missed the bus!** Which sentence shows stronger feeling? ____ 1710
neighbor, seems, dog. 1896	**Did the neighbor or anyone else ever see them hurt Fritzie** 1897
"What took so much time?" asked Betty. 2083	**María screamed don't sit on my painting** (Use an exclamation point.) _____ _____ 2084

equality 21	Underline *one* noun that is the name of an idea: **grocer farm tree honesty** 22
	Up to this point, you have studied three kinds of words: *nouns, pronouns,* and *verbs.* **I want to buy a pencil.** In this sentence, the word *pencil* is a _____. 210
No 397	**The crowd traveled** *on.* Because the word *on* modifies the verb **traveled,** it is an _____. 398
written 585	a. **We ... several themes this semester.** b. **We** *have* **... several themes this semester.** In which sentence would *wrote* be the correct verb? ____ 586
risen, flown 773	UNIT 4: **SUBJECT AND VERB MUST AGREE IN NUMBER** Lesson **26** **Recognizing Singular and Plural Subjects** [Frames 775-808]
proudly 961	Underline the correct modifier: **You must swing the bat more** (*vigorous, vigorously*). 962

It seems strange that people who use single pronouns correctly will make mistakes when they use pronouns in pairs.

> a. *He* **and** *I* **lost our way.**
> b. *Him* **and** *me* **lost our way.**

Which sentence is correct? ____

1150

---

a

1336

In this and the following frames, change each italicized sentence to an adverb clause. Select a clause signal that will make the meaning clear. Write the clause only.

I took the clock apart. **I couldn't put it together again.**

_____,

I couldn't put it together again.

1337

Looking at his
face, I wondered
if he was serious.

1523

Unfortunately, my birthday comes on December 26. *It is the day after Christmas.* (appositive word group)

_____

_____.

(Remember that an appositive word group does not ordinarily have a subject and a verb.)

1524

---

b

1710

Single words and groups of words that express strong feeling are often written as sentences and punctuated with exclamation points.

> **Horrors! A shark!**   **Oh, what a beautiful day!**

Punctuate the following:

> **Hurray____ A home run____**

1711

Fritzie?

1897

No he never actually saw them hurt the dog or mistreat him

1898

María
screamed, "Don't
sit on my painting!"

2084

Lesson **73** Unit Review

[Frames 2086-2114]

honesty	Underline *one* noun that is *not* the name of an idea: **happiness** **fairness** **motor** **beauty**
22	23

noun	If you said to a clerk, "I want to buy a pencil," he would probably ask you, "What kind?" If you said, "I want a red pencil," the clerk would immediately get you a pencil because the word _____ describes *what kind* of pencil you want.
210	211

adverb	a. **The crowd traveled** *on*. b. **The crowd traveled** *on* **the train.** In which sentence is the word *on* used as a preposition? ____
398	399

a	PRESENT SIMPLE PAST PAST WITH HELPER **take** **took** **(have) taken** We say, "They *took* the wrong road," but we say, "They *have* _____ the wrong road."
586	587

	Singular means "one"; **plural** means "more than one." The noun **road** is singular; the noun **roads** is _____.
	775

vigorously	a. **Bella was very** *serious* **about her plan.** b. **Bella spoke about her plan very** *serious*. Which sentence is *not* correct? ____
962	963

a 1150	We frequently use pronouns in pairs. When doubtful about which pronoun to use, "split the doubles" like this: **(She, Her) and (I, me) planned the debate.** SPLIT: *She* planned the debate. *I* planned the debate. Underline the same pronouns in the combined sentence: **(*She*, Her) and (I, *me*) planned the debate.** 1151
After (When, Although, If) I took the clock apart, 1337	*Mike plays the trombone.* **All the neighbors always close their windows.** _____, **all the neighbors always close their windows.** 1338
Unfortunately, my birthday comes on December 26, the day after Christmas. 1524	**Rip Van Winkle slept for twenty years.** *He is the main character.* (appositive word group) _____ _____. Note to student: You are now ready for Unit Test 7. 1525

Hurray!
A home run!
 	
1711
	Sentences that have the form of questions, commands, and requests can be punctuated with exclamation points if they show strong feeling.
	
	    a. **The cake is burning!**
	    b. **Don't sit on the baby!**
	
	Which sentence has the form of a command? ____ 1712

No, him. 1898	**However Fritzie frequently whined and cried and howled** 1899
	Do you remember how to place apostrophes in nouns to show ownership? Ask yourself the question "Whom (*or* What) does it belong to?" Then put the apostrophe right after the word that answers this question. **my *cousins* house** If the answer is *cousin*, put the apostrophe after the (*n*, *s*). 2086

motor 23	A noun is a word used to name a *person, place, thing,* or an _____. 24
red 211	*short* **pencil** *thin* **pencil** *blue* **pencil** *soft* **pencil** Each of these pairs of words gives you a different picture. The word that changes each picture is the (*first, second*) word of each pair. 212
b 399	a. **My friend came** *over* **the new road.** b. **My friend came** *over* **recently.** In which sentence is *over* used as a preposition? ____ 400
taken 587	Write the two past forms of **take:** **I** _____ **my test after Helen** *had* _____ **hers.** 588
plural 775	Underline two plural nouns: **box** **shoes** **pen** **house** **streets** 776
b 963	A few short adverbs can be used either with or without *–ly* to describe the action of a verb. **slow** *or* **slowly** **loud** *or* **loudly** **fair** *or* **fairly** **quick** *or* **quickly** **plain** *or* **plainly** **cheap** *or* **cheaply** a. **He talks too** *loud.* b. **He talks too** *loudly.* Are both the above sentences correct? (*Yes, No*) 964

She, I

1151

Now let's "split the doubles" in the sentence below:

Dad took (he, him) and (I, me) to the Dog Show.

SPLIT: Dad took *him* ....   Dad took *me* ....
Now underline the same pronouns in the combined sentence:

Dad took (*he, him*) **and** (*I, me*) **to the Dog Show.**

1152

Whenever (When, As, While) Mike plays the trombone,

1338

The grocer tries to please us. *We are steady customers.*

The grocer tries to please us _____

_____.

1339

Rip Van Winkle, the main character, slept for twenty years.

1525

UNIT 8: **AVOIDING SENTENCE FRAGMENTS AND RUN–ONS**

Lesson **53** No Fragments, Please!

[Frames 1527-1554]

---

b

1712

---

a. **Why do you say such things!**
b. **The milk is boiling over!**

Which sentence has the form of a question? ____

1713

However, howled.

1899

Would a dog howl like this if he were not being mistreated

1900

---

n

2086

---

my *cousins* **house**

If the answer is *cousins,* put the apostrophe after the (*n, s*).

2087

idea	In grammar, a word that is used to name a *person, place, thing*, or an *idea* is called a _____.
24	25

	thin **pencil**
first	In grammar, we say that the word *thin* modifies the noun **pencil.** In everyday language *to modify* means "to change."
	To *modify* your plans means to _____ your plans in some way.
212	213

	a. **Virginia had never flown** *before.*
a	b. **Virginia had never flown** *before* **this trip.**
	In which sentence is *before* used as an adverb? ____
400	401

took, taken	Underline the correct form of the verb:
	Someone must have (*took, taken*) the wrong coat.
588	589

	When we want to know whether a word is singular or plural, we ask, "What is its *number*?"
shoes, streets	**door window floor wall**
	All these nouns are singular in _____.
776	777

	a. **The bus goes** *slowly.*
Yes	b. **The bus stops too** *frequently.*
	In which sentence would it be all right to drop the *–ly* from the italicized adverb? ____
964	965

him, me

1152

Bob was looking for (he, him) and (she, her).

SPLIT: Bob was looking for *him*. Bob was looking for *her*.
Underline the correct pronouns:

Bob was looking for (*he, him*) and (*she, her*).

1153

---

because (since,
as) we are steady
customers.

1339

You rotate the tires. **They will last longer.**

_____,

they will last longer.

1340

Ordinarily, we should write our thoughts in complete sentences, not in parts of sentences.

<u>We</u> <u>went</u> **to a lake for two weeks.**

This is a complete sentence with both a subject and a

_____.

1527

---

a

1713

---

a. **Who cares what he does?**
b. **Who cares what he does!**

Both sentences are worded like questions.

Which shows stronger feeling? ____

1714

---

mistreated?

1900

When the Hunters heard this accusation they were of course quite puzzled

1901

---

s

2087

One *girls* picture was in the paper.

The picture belongs to one *girl*.
Therefore, we write (*girl's, girls'*).

2088

Lesson 2 Pronouns Come In Handy

[Frames 27-56]

---

change

If the design of a car is *modified,* is the car the same as it was before? (*Yes, No*)

213   214

---

a

A noun or pronoun that completes the meaning of a preposition is called its (*subject, object*).

401   402

---

taken

a. **Someone** *had* **... my keys.**
b. **Someone ... my keys.**

In which sentence would *took* be the correct verb? ____

589   590

---

number

Suppose that we have three chairs for five people, or five chairs for three people. Do the chairs and the people agree in number? (*Yes, No*)

777   778

---

a

In this and the following frames, underline the correct modifier. Be sure to choose the adverb (*–ly*) form when the word describes the action of the verb.

This paint dries more (*rapid, rapidly*).

965   966

him, her

1153

Mr. Chen thanked (he, him) and (I, me) for our help.

Underline the correct pronouns in the "split" sentences:

Mr. Chen thanked (*he, him*) for our help. Mr. Chen thanked (*I, me*) for our help.

1154

If (When, After, Because) you rotate the tires,

1340

The meeting will be held at night. *Parents can attend it.*

The meeting will be held at night _____

_____.

1341

---

verb

1527

A branch broken off a tree is not a tree. It is only a piece of a tree. In the same way, a piece broken off a sentence is not a complete sentence. It is only a piece of a sentence.

    a. We went to a lake for two weeks.
    b. We went to a lake. For two weeks.

In which line do you find a piece of a sentence? ____

1528

---

b

1714

    a. Keep off the street!
    b. Keep off the street.

Both sentences are worded like commands.

Which shows stronger feeling? ____

1715

---

accusation, were, course, puzzled.

1901

What an embarrassing situation

1902

---

girl's

2088

These *girls* picture was in the paper.

The picture belongs to several *girls*.
Therefore, we write (*girl's, girls'*).

2089

We have just studied the kind of word that names the persons, places, things, and ideas we talk about.

These name words are called _____.

27

No

214

blue **pencil**   *thin* **pencil**

When we say that the words *blue* and *thin* modify the noun **pencil,** we mean that they _____ our picture of the pencil.

215

---

object

402

A group of words that starts with a preposition and ends with its object is called a *prepositional* _____.

403

---

b

590

PRESENT   SIMPLE PAST   PAST WITH HELPER
  eat   ate   (have) eaten

We say, "Virginia *ate* her lunch," but we say, "Virginia *has* _____ her lunch."

591

No

778

Now suppose that we have three chairs for three people. Do the chairs and the people agree in number? (*Yes, No*)

779

---

rapidly

966

The tailor mended the hole very (*skillful, skillfully*).

967

him, me

1154

Underline the correct pronouns:

Mr. Chen thanked (*he, him*) and (*I, me*) for our help.

1155

---

so that parents
can attend it.

1341

I never met my grandmother. **I feel that I know her.**

_____,

I feel that I know her. (Try the clause signal *Although*.)

1342

---

b

1528

We went to a lake. *For two weeks.*

The italicized word group has been cut off from the sentence by a period and a capital letter.

For two weeks.

Does this cut-off word group have both a subject and a verb? (*Yes, No*)

1529

---

a

1715

In this and in each of the following frames, supply two end marks:

We have chocolate and vanilla____ Which do you prefer____

1716

---

situation!

1902

They loved Fritzie took good care of him and never hurt him

1903

---

girls'

2089

The *childrens* room has many books.

The room belongs to the *children*.
Therefore, we write (*children's, childrens'*).

2090

nouns 27	*Pete* **felt** *Pete's* **pocket to see if** *Pete* **had** *Pete's* **wallet with** *Pete.* This sentence sounds foolish because there are five nouns that all refer to _____. 28
change 215	**path** *narrow* **path** Adding the word *narrow* to the noun **path** makes your picture of the path (*more, less*) clear. 216
phrase 403	Lesson **14** **Prepositional Phrases Can Modify** [Frames 405-437]
eaten 591	Write the two past forms of **eat:** **I** _____ **only one piece of pie, but I could** *have* _____ **several pieces.** 592
Yes 779	A subject and a verb must agree in number, too—just like the chairs and the people. If the subject is singular, the verb must be singular. If the subject is plural, the verb must be plural. If we use a plural verb with a singular subject, do the subject and verb agree in number? (*Yes, No*) 780
skillfully 967	**My friends were quite** (*curious, curiously*) **about my grades.** 968

him, me 1155	**Ruth had a message for (she, her) and (I, me).** Underline the correct pronouns in the "split" sentences: **Ruth had a message for** (*she, her*). **Ruth had a message for** (*I, me*). 1156
Although (Though) I never met my grand- mother, 1342	**I didn't know the time.** *My watch had stopped.* **I didn't know the time** _____ _____. 1343
No 1529	*For two weeks.* Does this cut-off word group express a complete thought? (*Yes, No*) 1530
vanilla. prefer? 1716	**Have you seen their new car____ It's a total wreck____** 1717
Fritzie, him, him. 1903	**What was the cause of the howling** 1904
children's 2090	In this and the following frames, place the apostrophe correctly in each italicized word: **Louis got only one** *persons* **opinion.** 2091

Pete 28	*his* *he* *his* Pete **felt** ~~Pete's~~ **pocket to see if** ~~Pete~~ **had** ~~Pete's~~ **wallet with** *him* ~~Pete~~. Now the sentence is better because we use the noun *Pete* only _____. (How many times?) 29
more 216	A word that is used to modify a noun or pronoun is called an **adjective.** **The *loud* noise awoke us.** Because it modifies the noun **noise,** the word *loud* is an _____. 217

	Most prepositional phrases are used like adjectives and
	 adverbs to modify other words.
	
	        a. **a** *cream* **pitcher**
	        b. **a pitcher** *for cream*
	
	 Both the adjective *cream* in *a* and the prepositional
	 phrase *for cream* in *b* modify the noun _____.
	       405

ate, eaten
 	
 592
	Underline the correct form of the verb:
	
	      Jimmy *has* (*eaten, ate*) **all his salad.**
	
	       593

No 780	Most plural nouns end in **s** (*dogs, cars, books*) or **es** (*boxes, dishes, churches*). However, a small number of plural nouns do not end in **s** or **es.** Underline three plural nouns: **farm men children boy teeth school** 781
curious 968	**It rains rather** (*regular, regularly*) **during November.** 969

her, me 1156	Underline the correct pronouns: **Ruth had a message for** (*she, her*) **and** (*I, me*). 1157
because (since, as) my watch had stopped. 1343	*I was about to receive the medal.* **I suddenly awoke from my dream.** _____, **I suddenly awoke from my dream.** 1344

No
 	
1530
	To be a complete sentence, a group of words must pass two tests:
	    1. It must have both a subject and a verb.
	    2. It must express a complete thought.
	
	For two weeks.
	
	Does this word group pass either test? (*Yes, No*)
	
	1531

car? wreck! (*or* wreck.) 1717	**Gosh_____ What awful weather_____** 1718
howling? 1904	**Fritzie was very sensitive and a scolding would make him cry** 1905
person's 2091	**There are several** *doctors* **offices in this building.** 2092

once (one time) 29	*his* *he* *his* Pete felt ~~Pete's~~ pocket to see if ~~Pete~~ had ~~Pete's~~ wallet with *him* ~~Pete.~~ The words that we put in place of the nouns *Pete* and *Pete's* are called **pronouns**. A *pronoun* is a word used in place of a _____. 30
adjective 217	After looking at the balloons, the child chose a *red* one. The word *red* is an adjective because it modifies the pronoun _____. 218
pitcher 405	a. a *cream* **pitcher** b. A **pitcher** *for cream* Both the word *cream* in *a* and the prepositional phrase *for cream* in *b* are used as (*adjectives, adverbs*). 406
eaten 593	a. The boys . . . all the cookies. b. The boys *have* . . . all the cookies. In which sentence would *ate* be the correct verb? ____ 594
men, children, teeth 781	PLURAL: <u>Bees</u> <u>sting.</u> In this plural sentence, there is an **s** at the end of the (*subject, verb*). 782
regularly 969	You can live very (*comfortable, comfortably*) in one of these cabins. 970

her, me 1157	Instead of two pronouns, our pair sometimes consists of a noun and a pronoun. Just drop the noun, and try the pronoun by itself. This will tell you which pronoun to use. **Don will call for ~~Karen and~~ (I, me).** Underline the correct pronoun: NOUN DROPPED: **Don will call for** (*I, me*). 1158
As (When) I was about to receive the medal, 1344	*We bought a car.* **We first tried out several makes.** _____, **we first tried out several makes.** 1345
No 1531	A *fragment* means a piece of something that has been cut off or broken off—like a fragment of wood or glass. A word or word group that has been broken off from a sentence is a **sentence fragment**. It is a bad mistake in writing. Underline the sentence fragment: **We went to a lake. For two weeks.** 1532
Gosh! weather! 1718	**First, boil the milk____ Have you done that yet____** 1719
sensitive, cry. 1905	**The slightest push tap or shove would make him howl** 1906
doctors' 2092	**The car spattered both** *womens* **dresses.** 2093

noun	By using pronouns in place of nouns, we avoid (*repetition, discourtesy*).
30	31
one	Underline two adjectives in this sentence: **Elderly people often enjoy young children.**
218	219
adjectives	a. *winter* **clothing** b. **clothing** *for winter* The prepositional phrase *for winter* in *b* does the same job as the adjective _____ in *a*.
406	407
a	PRESENT SIMPLE PAST PAST WITH HELPER **fall** **fell** **(have) fallen** We say, "The picture *fell* down," but we say, "The picture *has* _____ down."
594	595
subject	SINGULAR: **A bee stings.** In this singular sentence, there is an **s** at the end of the (*subject, verb*).
782	783
comfortably	**The pitch was as (*swift, swiftly*) as a bullet.**
970	971

me

1158

Underline the correct pronoun:

Don will call for Karen and (*I, me*).

1159

Before we
bought a car,

1345

A bee stung me. *I was mowing the lawn.*

A bee stung me _____

_____.

1346

For two weeks.

1532

We went to a lake. *For two weeks.*

For two weeks is a prepositional phrase that modifies the
verb **went**.

Should a prepositional phrase be cut off from the word
that it modifies? (*Yes, No*)

1533

---

milk. yet?

1719

Do you expect to see Pat____ I have a message for her____

1720

---

push, tap,
howl.

1906

**If Mr. or Mrs. Hunter spoke loudly to the dog he would cry
mournfully**

1907

---

women's

2093

All the *boys* faces needed washing.

2094

repetition 31	a. **Susan Sontag wrote the** *story*. b. **Susan Sontag wrote** *it*. Is the italicized word a pronoun in sentence *a* or *b*? ____ 32
Elderly, young 219	The little words **a, an,** and **the** are a special kind of adjective. Don't include them when you pick out adjectives in this lesson. Underline two adjectives in this sentence: **The yellow tulips are a beautiful sight.** 220
winter 407	A prepositional phrase can also do the job of an adverb by describing the action of a verb. <div align="center">a. **drove** *cautiously* b. **drove** *with caution*</div>Both the adverb *cautiously* in *a* and the prepositional phrase *with caution* in *b* modify the verb _____. 408
fallen 595	Write the two past forms of **fall:** **The picture** _____ **just after I** *had* _____ **asleep.** 596
verb 783	<div align="center">PLURAL: **Bees sting.** SINGULAR: **A bee stings.**</div>Adding an s to the noun **Bee** makes it plural. Does adding an s to the verb **sting** make it plural? (*Yes, No*) 784
swift 971	**The fire engines came so** (*prompt, promptly*) **that little damage was done.** 972

me

1159

~~The Barts and~~ (we, us) attend the same church.

Underline the correct pronoun:

NOUN DROPPED: (*We, Us*) attend the same church.

1160

---

while (as, when) I was mowing the lawn.

1346

Lesson **46** Meet the Adjective Clause

[Frames 1348-1376]

No

1533

Underline the prepositional phrase that is written as a sentence fragment:

Mari Sandoz wrote a story. About the Sioux.

1534

Pat? her.

1720

Stop____ Don't you hear that train whistle____

1721

---

dog, mournfully.

1907

Yes the Hunters sometimes scolded their dog but they never hurt him

1908

---

boys'

2094

Childrens **meals should include milk.**

2095

b	a. **Susan Sontag wrote the** *story*. b. **Susan Sontag wrote** *it*. The pronoun *it* in sentence *b* takes the place of the noun _____ in sentence *a*.
32	33

yellow, beautiful	Some words can be used as either pronouns or adjectives.
	
	  a. **Rex ate both.**
	  b. **Rex ate both sandwiches.**
	
	In which sentence is **both** used as an adjective? _____

220	221

drove	a. **drove** *cautiously* b. **drove** *with caution* Both the word *cautiously* in *a* and the prepositional phrase *with caution* in *b* are used as (*adjectives, adverbs*).
408	409

fell, fallen	Underline the correct form of the verb: **The leaves** *have* (*fallen, fell*) **from the trees.**
596	597

No	Although adding an **s** to a noun always makes it plural, adding an **s** to a verb makes it _____.
784	785

promptly	**Claire didn't seem** (*happy, happily*) **about her invitation.**
972	973

We 1160	Underline the correct pronoun: **The Barts and (*we, us*) attend the same church.** 1161
	All the clauses in the previous two lessons explained *when, where, how, why* or *on what condition* the action of the sentence took place. Because these clauses do the job of adverbs, we call them _____ clauses. 1348
About the Sioux. 1534	Underline the prepositional phrases that are written as a sentence fragment: **I recognized my dog. By the spot on its ear.** 1535
Stop! whistle? (*or* whistle!) 1721	Lesson **60** Periods for Abbreviations [Frames 1723-1745]
Yes, dog, him. 1908	**As Mr. Hunter was talking to the police officers Fritzie came to investigate** 1909
Children's 2095	In this and the following frames, write between the parentheses the correct contraction for each pair of italicized words. *They are* (_____) **sure that** *you are* (_____) **not going.** 2096

story 33	a. I took *her* picture. b. I took *Nancy's* picture. Is the italicized word a pronoun in sentence *a* or *b*? ____ 34
b 221	a. *short* **pencil** *thin* **pencil** *blue* **pencil** *soft* **pencil** b. *this* **pencil** *that* **pencil** *two* **pencils** *some* **pencils** In which group do the italicized adjectives answer the question *What kind?* ____ 222
adverbs 409	a. **replied** *angrily* b. **replied** *with anger* The prepositional phrase *with anger* in *b* does the same job as the adverb _____ in *a*. 410
fallen 597	a. **The child** *had* **... into the bathtub.** b. **The child ... into the bathtub.** In which sentence would *fell* be the correct word? ____ 598
singular 785	We say, "The window*s* open," but we say, "The window open*s*." We say, "The mountain*s* rise," but we say, "The mountain _____." 786
happy 973	Lesson **33** Using *Good* and *Well* Correctly *page 67* [Frames 975-995]

we 1161	In this and the following frames, underline the correct pronoun or pronouns. Remember to use the same pronouns in pairs that you would use singly: **Miss Wanatee put (*he, him*) and (*I, me*) at the same desk.** 1162
adverb 1348	In this lesson we study clauses that do the job of adjectives. First, let us look at any ordinary adjective: **We need an *energetic* assistant.** The word *energetic* is an adjective because it modifies the noun _____. 1349

By the spot
on its ear.
 	
1535
	Sometimes a sentence fragment is cut off from the beginning of a sentence:
	    a. **From my bedroom window. I can see the park.**
	    b. **I can see the park. From my bedroom window.**
	In which line does the sentence fragment come first? ____
	
	1536

	Put a period after every abbreviated word. With a few exceptions, abbreviations should be avoided in ordinary writing. Here are some abbreviations that are correct to use: **Mr., Mrs. and Ms. (But Miss takes no period!)** Supply the missing periods: **Miss Brooks is the guest of Mr and Mrs Lasky.** 1723
police officers, investigate. 1909	**Fritzie playfully jumped on one of the police officers and Mr. Hunter pushed the dog back** 1910
They're, you're 2096	*Let us* (_____) **see if** *he will* (_____) **lend us his boat.** 2097

a. **I took** *her* **picture.**
b. **I took** *Nancy's* **picture.**

The pronoun *her* in sentence *a* takes the place of the noun

_____ in sentence *b*.

34

35

Here are other questions that adjectives can answer about nouns.

Which one(s)?   *How many?*   *How much?*

I like *these* **shoes.**

The adjective *these* answers the question "_____?"

222

223

---

a. **We ate** *under the tree.*
b. **The ground** *under the tree* **was dry.**

In which sentence does the prepositional phrase modify

the verb? _____

410

411

**(have) driven   (have) spoken   (have) taken   (have) fallen
(have) broken   (have) written   (have) eaten**

The helper form of every verb in this lesson ends with the

two letters _____.

598

599

We say, "The vegetable<u>s</u> grow," but we say, "The vegetable

_____."

786

787

The word **good** is an adjective. Like any other adjective, it can modify only a noun or a pronoun.

The road was *good.*

The adjective *good* modifies the noun _____.

975

him, me	(*He, him*) and (*I, me*) were waiting for a bus.
1162	1163

assistant	a. **We need an** *energetic* **assistant.** b. **We need an assistant** *who is energetic.* The clause *who is energetic* in sentence *b* does the same job that the adjective _____ does in sentence *a*.
1349	1350

a	a. **From my bedroom window. I can see the park.** b. **From my bedroom window I can see the park.** c. **I can see the park. From my bedroom window.** Which arrangement is correct? ____
1536	1537

Mr. Mrs.	Here are other correct abbreviations:
	
	    B. J. Thomas (after initials in names)
	    Dr. Brothers (only when used with a name)
	
	Supply the missing periods:
	
	    Dr Nolan is a cousin of C N Jackson.

1723	1724

police officers, back.	**Mr. Hunter gave Fritzie only a slight shove but the dog yelped loudly** (Are there both a subject and a verb after the conjunction *but*?)
1910	1911

Let's, he'll	*There is* (_____) **a car that** *I would* (_____) **like to drive.**
2097	2098

Nancy's 35	a. The *milk* **is sour.** b. *This* **is sour.** Is the italicized word a pronoun in sentence *a* or *b*? ____ 36
"Which ones?" 223	a. **The club has** *little* **money.** b. **I belong to** *three* **clubs.** c. **I joined** *that* **club.** In which sentence does the adjective answer the question *How many?* ____ 224
a 411	A prepositional phrase that is used as an adverb is called an **adverb phrase.** a. **We ate** *under the tree.* b. **The ground** *under the tree* **was dry.** In which sentence is the prepositional phrase an *adverb* phrase because it modifies the verb? ____ 412
–en 599	a. **driven spoken taken fallen broken written eaten** b. **drove spoke took fell broke wrote ate** Which group of verb forms should be used after the help- ing verb **have, has,** or **had?** ____ 600
grows 787	All the verbs in this lesson show *present* time. The prob- lem of subject-verb agreement does not arise when we use *simple past* verbs (except for the verb **be**). SIMPLE PAST: <u>The boy laughed.</u> If you changed the subject **boy** to **boys,** would you need to change the verb **laughed?** (*Yes, No*) 788
road 975	Can an adjective tell *how* about the action of a verb? (*Yes,* *No*) 976

He, I 1163	Were you able to get tickets for Peggy and (*I, me*)? 1164
energetic 1350	We need an assistant *who is energetic.* Because the clause *who is energetic* modifies the noun **assistant,** it is an _____ clause. 1351

b 1537	Here again are the two tests for a complete sentence:
	    1. It must have both a subject and a verb.
	    2. It must express a complete thought.
	A bowl of fruit stood on the table.
	Has this word group a subject and a verb? (*Yes, No*) 1538

Dr. C. N. 1724	These abbreviations are customary in stating times of the day: 8:00 A.M. 6:30 P.M. Supply the missing periods: **The zoo is open from 10:00 A M to 5:30 P M** 1725
shove, loudly. 1911	**The police officers laughed and went on their way** 1912
There's, I'd 2098	**Miss Valdez** *does not* (_____) **think that** *you have* (_____) **read the story.** 2099

b 36	a. **The** *milk* **is sour.** b. *This* **is sour.** The pronoun *This* in sentence *b* takes the place of the noun _____ in sentence *a*. 37
b 224	a. **The club has** *little* **money.** b. **I belong to** *three* **clubs.** c. **I joined** *that* **club.** In which sentence does the adjective answer the question *Which one?* ____ 225
a 412	A prepositional phrase that is used as an adjective is called an **adjective phrase.** a. **I went** *to the basement* **for some tools.** b. **The stairs** *to the basement* **were slippery.** In which sentence is the prepositional phrase an *adjective* phrase because it modifies a noun? ____ 413
a 600	Write the correct past form of each verb in parentheses: **Mr. Phillips had** _____ (*speak*) **to George about the excuse he had** _____ (*write*). 601
No 788	Adding an **s** to a verb that shows present time always makes it singular. However, a verb without an **s** can be either singular or plural, depending upon the subject. SINGULAR: *I* **want.** *He* **wants.** *She* **wants.** *It* **wants.** Do all the singular verbs end in **s**? (*Yes, No*) 789
No 976	WRONG: **This radio plays** *good.* This sentence is wrong because the adjective *good* cannot be used to tell *how* the radio _____. 977

me 1164	(*She*, *Her*) and (*I*, *me*) **tried out for the school play.** 1165
adjective 1351	Here is the adjective clause by itself: *who is energetic* What is the subject of the verb *is*? _____ 1352
Yes 1538	**A bowl of fruit stood on the table.** Does this word group express a complete thought? (*Yes*, *No*) 1539
A.M. P.M. 1725	Use abbreviations to state historical dates: **1000 B.C.** (for Before Christ) **A.D. 732** (for the Latin phrase Anno Domini, meaning "in the year of our Lord") **The period from 50 B C to A D 116 is known as the "Golden Age" of Latin literature.** 1726
way. 1912	**Well have you ever heard of a dog as sensitive as Fritzie** Note to student: You are now ready for Unit Test 9. 1913
doesn't, you've 2099	In this and the following frames, underline the correct word in each pair: **Why don't you borrow (*her's*, *hers*)?** 2100

milk 37	a. *Some* **were hungry.** b. **The** *children* **were hungry.** Is the italicized word a pronoun in sentence *a* or *b*? ___ 38
c 225	a. **The club has** *little* **money.** b. **I belong to** *three* **clubs.** c. **I joined** *that* **club.** In which sentence does the adjective answer the question *How much?* ___ 226
b 413	Now let's think, for a moment, about ordinary adverbs. **A bus** *finally* **came along.** The adverb *finally* modifies the verb ___. 414
spoken, written 601	Write the correct past form of each verb in parentheses: **The cows have** ___ (*eat*) **the apples that have** ___ (*fall*) **to the ground.** 602

No
 	
789
	Although we use the pronoun **you** in speaking to one person or to many, it always requires a plural verb.
	
	    SINGULAR: **You** (one person) **live near me.**
	    PLURAL: **You** (several persons) **live near me.**
	
	In both sentences, we use the plural verb ___.
	
	790

plays 977	An adjective cannot modify a verb. To modify a verb, we need to use an ___. 978

She, I	We didn't know whether the car had stopped for Peggy or (*I, me*).
1165	1166

who	**We need an assistant** *who is energetic.* The clause signal that starts the adjective clause in this sentence is _____.
1352	1353

Yes	Now we shall split the sentence in two: 　　WRONG: **A bowl of fruit. Stood on the table.** Does either word group have both a subject and a verb? (*Yes, No*)
1539	1540

B.C.　A.D.	In abbreviating the names of well-known organizations, you may either use periods or omit them. 　　**P.T.A.** *or* **PTA** (Parent-Teacher Association) 　　**R.O.T.C.** *or* **ROTC** (Reserve Officers' Training Corps) Supply the missing periods: 　　**We meet at 8:00 PM at the Y M C A every Monday.**
1726	1727

Well, Fritzie?	UNIT 10: **APOSTROPHES AND QUOTATION MARKS** Lesson **67** Apostrophes for Showing Ownership [Frames 1915-1948]
1913	

hers	(*Theirs, Their's*) **is an Irish terrier.**
2100	2101

a 38	a. **Kim and Dennis were absent from school.** b. *Both* **were absent from school.** How many nouns in sentence *a* does the word *Both* in sentence *b* take the place of? _____ 39
a 226	**I enjoy . . . movies.** Underline the adjective that could be used in the above sentence to answer the question *What kind?* **most those Western few** 227
came 414	*Finally* **a bus came along.** **A bus** *finally* **came along.** **A bus came along** *finally*. Is the adverb *finally* always next to the word **came**, which it modifies? (*Yes, No*) 415
eaten, fallen 602	Write the correct past form of each verb in parentheses: **Chester has** _____ (*take*) **the letter that he has** _____ (*write*) **to the mailbox.** 603

live
 	
790
	When both the subject and the verb are singular, or when both the subject and the verb are plural, we say that they agree in number.
	     a. **His** <u>sisters</u> <u>own</u> **the garage.**
	     b. **His** <u>sisters</u> <u>owns</u> **the garage.**
	
	In which sentence do the subject and verb agree? ____
	
	791

adverb 978	The word **well** can be used as an adverb to describe the action of a verb. RIGHT: **This radio plays** *well.* This sentence is right because we use the adverb _____ to tell *how* the radio **plays.** 979

me 1166	Will Uncle Steve take (*she, her*) and (*I, me*) to the fair? 1167
who 1353	**We need an assistant** *who is energetic.* The clause signal *who* is a pronoun because it refers to the noun _____. 1354
No 1540	**A bowl of fruit. Stood on the table.** Does either of these word groups express a complete thought? (*Yes, No*) 1541
P.M. Y.M.C.A. (*or* YMCA) 1727	In lists and schedules where the same words are repeated, certain abbreviations may be used to save space. ADDRESSES: **St.** (Street) **Rd.** (Road) **Rte.** (Route) **Ave.** (Avenue) **Blvd.** (Boulevard) **Bldg.** (Building) Is it proper to use these abbreviations in ordinary writing? (*Yes, No*) 1728
	There are two different ways of showing ownership or belonging: a. **The room of Robert** b. **Robert's room** Both of the above examples show that the **room** belongs to _____. 1915
Theirs 2101	**You left** (*your's, yours*) **in your locker.** 2102

two 39	*Both* **were absent from school.** The word *Both* is a _____. 40
Western 227	**We bought . . . tires.** Underline the adjective that could be used in the above sentence to answer the question *How many?* **several new those expensive** 228
No 415	*After several minutes,* **a bus came along.** The adverb phrase *after several minutes* modifies the verb **came** because it tells (*when, where, how*) the bus **came.** 416
taken, written 603	Write the correct past form of each verb in parentheses: **The man had** _____ (*drive*) **into a tree and had** _____ (*break*) **the bumper.** 604
a 791	Now let's look at a compound subject that has two parts: **June** *and* **Carla own the garage.** How many persons own the garage? _____ 792
well 979	a. **This radio plays** *good.* b. **This radio plays** *well.* Which sentence is correct? ____ 980

her, me 1167	The Wilsons and (*we, us*) shared the cost of the fence. 1168
assistant 1354	Let's try another sentence: **The road** *that we took* **was shorter.** The clause *that we took* modifies the noun _____. 1355
No 1541	**A <u>bowl</u> of fruit. <u>Stood</u> on the table.** How many sentence fragments do we have here? _____ 1542

No
 	
1728
	These abbreviations may be used for lists and schedules:
	
	GEOGRAPHICAL **NY** (New York) **Ft. Dodge** (Fort)
	NAMES: **WI** (Wisconsin) **Mt. Vernon** (Mount)
	                  TN (Tennessee) **Highland Pk.** (Park)
	Supply the missing periods:
	
	    Chairman: F S Stocker, Ft Wayne, IN
	
	1729

Robert 1915	**a. the room of Robert** **b. Robert's room** In example *a*, we show ownership by using an *of* phrase. In example *b*, we show ownership by adding ___ to the noun **Robert.** 1916
yours 2102	(*Its, It's*) **afraid of** (*its, it's*) **own shadow.** 2103

pronoun 40	**Most people like them.** The pronoun in this sentence is the word _____. 41
several 228	**We filled the jar with . . . water.** Underline the adjective that could be used in the above sentence to answer the question *How much?* **fresh some this salt** 229
when 416	*After several minutes,* **a bus came along.** How many words stand between the adverb phrase and the verb **came,** which it modifies? _____ 417
driven, broken 604	Lesson **20** Six More Irregular Verbs [Frames 606-634]
two 792	**June** *and* **Carla** **own the garage.** Because two persons own the garage, the subject of the verb **own** is (*singular, plural*). 793

b
 	
980
	Always use the adverb **well,** not the adjective **good,** to tell *how* about the action of a verb.
	
	    a. **These** **scissors** **cut** well.
	
	    b. **These** **scissors** **are** good.
	
	In which sentences does the verb show action? ____
	
	981

we 1168	**Neither the Roses nor** (*they, them*) **had heard the news.** 1169
road 1355	**The road** *that we took* **was shorter.** Because the clause *that we took* modifies the noun _____, it is an _____ clause. 1356

two
 	
1542
	Tests for a sentence:
	
	    1. It must have both a subject and a verb.
	    2. It must express a complete thought.
	
	If a group of words fails either one of these tests, it is not
	a sentence, but a sentence _____.
	1543

F. S.   Ft.
 	
1729
	Days of the week and months of the year may be abbreviated on lists and schedules, too, to save space.
	    DAYS: **Sat.** (Saturday) **Wed.** (Wednesday)
	    MONTHS: **Feb.** (February) **Dec.** (December)
	Supply the missing periods:
	    Track meet: 4:00 P M , Fri , Oct 21.
	1730

's 1916	To show ownership, we often put two nouns in a row. The first noun, with the apostrophe, shows the owner. The second noun, without the apostrophe, shows what is owned. **boy's bicycle woman's car dog's tail** In each of these examples, the owner is shown by the (*first, second*) word. 1917
It's, its 2103	(*Whose, Who's*) **the girl** (*whose, who's*) **model plane won?** 2104

them 41	**Most people like** *them.* Do you know whether the pronoun *them* refers to dogs, biscuits, or movies? *(Yes, No)* 42
some 229	In this and the following frames, underline three adjectives in each sentence. Omit the special adjectives *a, an,* and *the.* **Castles were cold, damp, and dark places.** 230
two 417	If a phrase answers a question like *When? Where?* or *How?* about the verb, it is an adverb phrase—wherever it may come. **We reached the fruit** *with a ladder.* The adverb phrase *with a ladder* modifies **reached** because it tells *(when, where, how)* we **reached** the fruit. 418
	Look at the simple past forms of these four verbs. Notice how similar they are: SIMPLE PAST: **flew grew knew threw** Do any of these simple past forms end in *–ed?* *(Yes, No)* 606
plural 793	**June** *and* **Carla own the garage.** Two singular subjects connected by the conjunction *and* require a *(singular, plural)* verb. 794
a 981	**These scissors cut (good, well).** The verb **cut** is an action verb. Therefore, to tell *how* the scissors **cut,** we would use the adverb _____. 982

| they | Dad settled the argument between my brother and (*I, me*). |
| 1169 | 1170 |

| road, adjective | Here is the adjective clause by itself:

that <u>we</u> <u>took</u>

The subject of the verb *took* is _____. |
| 1356 | 1357 |

| fragment | In this and the following frames, you will find two word groups. One of them is a correct sentence; the other is incorrect because it is a sentence fragment. In the blank space, write the letter of the complete sentence.

    a. **The driver of the other car.**
    b. **My friend drove the other car.** _____ |
| ,1543 | 1544 |

| P.M.   Fri.
Oct. | Abbreviate titles only when used with names:

TITLES: **Gov. Grasso** (Governor)   **Fr. Bradley** (Father)
            Pres. Taft (President)   **Sr. Mary Agnes** (Sister)
            Prof. Just (Professor)   **Rev. Jackson** (Reverend)
Supply the missing periods:

Committee: Prof Stone, Supt Curtis, Fr Brown, Dr King |
| 1730 | 1731 |

| first | a. **one** *boy's* **locker**   b. **several** *boys'* **lockers**

Look at the noun with an apostrophe in each example.

Does the apostrophe come before the *s* in each example? (*Yes, No*) |
| 1917 | 1918 |

| Who's, whose | (*Your, You're*) **friend knows that** (*your, you're*) **sorry.** |
| 2104 | 2105 |

No 42	a. **Most people like** *dogs*. b. **Most people like** *them*. One of these sentences is more definite than the other. The more definite sentence is the one with the italicized *(noun, pronoun)*. 43
cold, damp, dark 230	Underline three adjectives: **The little kitten has long, sharp claws.** 231
how 418	**We reached the fruit** *with a ladder*. How many words stand between the adverb phrase and the verb it modifies? _____ 419
No 606	SIMPLE PAST: **flew grew knew threw** Write the simple past form of each verb in parentheses: **Chuck** _____ *(grow)* **impatient with the puzzle and** _____ *(throw)* **it aside.** 607
plural 794	Now let's change the conjunction *and* to *or*: **June** *or* **Carla** <u>owns</u> **the garage.** The above sentence is another way of saying **June owns the garage, or Carla** _____ **the garage.** 795
well 982	Underline the correct modifier: **This pen writes** *(well, good)*. 983

we

1357

The road *that we took* **was shorter.**

The clause signal that starts the adjective clause in this sentence is _____.

1358

---

b

1544

Continue to write the letter of the complete sentence:

    a. **We won the first game.**
    b. **Won the first game of the season.**

The correct sentence is ____.

1545

Prof.   Supt.
Fr.   Dr.

1731

COMPANIES: **Pacific Power Co.** (Company)
              Briggs Mfg. Co. (Manufacturing Company)
              Robinson Bros. (Brothers)

Supply the missing periods:

    Sponsors: Arrow Oil Co and Proctor Bros of Dayton

1732

No

1918

---

    a. **one** *boy's* **locker**   b. **several** *boys'* **lockers**

In using apostrophes, the main problem is deciding whether to put the apostrophe before or after the final *s*.

In example *a*, the **locker** belongs to one *boy*.

In example *b*, the **lockers** belong to several _____.

1919

Your, you're

2105

(*Their, They're*) **owner must think that** (*their, they're*) **priceless.**

2106

noun

a. *Somebody* **borrowed Sam's pen.**
b. *Arthur* **borrowed Sam's pen.**

Which sentence is less definite because it contains a pronoun? _____

44

---

little, long, sharp

231

Underline three adjectives:

Most blond people have blue eyes.

232

---

two

419

I put the letter *in the envelope.*

The adverb phrase *in the envelope* modifies the verb

_____.

420

---

grew, threw

607

Write the simple past form of each verb in parentheses:

We _____ (*know*) **that you** _____ (*fly*) **to Dallas.**

608

---

owns

795

June *or* **Carla** owns **the garage.**

How many persons own the garage? _____

796

---

well

983

a. **Our car is . . . .**
b. **Our car runs . . . .**

In which sentence would it be a mistake to use the adjective **good?** _____

984

To make comparisons, we often use the words **than** and **as**.

Libby jumped higher than I jumped.

After the word **than,** we find a second subject and verb.

The pronoun **I** is the subject of the verb _____.

1172

---

that

1358

The road *that we took* **was shorter.**

The clause signal *that* is a pronoun because it refers to the noun _____.

1359

---

a

1545

a. **A trip through a glass factory.**
b. **A trip through a glass factory is interesting.**

The correct sentence is ____.

1546

Co.   Bros.

1732

Do not use an *and* sign (**&**) in place of the word *and* except in notes you might make for *your own* use only.

a. **Please give my regards to your mother & dad.**
b. **Please give my regards to your mother and dad.**

Which sentence would be correct for a personal letter? ____

1733

---

boys

1919

To decide whether to put the apostrophe before or after the final *s* is simple. Ask yourself this question: "Whom does the locker belong to?"

One *boys* **locker**

In this example, the **locker** belongs to one _____.

1920

Their, they're

2106

After each pair of sentences, write the letter of the sentence that is correctly punctuated and capitalized.

a. **Gordon said "that he slept like a log."**

b. **Gordon said that he slept like a log.** ____

2107

Two of the following words are nouns and two are pronouns.

Underline the two pronouns:

these   magazines   boats   several

Underline three adjectives:

Those handsome wallets cost five dollars.

A prepositional phrase that modifies a noun or pronoun is called an _____ phrase.

Here are the helper forms of these same verbs:

(have) flown   (have) grown   (have) known   (have) thrown

Each of these helper forms ends with the letter ____.

June _or_ Carla owns the garage.

Since either **June** or **Carla**—not both—owns the garage, the subject of the verb **owns** is (_singular, plural_).

Our car runs good.

This sentence is wrong because the adjective **good** cannot modify the (_noun, verb_) **runs.**

jumped 1172	Underline the correct pronoun: **We made more hits than** (*they, them*) **did.** 1173
road 1359	Here are the clause signals that start adjective clauses, There are not very many. ADJECTIVE CLAUSE SIGNALS: **who (whom, whose),** **which, that** Are these words different from the clause signals that start adverb clauses? (*Yes, No*) 1360
b 1546	a. **Suddenly let go of the ladder.** b. **Jeff let go of the ladder.** The correct sentence is ____. 1547
b 1733	a. **Hockey and basketball also interest me.** b. **Hockey & basketball also interest me.** Which sentence would be correct for an English theme? __ 1734
boy 1920	**one** *boys* **locker** Whom does the **locker** belong to? The answer to this question is *boy*, not *boys*. Therefore, put the apostrophe after *boy*, not after *boys*: **one** *boys* **locker** 1921
b 2107	a. **"Our team is the best," Clara boasted.** b. **"Our team is the best" Clara boasted.** ____ 2108

these, several 45	.?. can swim here. Underline two pronouns that would fit in the above sentence: **Leroy Anybody Everyone Boys** 46
Those, hand- some, five 233	Underline three adjectives: **Several people left the hot, stuffy room.** 234
adjective 421	A prepositional phrase that modifies a verb is called an _____ phrase. 422
–n 609	Write the helper form of each verb in parentheses: **The room** *had* _____(grow) **very warm, and I** *had* _____ (*throw*) **off my coat.** 610
singular 797	**June** *or* **Carla owns the garage.** Two singular subjects connected by the conjunction *or* require a (*singular, plural*) verb. 798
verb 985	In this and the following frames, underline two correct modifiers in each sentence. Choose the adjective *good* to modify a noun or pronoun. Choose the adverb *well* to describe the action of a verb. **The food was (***good, well***), and we ate (***good, well***).** 986

they 1173	**We made more hits than _they_ did.** We use the subject form of the pronoun because _they_ is the subject of the verb _____. 1174
Yes 1360	ADJECTIVE CLAUSE SIGNALS: **who (whom, whose), which, that** The pronoun **who** has two other forms: _____ and _____. 1361
b 1547	a. **The jet plane had four powerful engines.** b. **A jet plane with four powerful engines.** The correct sentence is ____. 1548
a 1734	In this and the following frames, first put a period after every abbreviation that is proper for ordinary writing. Then, on the blank line, write out in full any word that should not be abbreviated. **The party takes place at 8:00 P M on Fri, Apr 6.** _____ 1735
boy's 1921	**several _boys_ lockers** Whom do the **lockers** belong to? The lockers belong to several _____. 1922
a 2108	a. **The dentist said, "this will hurt for only a minute."** b. **The dentist said, "This will hurt for only a minute."** ____ 2109

Which **did you buy?**

Do you know whether *Which* refers to a candy bar, a coat, or a car? (*Yes, No*)

47

Several, hot,
stuffy

234

Many words can serve as either nouns or adjectives. If the word comes before another noun and tells *what kind,* it is an adjective.

> a. **The** *morning* **was very cool.**
> b. **I always read the** *morning* **paper.**

The word *morning* is an adjective in sentence _____.

235

---

adverb

422

Which kind of phrase is more likely to be separated from the word it modifies? An (*adjective, adverb*) phrase.

423

---

grown, thrown

610

Write the helper form of each verb in parentheses:

The Rosses must *have* _____ (*know*) **that they could**

have _____ (*fly*) **there.**

611

---

singular

798

> a. **Antonio** *and* **his sister . . . with the baby.**
> b. **Antonio** *or* **his sister . . . with the baby.**

Which sentence requires the singular verb **stays?** ____

799

---

good, well

986

We ate (*good, well*) **because the food was** (*good, well*).

987

did 1174	Usually we abbreviate (shorten) a comparison by omitting one or more words: **We made more hits than they did.** **We made more hits than they.** We abbreviated this comparison by omitting the verb ____. 1175
whom, whose 1361	ADJECTIVE CLAUSE SIGNALS: **who (whom, whose),** **which, that** Each of these adjective clause signals refers to a noun or another pronoun in the main part of the sentence. These signal words are therefore (*nouns, pronouns*). 1362
a 1548	a. **I planned to study my math before school.** b. **Planning to study my math before school.** The correct sentence is ____. 1549
P.M. Friday, April 1735	**Miss Jansen works for Mr A C Okura of NY** _____ 1736
boys 1922	**several** *boys* **lockers** This time, the answer to the question "Whom do the **lockers** belong to?" is *boys*, not *boy*. Therefore, put the apostrophe after *boys*, not after *boy*. **several** *boys* **lockers** 1923
b 2109	a. **The man said", This dog doesn't bite".** b. **The man said, "This dog doesn't bite."** ____ 2110

No 47	*Which* **did you buy?** Because the word *Which* might refer to a great many different things, it is a (*pronoun, noun*). 48
b 235	a. **Barry served** *lemon* **pie.** b. **The** *lemon* **improved the punch.** The word *lemon* is an adjective in sentence ____. 236
adverb 423	Sometimes an adjective phrase seems to answer the question *Where?* about a noun. However, it really modifies the noun by telling *which one(s)* we mean. **The leaves** *on this tree* **are falling.** The prepositional phrase *on this tree* tells which _____ we are talking about. 424

known, flown
 	
611
	PRESENT SIMPLE PAST PAST WITH HELPER
	  fly **flew** **(have) flown**
	  grow **grew** **(have) grown**
	  know **knew** **(have) known**
	  throw **threw** **(have) thrown**
	Do any of the above verb forms end in *–ed*? (*Yes, No*)
	
	612

b 799	a. **The teacher** *or* **a pupil . . . the attendance.** b. **The teacher** *and* **a pupil . . . the attendance.** Which sentence requires the singular verb **takes?** ____ 800
well, good 987	**A person whose health is** (*good, well*) **should sleep** (*good, well*). 988

did 1175	**We made more hits than** *they* **did.** **We made more hits than** *they.* When we omit the verb **did,** do we still use the same form of the pronoun? (*Yes,. No*) 1176
pronouns 1362	All the adjective clauses in this lesson start with a clause signal and end when the idea of the clause is completed. **The man** *who owns the truck* **lives across the street.** The adjective clause starts with the clause signal _____ and ends with the word _____. 1363
a 1549	a. **After the car drove away.** b. **The car drove away.** The correct sentence is ____. 1550
Mr. A. C. New York 1736	**The bus runs between Logan St and Evergreen Pk** _____ 1737
boys' 1923	Place your apostrophe so that the word *before* the apostrophe answers the question "Whom does it belong to?" **boy's boys'** If the answer to your question is **boy,** which of the above words would you choose? _____ 1924
b 2110	a. **Roy began, "It was Halloween. We kids were dressed up like astronauts."** b. **Roy began, "It was Halloween." "We kids were dressed up like astronauts."** 2111

pronoun 48	*She* **looked like a** *dancer.* In this sentence, one italicized word is a noun, and the other is a pronoun. The pronoun is the word _____. 49
a 236	a. **The** *candy* **spoiled my appetite.** b. **The tree was decorated with** *candy* **canes.** The word *candy* is an adjective in sentence ____. 237
leaves (ones) 424	**The leaves** *on this tree* **are falling.** The prepositional phrase *on this tree* modifies the noun **leaves.** It is therefore an (*adjective, adverb*) phrase. 425
No 612	Write the correct past form of each verb in parentheses. Whenever you see the helper **have, has,** or **had,** be sure to use the helper form that ends in *–n*. I _____ (*know*) **that Gina had** _____ (*throw*) **away her ticket.** 613
a 800	In this and the following frames, underline the verb that agrees with its subject. Remember that putting an **s** on a *present* verb always makes it singular. **The fire engines** (*hurry, hurries*) **to the fire.** 801
good, well 988	**The band was** (*good, well*), **and it played** (*good, well*). 989

Yes 1176	Underline the correct pronoun: **Phil has a larger collection than** (*I*, *me*). 1177
who ... truck 1363	When you remove an adjective clause from a sentence, a complete sentence should remain. **The man** (*who owns the truck*) **lives across the street.** When you read this sentence without the clause, are the remaining words a sentence? (*Yes, No*) 1364
b 1550	**a. I threw the fish back into the water.** **b. And threw the fish back into the water.** The correct sentence is ____. 1551
Street Park 1737	**The Emperor Augustus ruled Rome from 27 B C to A D 14.** _____ 1738
boy's 1924	**boy's boys'** If the answer to your question is **boys,** which of the above words would you choose? _____ 1925
a 2111	a. **"Did I get any mail today?" asked Mom.** b. **"Did I get any mail today," asked Mom?** ____ 2112

She 49	Underline two pronouns that you could use to refer to yourself or your belongings. **their I mine she** 50
b 237	We have now become acquainted with four different kinds of words: *nouns, pronouns, verbs,* and _____. 238
adjective 425	a. **Several people sat** *behind us.* b. **Everyone** *behind us* **was talking.** In which sentence is the prepositional phrase an adjective phrase because it modifies a pronoun? ____ 426
knew, thrown 613	Write the correct past form of each verb in parentheses: **Jack** _____ (*grow*) **nervous because he had never** _____(*fly*) **before.** 614
hurry 801	**The director** (*open, opens*) **the meeting.** 802
good, well 989	**I can paint** (*good, well*) **if the brush is** (*good, well*). 990

Underline the correct pronoun:

The storm delayed them more than it delayed (*we, us*).

1177

1178

Add a second parenthesis [)] after the word that ends the adjective clause. Remember: If you select the clause correctly, a complete sentence should remain.

The boy (whom we chose was new to the school.

1364

1365

---

a. **Besides being a good athlete.**
b. **June is also a good athlete.**

The correct sentence is ____.

1551

1552

It took Ramon 5 min and 12 sec to run one mile.

_____

1738

1739

---

this girls bicycle

Whom does the **bicycle** belong to? Answer: *girl*

Add the apostrophe:

this *girls* bicycle

1925

1926

---

a. **The officer asked, "How fast were you driving"?**

b. **The officer asked, "How fast were you driving?"** ____

2112

2113

I, mine 50	The *coat* **looks like** *mine*. In this sentence, the pronoun is the word _____. 51
adjectives 238	*To modify* means *to* _____ our picture or idea of something. 239
b 426	**A man** <u>*in another car*</u> **pointed** <u>*to our tire*</u>. a b Which prepositional phrase is an adverb phrase because it answers the question *Where?* about the verb? ____ 427
grew, flown 614	Write the correct past form of each verb in parentheses: **We** _____ (*throw*) **out the bread because it had** _____ (*grow*) **moldy.** 615
opens 802	**A dog or a cat** (*need, needs*) **to be trained.** 803
well, good 990	**If your work is** (*good, well*), **Ms. Brock will pay you very** (*good, well*). 991

us 1178	**The storm delayed them more than it delayed** *us*. We use the object form of the pronoun because *us* is the direct object of the verb _____. 1179
chose) 1365	Add a second parenthesis [)] after the word that ends the adjective clause: **The space (that separated the two houses was very narrow.** 1366
b 1552	a. **Which I carefully put in my pocket.** b. **I carefully put it in my pocket.** The correct sentence is ____. 1553
minutes seconds 1739	**Dr Rivera shares an office with another dr in the Webster Bldg** _____ 1740
girl's 1926	**these girls bicycles** Whom do the **bicycles** belong to? Answer: *girls* Add the apostrophe: **these** *girls* **bicycles** 1927
b 2113	a. **"Safe!" called the umpire.** b. **"Safe," called the umpire!** ____ Note to student: You are now ready for Unit·Test 10. *page 102* 2114

mine	**Every** *car* **has** *one*. Which word is a pronoun because it could refer to any one of a number of things?_____ 52
51	
change (or another word with the same meaning) 239	*gentle* **dog** In grammar, we say the adjective *gentle* _____ the noun **dog**. 240
b 427	In this and the following frames, each sentence contains one adjective phrase and one adverb phrase. **The boy** *in the next seat* **spoke** *to me*. a b The adverb phrase is (*a, b*). 428
threw, grown 615	Write the correct past form of each verb in parentheses: **If we had** _____ (*know*) **that Luisa** _____ (*fly*) **here, we would have picked her up at the airport.** 616
needs 803	**A dog and a cat** (*need, needs*) **to be trained.** 804
good, well 991	When the word *well* is used to mean the opposite of *sick*, it is an adjective. As an adjective, it means "in good health." **My uncle is** *well* **again.** The adjective *well* modifies the noun _____. 992

delayed 1179	Now let's abbreviate this comparison: **The storm delayed them more than it delayed** *us.* **The storm delayed them more than** *us.* We abbreviated this comparison by omitting the two words _____. 1180
houses) 1366	Add a second parenthesis [)] after the word that ends the adjective clause: **The blood (which flows from a wound washes away the germs.** 1367
b 1553	a. **Tells of an exciting adventure in a cave.** b. **The article tells of an exciting adventure in a cave.** The correct sentence is ____. 1554
Dr. doctor Building 1740	In this and the following frames, abbreviate each item as you might do to save space on a list or schedule: **Maple Road** _____ **Scott Avenue** _____ 1741
girls' 1927	**these neighbors dog** Whom does the **dog** belong to? Answer: *neighbors* Add the apostrophe: **these** *neighbors* **dog** 1928
a 2114	UNIT 11: **WHAT WORDS DO WE CAPITALIZE?** Lesson **74** Capitals for Geographical and Group Names [Frames 2116-2142]

one 52	*Jack* **bought** *one* **for** *Juanita.* In this sentence, the pronoun is the word _____. 53
modifies 240	Lesson **9** Adverbs Explain Verbs [Frames 242-277]
b 428	**The man** <u>*across the street*</u> **works** <u>*for a bank.*</u> a b The adverb phrase is (*a, b*). 429
known, flew 616	Notice how much alike the forms of these verbs are: PRESENT SIMPLE PAST PAST WITH HELPER **tear** **tore** **(have) torn** **wear** **wore** **(have) worn** Like the other four verbs in this lesson, the helper forms of these verbs end with the letter ____. 617
need 804	**Most children** (*enjoys, enjoy*) **this program.** 805
uncle 992	a. **My sister writes** *well.* b. **My sister is now** *well.* In which sentence is *well* used as an adjective? ____ 993

page 105

it delayed 1180	**The storm delayed them more than it delayed** *us.* **The storm delayed them more than** *us.* When we omit the words **it delayed,** do we still use the same form of the pronoun? (*Yes, No*) 1181
wound) 1367	ADJECTIVE CLAUSE SIGNALS: **who (whom, whose),** **which, that** **There are many plants which will bloom indoors.** The adjective clause starts with the word _____ and ends with the word _____. 1368
b 1554	Lesson **54** A Closer Look at Sentence Fragments [Frames 1556-1588]
Maple Rd. Scott Ave. 1741	**Sunday** _____ **Monday**_____ 1742
neighbors' 1928	**our doctors car** Whom does the **car** belong to? Answer: *doctor* Add the apostrophe: **our** *doctors* **car** 1929
	Capital letters are a helpful guide to the reader. **Have you ever seen John cook?** **Have you ever seen John Cook?** The meaning of these sentences depends on whether or not you capitalize the letter ____. 2116

one 53	A word used in place of a noun is a _____. 54
	What kind? Which one(s)? How many? How much? In the last lesson we learned that words that answer these questions about nouns are called _____. 242
b 429	*Through the telescope* **I could see the outline** *of a ship.* a b The adverb phrase is (*a, b*). 430
−n 617	PRESENT SIMPLE PAST PAST WITH HELPER **tear** **tore** **(have) torn** Write the correct past forms of **tear:** **My sleeve** _____ **in the same place that it had** _____ **before.** 618
enjoy 805	**The old house (***looks, look***) deserted.** 806
b 993	**Grandma Smith had an operation, but she is now** *well.* In this sentence, *well* is used as an (*adjective, adverb*). 994

Yes 1181	In any abbreviated comparison, think of the omitted word or words. This will tell you immediately which form of the pronoun to use. **I am two inches taller than .?. (is).** Think of the omitted word *is*. Which pronoun would fit in this sentence—**he** or **him?**____ 1182
which . . . indoors 1368	**The man who gave us our directions forgot to mention the turn.** The adjective clause starts with the word _____ and ends with the word _____. 1369
	To make sense, you must name what you are talking about. This is the subject part of your sentence. After you name what you are talking about, you must say something about it. This is the verb part of your sentence. **My dad closed the door and locked it.** How many verbs say something about the subject? _____ 1556
Sun. Mon. 1742	**January** _____ **February** _____ 1743
doctor's 1929	Remember that the word *before* the apostrophe should always name the owner or owners. a. the *lady's* rings b. the *ladies'* rings Look at the word before the apostrophe. Which example means the **rings** of *one* lady? ____ 1930
c 2116	**boy Harold** One of these nouns can be applied to *any* boy; the other noun names *one particular* boy that we might be talking about. The noun that names *one particular* boy is _____. 2117

pronoun	A pronoun is (*more*, *less*) definite than a noun.
54	55

adjectives	We need a different kind of word to explain more about the actions of verbs.
	
	        a. **The bus turned.**
	        b. **The bus turned** *sharply*.
	
	Which sentence gives you a clearer idea of the action of the verb **turned?** ____

242	243
a	**Ships** _from many countries_ **dock** _in San Francisco Bay._ a b The adverb phrase is (*a*, *b*).
430	431
tore, torn	PRESENT SIMPLE PAST PAST WITH HELPER **wear** **wore** **(have) worn** Write the correct past forms of **wear:** **Sandra** _____ **the same dress that she had** _____ **to the meeting.**
618	619
looks	**Rain and sunshine** (*make*, *makes*) **plants grow.**
806	807
adjective	**I slept ....** **Sue dances ....** **Ray bats ....** **The corn grows ....** To complete all these sentences, you would use the adverb (*good*, *well*).
994	995

he 1182	**I am two inches taller than** *he* **(is).** We use the subject form *he* because it is the subject of the omitted verb _____. 1183
who ... directions 1369	**Few city dogs get the exercise that they need.** The adjective clause starts with the word _____ and ends with the word _____. 1370
two 1556	**My <u>dad</u> <u>closed</u> the door and <u>locked</u> it.** Both the verb **closed** and the verb **locked** say something about the subject _____. 1557
Jan. Feb. 1743	**Father Brady** _____ **Professor Morris** _____ 1744
a 1930	**the** *lady's* **rings** This means the **rings** of *one* lady because the word before the apostrophe is _____. 1931
Harold 2117	a. **Canada** b. **country** The noun that names *one particular* country is _____. 2118

less 55	We have now studied two different kinds of words, _____ and _____. 56
b 243	**turned** *sharply* **turned** *suddenly* **turned** *slowly* Each pair of words gives you a different idea of *how* the bus **turned.** The word that changes your idea is the (*first, second*) word in each pair. 244
b 431	*During the week* **I read a book** *about Harriet Tubman.* a b The adverb phrase is (*a, b*). 432
wore, worn 619	Here are the simple past forms of the 13 verbs that you studied in this and the previous lesson: **drove spoke took fell broke wrote ate** **flew grew knew threw tore wore** Do any of these verbs have a past form that ends in *–ed*? (*Yes, No*) 620
make 807	**A book or a magazine** (*help, helps*) **to pass the time.** 808
well 995	Lesson **34** The Problem of *Sense* Verbs *page 111* [Frames 997-1028]

is 1183	**The doctor charged us more than** (*she charged*) . .?. . Think of the omitted words *she charged.* Which pronoun would fit in this sentence—**they** or **them**? _____ 1184
that . . . need 1370	**We called a doctor whom a neighbor had recommended.** The adjective clause starts with the word _____ and ends with the word _____ . 1371
dad 1557	WRONG: **My dad closed the door.** *And locked it.* The italicized word group is a fragment, not a sentence. It is a fragment because it lacks a (*subject, verb*). 1558
Fr. Brady Prof. Morris 1744	**Fisher Building** _____ **Ford Motor Company** _____ 1745
lady (*or* singular) 1931	**the** *ladies'* **rings** This means the **rings** of *more than one* lady because the word before the apostrophe is _____ . 1932
Canada 2118	a. **city** b. **Los Angeles** The noun that names *one particular* city is _____ . 2119

---

second

The **green** bus turned *sharply.*

The adjective *green* modifies the noun **bus.**

Which word modifies the verb **turned?** _____.

244

245

---

a

You often find two phrases in a row. The second phrase may modify the object of the first phrase, or it may modify the verb in another part of the sentence.

We learn much history *from the letters* *of soldiers.*
            a   b

Phrase *b* modifies (*learn, letters*).

432

433

No

Here are the helper forms of the same verbs:

(have) driven **(have) spoken** **(have) taken** **(have) fallen**
(have) broken **(have) written** **(have) eaten** **(have) flown**
(have) grown **(have) known** **(have) thrown** **(have) torn**
(have) worn

Each of these helper forms ends with the two letters ____ or the letter ____.

620

621

---

look   feel   taste   smell   hear

All these verbs are connected with our senses.

Each one of these verbs can mean an action we perform with parts of our bodies. For example, we **look** with our eyes, **feel** with our hands, and **smell** with our _____.

997

them 1184	So far, we have looked at comparisons made with the word **than.** Comparisons made with the word **as** are no different. **They can't stay as long as .?. (can stay).** Think of the omitted words *can stay.* Which pronoun would fit in this sentence—**we** or **us?** _____ 1185
whom ... recommended 1371	**The page which was missing from my book was found on the floor.** The adjective clause starts with the word _____ and ends with the word _____. 1372
subject 1558	When a sentence has two verbs that say different things about the same subject, don't cut off one of the verbs. a. I like our new house but miss my old friends. b. I like our new house. But miss my old friends. In which line do you find a sentence fragment? _____ 1559
Fisher Bldg. Ford Motor Co. 1745	Lesson **61** Commas in Compound Sentences [Frames 1747-1777]
ladies (*or* plural) 1932	a. All the *baby's* diets are carefully checked. b. All the *babies'* diets are carefully checked. c. All the *babie's* diets are carefully checked. Which sentence is correct? _____ 1933
Los Angeles 2119	boy country city Harold Canada Los Angeles We capitalize nouns that apply to (*any, a particular*) one of their kind. 2120

To make a sentence, you must first have a subject to talk about.

Herb   school   football   happiness

Does each of these words name a subject that you could make a sentence about? (*Yes, No*)

58

---

sharply

245

A word that modifies a verb is called an **adverb.**

The green bus turned *sharply.*

Because it modifies the verb **turned,** the word *sharply* is an _____.

246

---

letters

433

Remember: If a phrase can be moved to another part of the sentence, it modifies the verb.

I put the box *of matches* *on a high shelf.*
                    a   b

Phrase *b* modifies (*put, matches*).

434

–en, –n

621

A common mistake is to use the simple past form of these verbs, instead of the helper forms, after **have, has,** or **had.**

      a. **Dave** *has tore* **his shirt.**
      b. **Dave** *has torn* **his shirt.**

Which sentence is correct? ____

622

SINGULAR: **This watch runs.**

PLURAL: **These watches run.**

When we add an **s** to a verb that shows *present* time, we always make the verb (*singular, plural*).

810

---

noses

997

look   feel   taste   smell   hear

When these verbs are used to mean actions, we would use (*adjectives, adverbs*) to describe *how* these actions are performed.

998

we 1185	**My perfect score on the test surprised my teacher as well as** (*it surprised*) .?.. Think of the omitted words *it surprised*. Which pronoun would fit in this sentence—I or me? _____ 1186
which ... book 1372	**We finally found the man whose car had rolled into the street.** The adjective clause starts with the word _____ and ends with the word _____. 1373
b 1559	a. **Roy must pay a fine or lose his driver's license.** b. **Roy must pay a fine. Or lose his driver's license.** Which arrangement is correct? ____ 1560
	A compound sentence is made by joining two separate sentences. We use the conjunction **and, but,** or **or** to combine them. **We talked to Coretta King,** *and* **we asked many questions.** The conjunction that connects the two parts of this compound sentence is _____. 1747

b
 	
1933
	The words **man** and **woman** are singular; the words **men** and **women** are plural.
	
	     a. **the man's score**
	     b. **the men's score**
	
	Which means the score of *more than one* man? ____
	1934

a particular 2120	All the rules for capitals are based on one simple idea: Use a capital letter (or letters) for the special name of *one particular* person, group of people, place, or thing. a. **people** b. **Eskimos** The noun that is the name of *one particular* group of people is _____. 2121

Yes 58	**Herb school football happiness** Does any one of these words by itself make a complete sentence? *(Yes, No)* 59
adverb 246	**Pete studied.** This sentence tells you that Pete **studied**—nothing more. Here are questions you might ask about Pete's action: **When? Where? How? How often?** Any word that would answer one of these questions would be an *(adjective, adverb)*. 247
put 434	**She wrote the poem** <u>*on the back*</u> <u>*of an envelope.*</u> a b Phrase *b* modifies *(wrote, back)*. 435
b 622	It is simple to avoid this mistake. Whenever you need a helper form of one of these verbs, ask yourself if the verb has a form that ends in *–n* or *–en*. Does the verb **throw** have an *–n* or an *–en* form? *(Yes, No)* 623
singular 810	**This <u>man</u> <u>does</u> the typing.** This sentence is correct because the singular verb **does** agrees with the singular subject **man.** We know that **does** is singular because it ends in _____. 811
adverbs 998	**The customer** *looked* **carefully at his change.** In this sentence, *looked* means an action of the eyes. To describe this action, we use the adverb _____. 999

me 1186	Sometimes the meaning of a sentence depends on whether we use the subject or object form of a pronoun. a. **Dad helps my sister more than I** (*help her*). b. **Dad helps my sister more than** (*he helps*) **me**. In which sentence is the underlined pronoun the subject of the omitted verb? _____ 1187
whose ... street 1373	**A person who weighs 150 pounds on the earth would weigh only 25 pounds on the moon.** The adjective clause starts with the word _____ and ends with the word _____. 1374
a 1560	a. **My dog comes** *promptly.* b. **My dog comes** *when I call it.* Sentence *a* contains an adverb. Sentence *b* contains an adverb clause. Both the adverb and the adverb clause tell *when* about the verb _____, which they modify. 1561
and 1747	**I recognized Pauline,** *but* **she didn't recognize me.** The conjunction that connects the two parts of this compound sentence is _____. 1748
b 1934	a. **the women's pay** b. **the woman's pay** Which means the pay of *more than one* woman? _____ 1935
Eskimos 2121	Here is our first rule for using capitals: Capitalize geographical names that apply to *particular* countries, states, cities, streets, and so forth. **state Ohio** The noun that names *one particular* place is _____. 2122

No	**Herb laughed.**
	Now this is a sentence because we have added the word
	_____.
59	60

adverb	**Lena studied** _hard._
	The adverb _hard_ modifies the verb **studied.**
	Underline the question it answers:
	How? Where? When?
247	248

back	**I carried the letter** <u>_in my pocket_</u> <u>_for several days._</u>
	a b
	Phrase _b_ modifies (_carried, pocket_).
435	436

Yes	a. **The pitcher** _had thrown_ **a wild pitch.**
	b. **The pitcher** _had threw_ **a wild pitch.**
	Which sentence is correct? _____
623	624

s	a. **This <u>man</u> <u>does</u> not <u>type.</u>**
	b. **This <u>man</u> <u>do</u> not <u>type.</u>**
	Which sentence is correct because the subject and the
	verb agree in number? _____
811	812

carefully	**I** _felt_ **the hot stove cautiously.**
	In this sentence, _felt_ means an action of the hands.
	To describe this action, we use the adverb _____.
999	1000

a

a. **Dad helps my sister more than I** (*help her*).
b. **Dad helps my sister more than** (*he helps*) **me**.

In which sentence is the underlined pronoun the direct object of the omitted verb? ____

1187   1188

---

who ... earth

A family that lives on a houseboat can move very easily.

The adjective clause starts with the word _____
and ends with the word _____.

1374   1375

---

comes

My dog comes. *Promptly.*

Is it correct to cut off the adverb *promptly* from the verb **comes,** which it modifies? (*Yes, No*)

1561   1562

---

but

I call for Bob, *or* **Bob calls for me.**

The conjunction that connects the two parts of this compound sentence is _____.

1748   1749

---

a

The word **child** is singular; the word **children** is plural.

     a. **Here are the** *childrens'* **magazines.**
     b. **Here are the** *children's* **magazines.**

The *magazines* belong to the *children*.

Which sentence is correct? ____

1935   1936

Ohio

     a. **country**   **state**   **city**   **street**
     b. **france**   **oregon**   **denver**   **broadway**

In which group should the words be written with capital letters? ____

2122

2123

laughed 60	**Herb laughed.** The word **laughed** tells what **Herb** did. Any word that tells what someone or something *does* is called a **verb.** The word **laughed** in this sentence is a _____. 61
How? 248	**Lena studied** *yesterday.* The adverb *yesterday* modifies the verb **studied.** Underline the question it answers: **How?** **Where?** **When?** 249
carried 436	**You can see cottages** *across the lake* *on clear days.* a b Phrase b modifies (*can see, lake*). 437
a 624	You know that after any form of **have (has, had)** you must use the helper form of the verb. After any form of **be (is, am, are—was, were, been)**, you must use the helper form, too. Use the helper form of the verb after any form of the helping verb *have* or _____. 625
a 812	We can make one word of **does not** by writing **doesn't.** We can make one word of **do not** by writing **don't.** The verb **don't** can be either singular or plural—for example, "I don't" (singular), "We don't" (plural). The verb **doesn't,** however, is always _____. 813.
cautiously 1000	**Maggie** *tasted* **her first oyster hesitantly.** In this sentence, *tasted* means an action of the mouth. To describe this action, we use the adverb _____. 1001

b

1188

a. **Dad helps my sister more than** *I* (*help her*).
b. **Dad helps my sister more than** (*he helps*) *me*.

Which sentence means that your dad gives more help to your sister than you do? ____

1189

---

that ...
houseboat

1375

We were asked to write a theme about any person whom we admired.

The adjective clause starts with the word _____

and ends with the word _____.

1376

No

1562

My dog comes. *When I call it.*

Is it correct to cut off the adverb clause *when I call it* from the verb **comes**, which it modifies? (*Yes, No*)

1563

---

or

1749

The three conjunctions that can join two sentences into a

compound sentence are _____, _____, and ____.

1750

---

b

1936

a. **Some** *children's* **games are very interesting.**
b. **Some** *childrens'* **games are very interesting.**

Which sentence is correct? ____

1937

---

b

2123

Copy and add capital letters to the two words which should be capitalized:

We left detroit and crossed the river to canada.

_____

2124

verb 61	**Herb laughed.** Underline two other verbs that could tell what **Herb** did: **shouted** **tall** **stumbled** **soon** 62
When? 249	**Lena studied** *there*. The adverb *there* modifies the verb **studied.** Underline the question it answers: **How often?** **Where?** **How?** 250
can see 437	Lesson **15** **Conjunctions Do the Connecting** [Frames 439-470]
be 625	a. **This wedding dress** *was wore* **by my grandmother.** b. **This wedding dress** *was worn* **by my grandmother.** Which sentence is correct? ____ 626
singular 813	Use **doesn't** only where you can use the words **does not.** Use **don't** only where you can use the words _____. 814
hesitantly 1001	**look** **feel** **taste** **smell** These verbs have a second meaning. This meaning has nothing to do with actions of our eyes, hands, noses, and mouths. **The pie** *looks* **good.** Does a pie have eyes with which to look at something? (*Yes, No*) *page 123* 1002

[Frames 1378-1401]

a

1189

a. **Dad helps my sister more than** *I* (*help her*).
b. **Dad helps my sister more than** (*he helps*) *me*.

Which sentence means that your dad helps both your sister and you but that he helps her more? ____

1190

whom . . . admired

1376

Lesson 47 Using *Who* and *Whom* Correctly

No

1563

A word group and the word it modifies should always be (*in the same sentence, in different sentences*).

1564

and, but, or

1750

<u>We talked</u> to Coretta King, *and* <u>we asked</u> many questions.

In a compound sentence, are there a subject and a verb both *before* and *after* the conjunction? (*Yes, No*)

1751

a

1937

In this and the following frames, add the apostrophe in each italicized word. Be sure to ask your question in exactly these words: "Whom (*or* What) does it belong to?" Using other words can give you the wrong answer.

One *boys* locker wouldn't open.

1938

Detroit, Canada

2124

Also capitalize the complete names of *particular* oceans, lakes, rivers, mountains, parks, and so forth.
When a word such as **ocean, lake, river,** or **park** is part of the complete name, this word should be capitalized, too.

a. **Columbia River**   b. **Columbia river**

Which example is correctly capitalized? ____

2125

shouted,
stumbled

Herb laughed.

Whom or what is this two-word sentence about? _____

Where?

a. **Our boat leaks** *now.*
b. **Our boat leaks** *badly.*
c. **Our boat leaks** *everywhere.*

All the italicized words are adverbs because they modify

the verb _____.

Wendy and Stan washed the dishes.

This sentence has two (*subjects, verbs*).

---

b

The following frames review the irregular verbs in this and the previous lesson. In each frame, write the correct past forms of the verbs in parentheses:

My Uncle Mac _____ (*drive*) to Milwaukee and

_____ (*fly*) **back.**

---

do not

My dad *don't* **smoke.**

In this sentence, could you use the words *do not* instead of *don't*? (*Yes, No*)

No

These melons *feel* **ripe.**

Does a melon have hands with which to feel something? (*Yes, No*)

Ann writes to Verna as often as (*she, her*).

To say that Ann writes to Verna as often as another girl writes to Verna, choose the pronoun (*she, her*).

1191

I have a cousin *who visits my sister.*

The adjective clause *who visits my sister* modifies the noun _____.

1378

---

in the same
sentence

1564

If a clause is cut off from the word it modifies, it becomes a sentence fragment. Let's see why:

WRONG: **My dog comes.** *When I call it.*

Although the clause *When I call it* has a subject and a verb, does it make sense by itself? (*Yes, No*)

1565

Yes

1751

If you don't find a subject and a verb after the conjunction, is it a compound sentence? (*Yes, No*)

1752

---

boy's

1938

(Whom do the **parents** belong to?)

Several *students* **parents visited our class.**

1939

---

a

2125

a. **Yellowstone national park**   b. **Yellowstone National Park**

Which example is correctly capitalized? ____

2126

Herb 63	The word that names *whom* or *what* a sentence is about is called the **subject** of the sentence. **Herb laughed.** **Rosa laughed.** **Judy laughed.** Each of these sentences has a different _____. 64
leaks 251	Adverbs, like adjectives, can answer the question *How much?* a. **Our boat leaks** *now.* b. **Our boat leaks** *badly.* c. **Our boat leaks** *everywhere.* In which sentence does the italicized adverb answer the question *How much?* ____ 252
subjects 439	**Wendy** and **Stan** <u>washed</u> the dishes. The two subjects, **Wendy** and **Stan**, are connected by the word _____. 440
drove, flew 627	Keep your eyes open for forms of the helping verbs **have (has, had)** and **be (is, am, are—was, were, been)**. Be sure to use the helper form (*–n* or *–en*) after them. **The children _____ (*grow*) sleepy soon after they had _____ (*eat*) their dinner.** 628
No 815	a. **My dad** *don't* **smoke.** b. **My dad** *doesn't* **smoke.** Which sentence is correct? ____ 816
No 1003	**My apple** *tastes* **sour.** Does an apple have a mouth with which to taste something? (*Yes, No*) 1004

she 1191	**Ann writes to Verna as often as** (*she, her*). To say that Ann writes to Verna as often as Ann writes to another girl, choose the pronoun (*she, her*). 1192
cousin 1378	**I have a cousin** *who visits my sister*. The clause signal *who* is a pronoun. It refers to the noun _____ . 1379
No 1565	WRONG: *When I call it.* This clause by itself doesn't satisfy you. You want to hear *what happens*. When you write a clause as though it were a complete sentence, you produce a sentence _____ . 1566
No 1752	**We talked to Coretta King** *and* **we asked many questions.** Listen to yourself say this sentence. Notice where your voice pauses. Your voice pauses after the noun _____ . 1753
students' 1939	(Whom did the **handkerchief** belong to?) **A** *mans* **handkerchief is the only clue.** 1940
b 2126	Copy and add capital letters to the three words which should be capitalized: **The Erie canal connects the Hudson river with lake Erie.** _____ 2127

subject 64	**Herb laughed.** **Herb shouted.** **Herb stumbled.** Each of these sentences has a different _____. 65
b 252	a. **Our boat leaks** *now.* b. **Our boat leaks** *badly.* c. **Our boat leaks** *everywhere.* In which sentence does the italicized adverb answer the question *When?* ____ 253
and 440	**Stan washed and dried the dishes.** This sentence has two (*subjects, verbs*). 441
grew, eaten 628	**These strawberries are _____ (*grow*) in California** **and are _____ (*fly*) to the East.** 629
b 816	a. **The bus** *doesn't* **stop here.** b. **The bus** *don't* **stop here.** Which sentence is correct? ____ 817
No 1004	Do you remember that there are two kinds of verbs— *action* verbs and *linking* verbs? The job of a *linking* verb is to connect a word that follows it with the subject. **The pie is good.** What is the linking verb that connects the adjective **good** with the subject **pie?** ____ 1005

her 1192	In this and the following frames, underline the correct pronoun in each comparison. Be sure to think of the missing words before making your choice. **We made two more touchdowns than** (*they, them*). 1193
cousin 1379	Here is the adjective clause by itself: *who visits my sister* The subject of the verb *visits* is the pronoun _____. 1380
fragment 1566	a. **I am interested in stamps. Although I don't collect them.** b. **I am interested in stamps although I don't collect them.** Which arrangement is correct? ____ 1567
Coretta King 1753	In a compound sentence, put a comma after the first part of the sentence, where your voice pauses. This comma separates the two parts of the sentence and makes the sentence easier to read. **We talked to Coretta King,** *and* **we asked many questions.** The comma comes (*before, after*) the conjunction **and.** 1754
man's 1940	(Whom do the **children** belong to?) **My two** *sisters* **children are all boys.** 1941
Canal, River, Lake 2127	Capitalize the word **street, avenue, road, drive, boulevard,** and so forth, when it is part of the complete name. **Main Street Sanford Avenue Wilshire Boulevard** Supply capitals for the four words that need them. **Our school is at the corner of curtis street and pine road.** 2128

verb 65	He laughed. She shouted. We stumbled. Can pronouns, as well as nouns, be the subjects of sentences? *(Yes, No)* 66
a 253	a. **Our boat leaks** *now.* b. **Our boat leaks** *badly.* c. **Our boat leaks** *everywhere.* In which sentence does the italicized adverb answer the question *Where?* ____ 254
verbs 441	**Stan <u>washed</u> and <u>dried</u> the dishes.** The two verbs, **washed** and **dried**, are connected by the word _____. 442
grown, flown 629	**Ross must have** _____ *(know)* **that his shirt was** _____ *(tear).* 630
a 817	a. **He ... like cats.** b. **They ... like cats.** In which sentence would **don't** be correct because the words **do not** would fit in? ____ 818
is 1005	**These melons are ripe.** What is the linking verb that connects the adjective **ripe** with the subject **melons?** _____ 1006

they 1193	**This coat fits you better than** (*she, her*). 1194
who 1380	**Who** (like **he**) is the subject form of the pronoun. **Whom** (like **him**) is the object form of the pronoun. When the pronoun is the subject of the verb, you would choose (*who, whom*). 1381
b 1567	a. **Ellen wrote a poem, which the teacher read to the class.** b. **Ellen wrote a poem. Which the teacher read to the class.** Which arrangement is correct? ____ 1568
before 1754	The comma in a compound sentence helps you to read it more easily and to get the right meaning. **Jim apologized to Sue and his mother was pleased.** Because the comma is missing from this sentence, you might get the idea that Jim apologized to two persons— **Sue** and _____. 1755
sisters' 1941	(Whom do the **records** belong to?) **Each** *pupils* **records are kept in the office.** 1942
Curtis Street, Pine Road 2128	Copy and add capital letters to the four words which should be capitalized: **Our street will be paved from madison avenue to sunset drive.** 2129

Yes 66	a. Herb laughed. b. They shouted. c. Judy stumbled. In which sentence is the subject a pronoun? ____ 67

c
 	
254
	Now, for just a few frames, let's go back to adjectives.
	
	    a. **My aunt lives in the** *white* **house.**
	    b. **Sarah Caldwell conducted** *several* **pieces.**
	    c. **Harriet Tubman showed** *great* **courage.**
	
	Is each italicized adjective right next to the word it modifies? (*Yes, No*)
	
	255

and 442	**Wendy or Stan washed the dishes.** Here the two subjects, **Wendy** and **Stan**, are connected by the word _____. 443
known, torn 630	**The clerk _____ (***throw***) away the cookies that had _____ (***fall***) on the floor.** 631
b 818	**.?.** *don't* **look fresh.** Underline two items that could be used correctly as the subject of the above sentence. Remember that *don't* means *do not*. **The lettuce The carrots It They** 819
are 1006	The most common linking verb is **be** (*is, am, are—was, were, been*). **These melons are ripe.** Two of the following verbs could be used in place of the linking verb **are** in the above sentence. Underline these two verbs: **look walk feel fix** 1007

her 1194	Dad doesn't have as much patience as (*she, her*). 1195
who 1381	When the pronoun is the object of the verb, you would choose (*who, whom*). 1382
a 1568	Don't cut off an –*ing* word group from the sentence that contains the word it modifies. WRONG: **Pedro burst into the house. Waving his report card proudly.** The sentence fragment is the (*first, second*) word group. 1569
(his) mother 1755	Punctuate this compound sentence: **The air was cold but the water was warm.** 1756
pupil's 1942	**The two *mens* fingerprints were compared.** 1943
Madison Avenue, Sunset Drive 2129	Here is another rule for using capital letters: Capitalize nouns and adjectives that apply to *particular* nationalities, languages, races, and religious groups. **Canadian French Black Catholic** Which word is the name of both a nationality and a language? _____ 2130

b 67	**Herb laughed.** **Herb shouted.** **Herb stumbled.** In all these sentences, do the verbs show action that you might plainly see? *(Yes, No)* 68
Yes 255	a. **My aunt lives in the** *white* **house.** b. **Sarah Caldwell conducted** *several* **pieces.** c. **Harriet Tubman showed** *great* **courage.** Can the italicized adjectives be moved to other positions in these sentences? *(Yes, No)* 256
or 443	**We listened but heard nothing.** This sentence has two *(subjects, verbs)*. 444
threw, fallen 631	**The car could be** _____ *(drive)* **even though the** **windshield was** _____ *(break)*. 632
The carrots, They 819	**.?. *don't* fit well.** Underline two items that could be used correctly as the subject of the above sentence: **The coat The sleeves My shoes The collar** 820
look, feel 1007	**These melons are ripe.** Underline two more verbs that could be used in place of the linking verb **are**: **plant taste find smell** 1008

she 1195	**Although Cliff has collected stamps for only a short time, he already has more stamps than** (*I, me*). (Are you thinking of the missing words?) 1196
whom 1382	**I have a cousin** *who* *visits* **my sister.** In the adjective clause, we use the subject form *who* because it is the subject of the verb _____. 1383
second 1569	Here is the *–ing* word group by itself: FRAGMENT: *Waving his report card proudly.* Does this *–ing* word group have both a subject and a verb? (*Yes, No*) 1570
cold, but 1756	Punctuate this compound sentence: **You must hire a guide or you might lose your way.** 1757
men's 1943	**Judy Blume writes** *childrens* **books.** 1944
French 2130	**Cuban Black Baptist** Which word is the name of a particular race? _____ 2131

Yes
 	
68
	There are other actions that are not so easy to see because they occur within a person's mind.
	
	    a. **Herb jumped.**
	    b. **Herb thought.**
	
	In which sentence does the verb express an action of the mind? ____
	
	69

No 256	An adjective usually cannot be moved from its position before the noun it modifies. Now look at an adverb: **Don visits me** *frequently*. The word *frequently* is an adverb because it modifies the verb _____. 257
verbs 444	**We listened but heard nothing.** The two verbs, **listened** and **heard**, are connected by the word _____. 445
driven, broken 632	**Some of us** _____ (*know*) **that the poem had been** _____ (*write*) **by Phillis Wheatley.** 633
The sleeves, My shoes 820	When you use **doesn't** or **don't** to ask a question, look ahead to see whether the subject is singular or plural. If the subject is singular, use (*doesn't, don't*). 821
taste, smell 1008	**These melons (look, feel, taste, or smell) ripe.** Whichever one of these verbs you used would connect the adjective **ripe** with the subject _____. 1009

I 1196	Bobby is jealous because he thinks his parents like the baby more than (*he, him*). 1197
visits 1383	Now we shall change the meaning of our clause: **I have a cousin** *whom my sister visits.* In the adjective clause, the subject of the verb *visits* is not *whom*, but _____. 1384
No 1570	FRAGMENT: *Waving his report card proudly.* Does this *–ing* word group make sense by itself? (*Yes, No*) 1571
guide, or 1757	A sentence is not compound unless there are a subject and a verb both *before* and *after* the conjunction. Look carefully at this sentence: **We talked to Coretta King** *and* **asked many questions.** After the conjunction *and,* do you find both a subject and a verb? (*Yes, No*) 1758
children's 1944	In each of the remaining frames, there are two italicized words that require apostrophes. **My** *mothers* **job was to collect all the** *members* **dues.** 1945
Black 2131	**Polish Indian Jewish** Which adjective applies to a particular religious group? _____ 2132

b	Underline two verbs that express actions of the mind: **played agreed wondered pitched**
69	70
visits	a. **Don visits me** *frequently*. b. **Don** *frequently* **visits me.** c. *Frequently* **Don visits me.** Is an adverb always next to the verb it modifies? (*Yes, No*)
257	258
but	Words used to connect words or groups of words are called **conjunctions.** The most common conjunctions are **and, but,** and **or.** We use conjunctions to _____ words or groups of words.
445	446
knew, written	Ms. Daly had _____ (*speak*) to me about the test I had _____ (*take*) on Monday.
633	634
doesn't	a. ...that cake look good? b. ...those cookies look good? In which sentence would it be a mistake to use the plural verb **Don't?** ____
821	822
melons	Every linking verb is followed by a word that refers back to the subject. Early in this book, we learned that this word is called a **subject complement.** **These melons are ripe.** The subject complement **ripe** describes the _____.
1009	1010

him 1197	Canada has as high a standard of living as (*we, us*). 1198
sister 1384	*whom my <u>sister</u> <u>visits</u>* Now let's straighten out this clause, remembering that *whom* stands for *cousin*. *my <u>sister</u> <u>visits</u> whom* The clause signal *whom* is the direct _____ of the verb *visits*. 1385
No 1571	a. Knowing nothing about the party. I walked into the room. b. Knowing nothing about the party, I walked into the room. Which arrangement is correct? ____ 1572
No 1758	<u>We</u> <u>talked</u> to Coretta King *and* <u>asked</u> many questions. After the conjunction *and*, we do not find both a subject and a verb. We find only a (*subject, verb*). 1759
mother's, members' 1945	Two other *boys* scores were higher than *Carls* score. 1946
Jewish 2132	Copy and add capital letters to the three words which should be capitalized: Early spanish explorers learned much about farming from the indians. 2133

agreed, wondered	Underline two verbs that express actions of the mind: **hoped pushed feared returned**
70	71

No	You will often find an adverb several words away from the verb it modifies. *Recently* **one of my friends** *moved.* How many words come between the adverb and the verb it modifies? _____
258	259

connect (*or* join)	You will have no trouble spelling the first and last syllable of the word *con-junc-tion.* Fill in the middle syllable: *con*_____*tion.*
446	447

spoken, taken	Lesson **21** Verbs of the *Ring–Rang–Rung* Pattern
634	[Frames 636-661]

a	Underline the correct verb: (*Doesn't, Don't*) **that window open?**
822	823

melons	These melons look ripe. These melons taste ripe. These melons feel ripe. These melons smell ripe. In each of these sentences, too, the subject complement **ripe** describes the subject _____.
1010	1011

We are not at home as much as (*they, them*).

1199

---

object

1385

It is very easy to decide whether to use *who* or *whom* as an adjective clause signal.

<u>who</u> <u>visits</u> *my sister*

If the verb has no other possible subject, use ＿＿＿＿＿.

1386

---

b

1572

When appositives are cut off from the words they explain, they, too, become fragments.
WRONG: **We spoke to Ann Fry.** *The owner of the lot.*
The appositive word group *The owner of the lot* belongs

in the same sentence with the name ＿＿＿＿＿＿＿＿＿＿, which it explains.

1573

---

verb

1759

We talked to Coretta King *and* **asked many questions.**

Is this sentence compound? (*Yes, No*)

1760

---

boys', Carl's

1946

My youngest *sisters* **hobby is collecting movie** *actors* **pictures.**

1947

Spanish, Indians

2133

Copy and add capital letters to the three words which should be capitalized:

Many american and european composers have been influenced by black music.

2134

<table>
<tr>
<td>hoped, feared

71</td>
<td>A verb that expresses action of any kind—whether you can see it or not—is called an **action verb.**

slipped   dreamed   escaped   understood

Are all these verbs *action verbs? (Yes, No)*

72</td>
</tr>
<tr>
<td>four

259</td>
<td>In this and the following frames, you will find one or more words separating the adverb from the verb it modifies.

Circle the verb and underline the adverb that modifies it:

Suddenly the chair collapsed.

260</td>
</tr>
<tr>
<td>junc

447</td>
<td>Underline two conjunctions in this sentence:

Any boy or girl will understand and enjoy this story.

448</td>
</tr>
<tr>
<td></td>
<td>All five verbs in this lesson follow the same pattern:

PRESENT: **r<u>i</u>ng   s<u>i</u>ng   sw<u>i</u>m   dr<u>i</u>nk   beg<u>i</u>n**
SIMPLE PAST: **r<u>a</u>ng   s<u>a</u>ng   sw<u>a</u>m   dr<u>a</u>nk   beg<u>a</u>n**

When we change these verbs from present to simple past,

the *i* in each verb changes to ____.

636</td>
</tr>
<tr>
<td>Doesn't

823</td>
<td> WAS AND WERE Here are two sentences that show *present* time:

    SINGULAR: **The car stops.**
    PLURAL: **The cars stop.**

When we change the subject from singular to plural, do we need to change the verb? (*Yes, No*)

824</td>
</tr>
<tr>
<td>melons

1011</td>
<td>**These melons look ripe.**   **These melons taste ripe.**
These melons feel ripe.   **These melons smell ripe.**

The subject **melons** is a noun. Therefore, the subject complement **ripe,** which describes it, must be an (*adverb, adjective*).

1012</td>
</tr>
</table>

they	**Although Gerald worked a shorter time, Mrs. Diaz paid him just as much as** (*I, me*).
1199	1200

who	*whom my sister visits* If the verb has another word as its subject, use _____.
1386	1387

Ann Fry	Here is the appositive phrase by itself: FRAGMENT: *The owner of the lot.* Does this word group have both a subject and a verb, or does it express a complete thought? (*Yes, No*)
1573	1574

No	**We talked to Coretta King** *and* **asked many questions.** This sentence is not compound. The *and* does not connect two sentences, each with its own subject and verb. The conjunction *and* connects the two verbs **talked** and _____.
1760	1761

sister's, actors'	**All the** *childrens* **parents met in the** *schools* **auditorium.**
1947	1948

American, European, Black	In this and the following frames, copy only the words in which the small letters should be changed to capitals. Add the necessary capitals. (The number after each sentence tells how many words need to be capitalized.) **The catholic church on dorset avenue has many chinese** **members. (4)** _____
2134	2135

Yes 72	To identify the subject and verb of a sentence, we shall underline the subject with one line and the verb with two lines. Underline the subject and verb in this sentence: **Parrots talk.** 73
suddenly (collapsed) 260	Circle the verb and underline the adverb that modifies it: **I shook the rug vigorously.** 261
or, and 448	Underline two conjunctions in this sentence: **The sandwiches and desserts are cheap but good.** 449
a 636	Underline three verbs that show past time: **ring sang swam drink began** 637

Yes
 	
824
	Now we shall change these same sentences to show *past* time:
	
	      SINGULAR: **The car stopped.**
	      PLURAL: **The cars stopped.**
	
	When we change the subject from singular to plural, do we still need to change the verb? (*Yes, No*)
	
	825

adjective 1012	**These melons are ripe.** We have seen that the verbs **look, feel, taste,** and **smell** could be used as linking verbs in the above sentence. In different sentences, could these same verbs be used to show actions of our eyes, hands, noses, and mouths? (*Yes, No*) 1013

me 1200	Lesson **41** **Four Pronoun Problems** |Frames 1202-1232|

whom 1387	(*who, whom*) <u>wrote this story</u> Because the verb *wrote* has no other subject, we choose _____. 1388

No 1574	a. **We spoke to Ann Fry. She owns the lot.** b. **We spoke to Ann Fry. The owner of the lot.** Which arrangment is wrong because it contains a sentence fragment? ____ 1575

asked 1761	**We talked to Coretta King, *and* we asked many questions.** **We talked to Coretta King *and* asked many questions.** Only one of these sentences requires a comma. A comma is used only when the conjunction connects two (*sentences, verbs*). 1762

children's, school's 1948	Lesson **68** **Apostrophes for Missing Letters** |Frames 1950-1974|

Catholic, Dorset Avenue, Chinese 2135	**The map shows you that minnesota extends farther north than maine or any other state. (2)** _____ 2136

<u>Parrots</u> <u>talk</u> 73	Most sentences contain more than just two words. But no matter how long a sentence may be, it always contains a *subject* and a _____. 74
(shook) <u>vigorously</u> 261	Circle the verb and underline the adverb that modifies it: **Ella gives concerts everywhere.** 262
and, but 449	The word *compound* means "having two or more parts." **<u>Wendy</u> and <u>Stan</u> <u>washed</u> the dishes.** When the same verb has two or more subjects, we say that the subject is *com*_____. 450

sang, swam, began
 	
637
	SIMPLE PAST: r<u>a</u>ng s<u>a</u>ng sw<u>a</u>m dr<u>a</u>nk beg<u>a</u>n
	PAST WITH HELPER:
	        (have) r<u>u</u>ng (have) s<u>u</u>ng (have) sw<u>u</u>m
	        (have) dr<u>u</u>nk (have) beg<u>u</u>n
	Do we use the same form of these verbs for the simple past and for the past with helper? (*Yes, No*)
	
	638

No 825	We needed to change the verb to make it agree with its subject only when it showed (*present, past*) time. 826
Yes 1013	**look feel taste smell** Each of these verbs, then, can be used as either an *action* verb or a _____ *ing* verb. 1014

DUPLICATING THE SUBJECT

A pronoun is used *in place of* a noun.

    a. **Nadia won a gold medal.**
    b. **She won a gold medal.**

In which sentence is the subject a pronoun? ___

1202

---

who

1388

(*who, whom*) *the* <u>police</u> <u>arrested</u>

Because the verb *arrested* already has a subject, we choose _____.

1389

---

b

1575

In this and the following frames, you will find two separate word groups. If both word groups are separate sentences, write *Correct* on the blank line.

EXAMPLE: **We fished all morning. We didn't catch a single fish.**

_____ *Correct* _____ (*Turn to the next frame.*)

1576

---

sentences

1762

a. **The** <u>batter</u> <u>swung</u> **at the ball three times** *but* **he never even** <u>came</u> **close to it.**
b. **The** <u>batter</u> <u>swung</u> **at the ball three times** *but* **never even** <u>came</u> **close to it.**

In which sentence should you put a comma before the conjunction *but*? ___

1763

In addition to showing ownership, the apostrophe is used to show where letters have been omitted from words.

    a. **The** *boys'* **mothers are invited.**
    b. **This window** *doesn't* **open.**

The apostrophe does not show ownership in sentence ___.

1950

Minnesota,
Maine

2136

Moslems, jews, and christians all consider jerusalem a holy city. (3)

_____

2137

verb 74	All the words with which we build up a sentence are attached to either the subject or the verb. *A handsome, tall* <u>**boy**</u> <u>**spoke**</u>. In this sentence, the added italicized words go with the (*subject, verb*). 75
(gives) <u>everywhere</u> 262	Circle the verb and underline the adverb that modifies it: **Often he skipped his breakfast.** 263
compound 450	When the same subject has two or more verbs, we say that the verb is *compound*. a. **Our dog ran away but returned.** b. **Our dog and cat ran away.** Which sentence contains a compound verb? ____ 451

No
 	
 638
	SIMPLE PAST: <u>r**a**ng</u> s**a**ng sw**a**m dr**a**nk beg**a**n
	PAST WITH HELPER:
	         (have) r<u>u</u>ng (have) s<u>u</u>ng (have) sw<u>u</u>m
	         (have) dr<u>u</u>nk (have) beg<u>u</u>n
	
	When we change these verbs from simple past to past with helper, the *a* in each verb changes to ____. 639

present 826	Generally, there is no problem of subject-verb agreement when we use *simple past* verbs. The only exception is the simple past of the verb **be**—*was* and *were*. a. **The <u>story</u> <u>was</u> interesting.** b. **The <u>stories</u> <u>were</u> interesting.** The verb **was** is singular; the verb _____ is plural. 827
linking 1014	**look feel taste smell hear** Suppose that you use one of these verbs as an action verb. To tell *how* the action was performed, you would use an (*adjective, adverb*). 1015

b 1202	WRONG: **Nadia** *she* **won a gold medal.** The noun **Nadia** makes it clear whom the sentence is about. Does the pronoun *she* serve any useful purpose? (*Yes, No*) 1203
whom 1389	Underline the correct clause signal: (*who, whom*) <u>guard</u> the President 1390
  1576	If one word group is a fragment, connect the two word groups by writing the last word of the first word group and the first word of the second word group with a small letter. EXAMPLE: **We fished all morning. Without catching a single fish.** <u>*morning without*</u> (*Turn to the next frame.*) 1577
a 1763	a. **Eleanor can design the costumes** *or* **work with the stage crew.** b. **Eleanor can design the costumes** *or* **she can work with the stage crew.** In which sentence should you put a comma before the conjunction *or*? ____ 1764
b 1950	As a shortcut, we often omit one or more letters from certain words. Then we attach the shortened word to another word, thus making a two-in-one word. **does not** *becomes* **doesn't** In **doesn't,** the apostrophe takes the place of the missing letter ____. 1951
Jews, Christians, Jerusalem 2137	**The Sahara desert extends from the Atlantic ocean to the Red sea. (3)** _____ 2138

subject 75	**Lana spoke** *enthusiastically about her work.* In this sentence, the added italicized words go with the (*subject, verb*). 76
<u>often</u> (skipped) 263	Circle the verb and underline the adverb that modifies it: **Leroy carried the baby clumsily.** 264

a
 	
451
	Any basic part of a sentence can be compound: the subject, verb, direct object, or subject complement.
	
	    a. **I washed my hands.**
	    b. **I washed my hands and face.**
	
	Which sentence contains a compound direct object? ____
	
	452

u 639	a. **rang sang swam drank began** b. **rung sung swum drunk begun** Which words would you use after forms of the helping verbs **have** and **be**? ____ 640
were 827	We say, "I *was* invited," but we say, "We _____ invited." 828
adverb 1015	**look feel taste smell sound** Now suppose that you use one of these verbs as a linking verb. The subject complement that follows it and describes the subject would need to be an (*adjective, adverb*). 1016

No 1203	Don't duplicate the subject by using both a noun and a pronoun to refer to the same person or thing. Use either the noun or the pronoun—not both. **a. Chuck he struck out.** **b. Chuck struck out.** Which one is wrong because it duplicates the subject? ____ 1204
who 1390	Underline the correct clause signal: *(who, whom) the President appointed* 1391
1577	Now continue for yourself: **The headlights were too bright. They blinded the other driver.** _____ 1578
b 1764	**Nancy Lopez sank the putt, and** *she* **won the tournament.** If you dropped the word *she,* would you still keep the comma? *(Yes, No)* 1765
o 1951	*To contract* means "to get shorter." It is the opposite of the verb *to expand.* For this reason, we call these shortened words **contractions.** **a. we're** **b. we are** Which example is a *contraction?* ____ 1952
Desert, Ocean, Sea 2138	**Words in the english language are more difficult to spell than words in spanish or most other languages. (2)** _____ 2139

verb 76	**Jimmy looked** *enviously at my strawberry shortcake.* In this sentence, the added italicized words go with the (*subject, verb*). 77˙
(carried) clumsily 264	Now we shall do something else: **The fire engines arrived .⸮. . (How?)** Underline the adverb that you could add to answer the question in parentheses: **here later fast soon** 265
b 452	a. **At first the dog was nervous.** b. **At first the dog was nervous and timid.** Which sentence contains a compound subject complement? ___ 453
b 640	**ring sing swim drink begin** Whenever you use one of these words after any form of **have (has, had)** or **be (is, am, are—was, were, been).** you should change the *i* to (*a, u*). 641
were 828	We say, "The egg *was* fresh," but we say, "The eggs _____ fresh." 829
adjective 1016	a. **The cloth** *felt* **rough.** b. **John** *felt* **the cloth roughly.** In one sentence, *felt* is an action verb; in the other, *felt* is a linking verb. In which one does *felt* mean an action of the hands? ___ 1017

a 1204	**This dog it wouldn't bite anybody.** Since **This dog** is the subject of the sentence, the pronoun _____ should be omitted. 1205
whom 1391	*whom the <u>President</u> <u>appointed</u>* We use the object form *whom* because the verb *appointed* already has a subject. The subject of the verb *appointed* is _____. 1392
Correct 1578	**Hannah bought all the parts. And built the set herself.** _____ 1579
No 1765	a. **I set the alarm, but forgot to wind the clock.** b. **I set the alarm, but I forgot to wind the clock.** In which sentence is the comma used correctly? ____ 1766
a 1952	In a *contraction,* the apostrophe shows where one or more letters have been omitted. **we're** *means* **we are** In the contraction **we're**, the apostrophe takes the place of the missing letter ____. 1953
English, Spanish 2139	**A man with an irish terrier walks through woodside park every afternoon. (3)** _____ 2140

verb 77	*The thin paper* **bag tore.** In this sentence, the added italicized words go with the (*subject, verb*). 78
fast 265	**Tina waited . ? . for her friends. (Where?)** Underline the adverb that would answer the question in parentheses: **eagerly often impatiently there** 266

b
 	
453
	Besides connecting words, the conjunctions **and, but,** and **or** can also connect two sentences into a single sentence.
	
	    a. **My friend came over, and we worked on math.**
	    b. **My friend came over and helped me with math.**
	
	The conjunction **and** connects two sentences in _____.
	
	454

u 641	a. **The tardy bell** *has rang.* b. **The tardy bell** *has rung.* Which sentence is correct? _____ 642
were 829	**Vicky was late.** If we changed the subject to **Vicky and her sister,** we would change the singular verb **was** to the plural verb _____. 830
b 1017	**John** *felt* **the cloth roughly.** In this sentence, the verb *felt* means an action of the hands. To describe this action, we use the (*adjective, adverb*) **roughly.** 1018

it 1205	## ORDER OF COURTESY A courteous person serves others first and allows others to pass through a door ahead of him. It is also good manners to mention others first and yourself last. **a. I and Carl stayed home.** **b. Carl and I stayed home.** Which sentence shows better manners? ____ 1206
President 1392	Underline the correct clause signal: *(who, whom) invented the electric light* 1393
parts and 1579	**After Doris painted the chair. It looked as good as new.** _____ 1580
b 1766	**a. The plane ran out of gas, and landed on a golf course.** **b. The plane ran out of gas, and it landed on a golf course.** From which sentence should the comma be dropped? ____ 1767
a 1953	**we'll** *means* **we will** In the contraction **we'll**, the apostrophe takes the place of the two missing letters _____. 1954
Irish, Woodside Park 2140	**There is a lutheran college on hickory lake in Milford county. (4)** _____ *page 156* 2141

subject 78	Underline the action verb with two lines: **Frank <u>left</u> in a great hurry.** 79
there 266	**I mow the lawn .?. . (When?)** Underline the adverb that would answer the question in parentheses: **hastily willingly early usually** 267
a 454	a. **We <u>looked</u> for Diana, but Diana <u>had gone</u> home.** b. **We <u>looked</u> for Diana but <u>could</u> not <u>find</u> her.** In which sentence does the conjunction **but** connect two sentences? _____ 455
b 642	a. **We** *had* **just** *sang* **our school song.** b. **We** *had* **just** *sung* **our school song.** Which sentence is correct? _____ 643
were 830	a. **A few sandwiches . . . left over.** b. **One sandwich . . . left over.** In which sentence would **were** be correct? _____ 831
adverb 1018	**The cloth** *felt* **rough.** In this sentence, *felt* is a linking verb. It connects the adjective **rough** with the subject _____. 1019

b

1206

a. **Chris played against me and her.**
b. **Chris played against her and me.**

Which sentence shows better manners? ____

1207

---

who

1393

Underline the correct clause signal:

(*who, whom*) *the voters trust*

1394

---

chair, it

1580

Anita sprained her wrist. The coach put Kim into the game.

_____

1581

---

a

1767

The comma may be omitted when a compound sentence is short.

a. **We visit them, and they visit us.**
b. **We visit them during the Christmas holiday, and they visit us every summer.**

From which sentence might you omit the comma? ____

1768

---

wi

1954

I'd *means* **I would**

In the contraction I'd, the apostrophe takes the place of the four missing letters _____.

1955

Lutheran,
Hickory Lake,
County

2141

The Suez canal shortens the distance between the United states and the Indian ocean by more than 6,000 miles. (3)

_____

2142

left

Underline the subject with one line:

The shaky old chair finally collapsed.

79

Jose .?. postponed his visit to the dentist. (How often?)

early

Underline the adverb that would answer the question in parentheses:

sometimes   foolishly   finally   recently

267

---

a

a. **You can go alone or come with us.**

b. **You can go alone, or we can pick you up.**

In which sentence does the conjunction or connect two sentences? _____

455

---

b

We *swam* **in that lake many times.**

If you added the helper *have* to the verb, you would need to change *swam* to _____.

643

---

a

In English, the pronoun **you** always requires a plural verb. Always say, "You *were* ..." even though you are speaking to one person.

You *were* **in your room.**

Would this sentence be correct if you were speaking to only one person? (*Yes, No*)

831

---

cloth

In this and the following frames, underline the correct modifier. If the verb shows action, choose the adverb. Otherwise, choose the adjective.

The cashier looked (*suspicious, suspiciously*) **at the check.**

1019

b 1207	a. **Miss Chu's class and we are putting on a play.** b. **We and Miss Chu's class are putting on a play.** Which sentence shows better manners? ____ 1208
whom 1394	In this and the following frames, write *who* or *whom,* depending on whether or not the clause signal is the subject of the clause. **The president** _____ *ran the meeting* **was capable.** 1395
Correct 1581	**I spent an hour in the library. Looking up material about Chief Joseph.** _____ 1582
a 1768	In this and the following frames, add a comma wherever the conjunction **and, but,** or **or** connects the two parts of a compound sentence. If the sentence is not compound, make no change. **The equipment was expensive and we lacked the money to buy it.** 1769

woul
 	
1955
	Do you know how to spell all the following contractions?
	
	  it's (it i̶s) **you've (you h̶a̶ve)** **we'd (we w̶o̶u̶ld)**
	  let's (let u̶s) **they're (they a̶re)** **there's (there i̶s)**
	
	In which contraction does the apostrophe take the place of the largest number of letters? _____
	
	1956

Canal, States, Ocean 2142	Lesson **75** **Capitals for Organizations and Institutions**

|Frames 2144-2172|

chair 80	Underline the subject with one line and the verb with two lines: **The blue lake sparkled in the sun.** 81
sometimes 268	**They moved the furniture .?. . (How much?)** Underline the adverb that would answer the question in parentheses: **today slightly back carelessly** 269
b 456	A sentence made by connecting two or more simple sentences with the conjunction **and, but, or or** is a **compound sentence.** A sentence is not compound unless it has a subject and a verb both *before* and *after* the conjunction. **The <u>crowd</u> <u>stood</u> patiently *and* <u>waited</u> in the rain.** Is this sentence compound? (*Yes, No*) 457
swum 644	**Wendy *drank* all her milk.** If you added the helper *has* to the verb, you would need to change *drank* to _____. 645
Yes 832	Underline the correct verb: **You (*was, were*) the one who wanted to go.** 833
suspiciously 1020	**The check looked (*suspicious, suspiciously*) to the cashier.** 1021

a	## "WE BOYS" AND "US GIRLS" Some people do not know whether to use **we** or **us** in expressions like "we boys" and "us girls." (*We, Us*) **boys can paint the fence.** If you omitted the noun **boys,** which pronoun would you use? _____
1208	1209

who	**The president** _____ *we elect* **should be capable.**
1395	1396

library, looking	**Uncle Ted served venison stew. Which my dad doesn't like.** _____
1582	1583

expensive, and	**Diane dived off the raft and swam to the boat.**
1769	1770

we'd	The contraction of **it is** is _____. The contraction of **you have** is _____.
1956	1957

Capitalize the complete names of particular companies, stores, buildings, hotels, theaters, and so forth.

Ohio Oil Company   **Chrysler Building**   **Wayside Hotel**
Turner Garage   **Melody Record Shop**   **Capitol Theater**

Are words such as **company, building, hotel,** and **theater** capitalized when they are parts of names? (*Yes, No*)

2144

<u>lake</u> <u>sparkled</u>	A sentence is built around a _____ and a
	_____.
81	82

	You can often turn an adjective into an adverb by adding **–ly** to it.
slightly	**proud—proudly polite—politely** **timid—timidly serious—seriously**
	The adverb is the (*first, second*) word in each pair.
269	270

	a. **The <u>boys</u> <u>pushed</u> hard and <u>moved</u> the rock.**
No	b. **The <u>boys</u> <u>pushed</u> hard, and the <u>rock</u> <u>moved</u>.**
	Which sentence is compound? _____
457	458

	The game *began* to get very exciting.
drunk	If you added the helper *had* to the verb, you would need
	to change *began* to _____.
645	646

	When you use **was** or **were** to ask a question, look ahead to see whether the subject is singular or plural.
were	a. ...your dad at home? b. ...your parents at home?
	In which sentence would it be a mistake to use the singu-
	lar verb **Was?** _____
833	834

	The house smelled (*musty, mustily*) until we opened the
suspicious	**window.**
1021	1022

We 1209	**Our neighbor drove** (*we, us*) **girls to school.** If you omitted the noun **girls**, which pronoun would you use? _____ 1210
whom 1396	**Daniel K. Inouye is a man** _____ *everyone respects.* 1397
stew, which 1583	**Basketball takes brains. You have to make quick decisions.** _____ 1584
No comma 1770	**The mountain looks very close but it is over twenty miles away.** 1771
it's you've 1957	The contraction of **let us** is _____. The contraction of **there is** is _____. 1958
Yes 2144	a. **Terry works for the Beacon drug company.** b. **Terry works for the Beacon Drug Company.** Which sentence is correct? ____ 2145

subject, verb 82	The verb says something about the _____ of the sentence. 83
second 270	The adverb form of the adjective *clever* is _____. 271
b 458	**We waved and shouted at the passing ship.** Are there both a subject and a verb after the conjunction **and?** (*Yes, No*) 459
begun 646	**I had** *drunk* **too much ice water.** If you dropped the helper *had,* you would need to change the verb *drunk* to _____. 647
b 834	Underline the correct verb: (*Was, Were*) **your keys in that drawer?** 835
musty 1022	**Mother felt** (*unhappy, unhappily*) **about the scratch on the new car.** 1023

us 1210	When you use expressions like "we boys" or "us girls," use the same pronoun you would use if the word *boys* or *girls* were omitted. Underline the correct pronoun: **Only two of** (*we, us*) ~~boys~~ **got a chance to play.** 1211
whom 1397	**Daniel K. Inouye is a man** _____ *tries to help others.* 1398
Correct 1584	**Lois was walking with her dog. A black cocker spaniel.** _____ 1585
close, but 1771	**You should visit Marjorie or send her a "get well" card.** 1772
let's there's 1958	**The contraction of they are** is _____. **The contraction of we would** is _____. 1959
b 2145	a. **Elvira's office is in the Citizens' Bank Building.** b. **Elvira's office is in the Citizens' bank building.** Which sentence is correct? ____ 2146

subject 83	Most verbs are action words. Verbs like *write, speak, bring,* and *carry* indicate actions of the (*mind, body*). 84
cleverly 271	The adverb form of the adjective *slight* is _____. 272
No 459	**We waved and shouted at the passing ship.** Is this a compound sentence? (*Yes, No*) 460
drank 647	**Our pitcher** *had begun* **to lose control.** If you dropped the helper *had,* you would need to change the verb *begun* to _____. 648
Were 835	In this and the following frames, underline the verb that agrees with its subject: **Our seats (*were, was*) close together.** 836
unhappy 1023	**This chocolate pie tastes (*delicious, deliciously*).** 1024

us 1211	Underline the correct pronoun: (*We*, *Us*) ~~girls~~ can meet at our house. 1212
who 1398	This story was written by an author _____ *understands* children. 1399
dog, a 1585	The party was a success. Everyone had a good time. _____ 1586
No comma 1772	You must get up early or you will miss the sunrise. 1773
they're we'd 1959	Very many contractions are made by shortening the adverb *not* to *n't*. isn't doesn't aren't haven't In each of these contractions, the apostrophe takes the place of the missing letter ____. 1960
a 2146	The ʌ theater will open next week. If you inserted the name **Rosedale** before the noun **theater**, would you capitalize the noun **theater**? (*Yes*, *No*) 2147

body 84	Verbs like *decide*, *worry*, *want*, and *expect* indicate actions of the (*mind*, *body*). 85
slightly 272	Underline the adverb: **A foolish person talks foolishly.** 273

No
 	
460
	If a sentence is compound, you can break it into two separate sentences, each with a subject and a verb.
	
	    a. **My eyes were closed, but I wasn't sleeping.**
	    b. **I closed my eyes and pretended to be asleep.**
	
	Which sentence is compound? ____
	
	461

began
 	
648
	Remember that after all forms of **be (is, am, are—was, were, been),** you must also use the helper form.
	
	    a. **The tardy bell** *was rang* **too early.**
	    b. **The tardy bell** *was rung* **too early.**
	
	Which sentence is correct? ____
	
	649

were 836	**Linda** (*don't*, *doesn't*) **waste her money.** 837
delicious 1024	**We could smell gas very** (*distinct*, *distinctly*) **in the kitchen.** 1025

We 1212	Underline the correct pronoun: **Some of** (*we, us*) **students read Leslie Silko's story.** 1213
who 1399	**Don't accept a ride from anyone** _____ *you don't know.* 1400
Correct 1586	**Our dog Jiggs feels hurt. When we don't pay attention to him.** _____ 1587
early, or 1773	**A dachshund's body is long and its legs are very short.** 1774

o
 	
 1960
	People sometimes forget that the apostrophe takes the place of the missing o in such words as **isn't** and **doesn't**. As a result, they put the apostrophe in the wrong place.
	
	     a. wasn't aren't hasn't doesn't
	     b. was'nt are'nt has'nt does'nt
	 In which group are the contractions spelled correctly? ___
	
	 1961

Yes 2147	**The Dorset Hotel is very modern.** If you dropped the name **Dorset,** would you still write **Hotel** with a capital letter? (*Yes, No*) 2148

Lesson 4 Spotting the Verb and Its Subject

[Frames 87-113]

---

foolishly

273

a. **What kind?   Which one(s)?   How many?**
b. **When?   Where?   How?   How often?**

Adverbs would answer the questions in group (*a*, *b*).

274

---

a

461

Put a comma before the conjunction **and, but,** or **or** that connects the two parts of a compound sentence.

a. **I looked in my drawer and found my wallet.**
b. **I looked in my drawer and my wallet was there.**

Which sentence is compound and therefore requires a comma before **and?** ____

462

---

b

649

a. **The songs** *were sang* **without accompaniment.**
b. **The songs** *were sung* **without accompaniment.**

Which sentence is correct? ____

650

---

doesn't

837

We (*were, was*) **just about to eat dinner.**

838

---

distinctly

1025

The color looks (*different, differently*) **in the daylight.**

1026

us	(*Us, We*) eighth-graders will serve as ushers.
1213	1214

whom	When the clause signal is the subject of the clause, always choose (*who, whom*).
1400	1401

hurt when	**Suddenly Sandy rushed to the kitchen. Remembering the cake in the oven.** _____
1587	1588

long, and	**We tried every brand of dog food but Pepper wouldn't eat any of them.**
1774	1775

a	In all the **n't** words, remember to put the apostrophe in place of the missing **o**. The contraction of **are not** is _____. The contraction of **did not** is _____.
1961	1962

No	Capitalize the complete names of particular schools, colleges, churches, hospitals, libraries, and so forth. **King High School** **Bethel Church** **Franklin Library** **Albion College** **Dover Art Club** **Fremont Hospital** Are words such as **school, church, library,** and **hospital** capitalized when they are parts of names? (*Yes, No*)
2148	2149

Verbs generally show by their spelling whether they mean *present* or *past* time.

> a. We *live* in Texas.
> b. We *lived* in Texas.

In which sentence does the verb show *present* time? _____

87

---

b

274

> a. always, never, recently, forever
> b. here, there, away, aside, everywhere
> c. steadily, happily, successfully, cheerfully

All the above words can be used as adverbs. In which group would the words answer the question *How?* _____

275

---

b

462

a. You can bring your own lunch, or buy it in the cafeteria.
b. I must get enough sleep, or I feel tired the next day.

One of these sentences is not compound. A comma, therefore, should not be used.

The comma should be omitted in sentence _____.

463

---

b

650

Write the missing forms of these verbs:

PRESENT	SIMPLE PAST	PAST WITH HELPER
drink	drank	(have) _____
begin	began	(have) _____
swim	swam	(have) _____

651

---

were

838

This cover (*doesn't, don't*) fit the jar.

839

---

different

1026

His plan sounded rather (*dishonest, dishonestly*) to me.

1027

We	Most of (*us, we*) boys attend every game.
1214	1215

[Frames 1403-1421]

who	Lesson **48** Using *Who, Which,* and *That* Correctly
1401	[Frames 1403-1421]

kitchen, remembering	Lesson **55** Sentences That Forget to Stop
1588	[Frames 1590-1617]

food, but	Many people must work at night and sleep during the day.
1775	1776

aren't didn't	**can't** *means* **cannot**
	In the contraction **can't,** the apostrophe takes the place of two missing letters: ____ and ____.
1962	1963

Yes	a. **I attend the Preston Junior High School.**
	b. **I attend the Preston junior high school.**
	Which sentence is correct? ____
2149	2150

a	a. We *take* several magazines. b. We *took* several magazines. In which sentences does the verb show *past* time? ____
87	88

c	Do you always find an adverb next to the word it modifies? (*Yes, No*)
275	276

a	The teacher paused at my desk, and *she* looked at my composition. If you omitted the subject *she* in the second part of the sentence, would the sentence still be compound? (*Yes, No*)
463	464

drunk begun swum	Write the correct past form of **ring:** The fire alarm had been _____ by mistake.
651	652

doesn't	My dad and my mother (*was, were*) in the living room.
839	840

dishonest	You can taste the lemon very (*definite, definitely*) in this cake.
1027	1028

THEM OR THOSE?

Never use the pronoun **them** to point something out. The proper word for pointing out is **those**.

> a. *Them* **are my books.**
> b. *Those* **are my books.**

Which sentence is correct? ____

1216

CLAUSE SIGNALS: **who (whom, whose), which, that**

Use **who** and **whom** to refer to persons.
Use **which** to refer to things and animals.

Underline the correct clause signal:

The chef (*who, which*) **prepared our lunch was Señor Gomez.**

1403

A person who writes a sentence fragment mistakes a piece of a sentence for a complete sentence.

> a. **Knowing several people in this town.**
> b. **I knew several people in this town.**

Which is a sentence fragment? ____

1590

No comma

1776

A package must be properly wrapped or the post office will not accept it.

1777

---

n, o

1963

One **n't** contraction is different from all the others:
won't (wi̶l̶l̶ n̶o̶t)

There is the usual apostrophe to take the place of the missing **o** in **not**.

However, the letters **ill** in **will** disappear completely, and after the **w** we find the letter ____.

1964

---

a

2150

> a. **My brother just graduated from high school.**
> b. **My brother just graduated from Kirk high school.**

In which sentence should the words **high school** be capitalized because they are part of the name of a particular school? ____

2151

b 88	When you change a sentence from present time to past time, or from past time to present time, the verb generally changes its spelling. PRESENT: **My friend usually** *rides* **to school.** If you changed this sentence to *past* time, you would need to change the verb *rides* to _____. 89
No 276	Many adverbs, especially those that tell *how*, end with the letters (*–tion, –ly, –ing*). 277
No 464	**The teacher paused at my desk, and** *she* **looked at my composition.** If you omitted the subject *she* in the second part of the sentence, would you keep the comma before *and*? (*Yes, No*) 465
rung 652	Write the correct past form of **drink:** **Someone has** _____ **all my lemonade.** 653
were 840	**This tie and this shirt** (*don't, doesn't*) **match.** 841
definitely 1028	Lesson **35** How to Make Comparisons [Frames 1030-1062]

b	The pronoun **them** is the object form of **they**. It should be used for direct objects and for objects of prepositions, not to point something out.
	
	    a. I left *them* at school.
	    b. *Them* are not mine.
	
	In which sentence is *them* used correctly? _____

1216	1217

who	Remember:
	
	  who and **whom**.........persons
	  which.....................things and animals
	
	Underline the correct clause signal:
	
	Our neighbors have a crow (*who, which*) **can talk.**

1403	1404

a	Some people make the opposite error. They reach the end of a sentence and keep right on going into the next. First, let us look at two separate sentences: We took our seats. The show began. These are two separate sentences, each with a subject and a _____ .
1590	1591

wrapped, or	Lesson **62** **Commas After Introductory Word Groups** [Frames 1779-1806]
1777	

o	The contraction of **will not** is _____ .
1964	1965

b	**a Methodist church** This is not the name of a *particular* church at a *particular* location. It could mean *any* Methodist church anywhere in the world. Is the word **church** capitalized? (*Yes, No*)
2151	2152

rode

89

PAST: **The catcher** *stood* **behind the plate.**

If you changed this sentence to *present* time, you would need to change the verb *stood* to _____.

90

–ly

277

Lesson **10** Adverbs
That Control the Power

[Frames 279-312]

No

465

Carlos kept his old friends and ∧ made several new ones.

If you added the subject **he** at the point indicated by the caret (∧), would you add a comma before the conjunction **and?** (*Yes, No*)

466

---

drunk

653

Write the correct past form of **begin:**

One of the engines had _____ **to miss.**

654

---

don't

841

Lesson **28** Don't Let Phrases Fool You!

[Frames 843-872]

A plane is *fast.*

In this sentence, do we compare a plane with any other means of travel? (*Yes, No*)

1030

a	a. Are *them* too big for me? b. I didn't look at *them*. In which sentence is *them* used correctly? ____ 1218
which 1404	a. Dan has a rifle ... is 100 years old. b. Dan has a great-uncle ... is 100 years old. In which sentence would **which** be correct? ____ 1405
verb 1591	<u>We</u> <u>took</u> our seats. The <u>show</u> <u>began</u>. We show the end of a sentence by putting down an end mark—a period, a question mark, or an exclamation point. Then we start the next sentence with a _____ letter. 1592
	I saw Andrew Young *at the game in the Astrodome.* This sentence consists of two word groups. The first word group tells *what happened*. The second word group tells only *where* it happened. The more important word group comes (*first, last*). 1779
won't 1965	In this and the following frames, write between the parentheses the correct contraction for each pair of italicized words. Remember that the apostrophe goes in where the letter or letters come out. *Let us* (_____) **see if** *it is* (_____) **ready.** 1966
No 2152	**Westport Methodist Church** This is the name of a *particular* Methodist church at a *particular* location. Is the word **church** capitalized? (*Yes, No*) 2153

stands 90	If you are doubtful about which word in a sentence is the verb, change the sentence from present to past time or from past to present time to see which word changes. The word that changes is the (*subject, verb*). 91
	There are two kinds of words that modify other words. One kind is called *adjectives,* and the other kind is called _____. 279
Yes 466	*Compound* means "having _____ or more parts." (How many?) 467
begun 654	Write the correct past form of each verb in parentheses: **The dismissal bell _____ (*ring*) before we had _____ (*sing*) our song.** 655
	<u>One <u>was</u> very noisy.</u> The subject **One** is singular; the verb **was** is singular, too. We say, therefore, that the subject and the verb _____ in number. 843
No 1030	**A plane is *faster* than a train.** When we compare a plane with *one* other means of travel, we change the word *fast* to _____. 1031

b
 	
1218
	Underline the correct word:
	
	    (*Them, Those*) **belong to our neighbor.**
	
	                                          1219

a
 	
1405
	a. **Mr. Prentis has a pupil ... is always slow.**
	    b. **Mr. Prentis has a watch ... is always slow.**
	
	In which sentence would **which** be correct? ____
	
	                                          1406

capital 1592	A period (or a question mark or an exclamation point) is a stop signal. It tells the reader that the sentence has ended. A comma tells the reader only to pause—that more of the sentence is coming. You know that a sentence ends when you see a (*comma, period*). 1593

first
 	
1779
	a. **I saw Andrew Young** *at the game in the Astrodome.*
	    b. *At the game in the Astrodome,* **I saw Andrew Young.**
	
	In which sentence does the modifying word group come before the main statement? ____
	
	                                          1780

Let's, it's 1966	**It** *does not* (_____) **seem to me that** *they are* (_____) **trying to win.** 1967

Yes
 	
2153
	a. **a Methodist Church**
	    b. **Westport Methodist Church**
	
	In which example is it a mistake to capitalize the word **church?** ____
	
	                                          2154

verb 91	Underline the verb with two lines: **<u>I</u> generally see my dentist twice a year.** 92
adverbs 279	Both adjectives and adverbs make the pictures and ideas we get from words (*more, less*) clear and exact. 280
two 467	Words that connect words or groups of words are called _____. 468
rang, sung 655	Write the correct past form of each verb in parentheses: **Before we had _____ (*swim*) across the stream, it _____ (*begin*) to rain.** 656
agree 843	**One <u>was</u> very noisy.** Do you know whether the subject **One** refers to a motor, a child, a record, or a room? (*Yes, No*) 844
faster 1031	**A plane is the *fastest* means of travel.** There are many means of travel—horses, cars, boats, buses, trains, and so forth. In this sentence, are we comparing a plane with *more than one* other means of travel? (*Yes, No*) 1032

Those 1219	Neither should you use **them** as an adjective to point out the noun that follows it. Underline the correct word: (*Those, Them*) **flowers belong to our neighbor.** 1220
b 1406	a. **This is the light ... directs the traffic.** b. **This is the officer ... directs the traffic.** In which sentence would **which** be correct? ____ 1407

period
 	
1593
	When one sentence runs into another, the result is called a **run-on sentence.** It is a bad mistake in writing.
	
	    a. **We took our seats. The show began.**
	    b. **We took our seats, the show began.**
	
	Which is a run-on sentence? ____
	
	1594

b 1780	The word **introductory** means "leading into." An introductory paragraph leads into the story. An introductory remark leads into the speech. An introductory phrase or clause leads into the main statement. An introductory word group comes (*before, after*) the main statement of a sentence. 1781
doesn't, they're 1967	*I would* (_____) **like to know if** *you are* (_____) **going to the game.** 1968
a 2154	**The St. Agnes Catholic** *Church* **is not the only Catholic** *Church* **in our town.** Because it is not part of the name of a *particular* church building, the (*first, second*) italicized word should not be capitalized. 2155

see == 92	Underline the verb with two lines: **The <u>boy</u> in the back seat knows all the answers.** 93
more 280	We call a person who drives a *driver;* one who bakes, a *baker;* one who pitches, a *pitcher.* In the same way, we call a word that modifies another word a *modifier.* Both adjectives and adverbs are _____. 281
conjunctions 468	The three most common conjunctions are the words _____, _____, and _____. 469
swum, began 656	The verb **bring** looks very similar to **ring** and **sing,** but it behaves quite differently. PRESENT SIMPLE PAST PAST WITH HELPER **bring** **brought** **(have) brought** Do we use the same past form of **bring** for both the simple past and for the past with helper? (*Yes, No*) 657
No 844	To make clear what **One** refers to, we shall add a preposi-tional phrase. **One** *of the motors* **was very noisy.** The prepositional phrase starts with the preposition _____ and ends with its object _____. 845
Yes 1032	**A plane is the** *fastest* **means of travel.** When we compare a plane with *more than one* other means of travel, we use the adjective _____. 1033

Those 1220	Underline the correct word: **I had never seen** (*those, them*) **boys before.** 1221
a 1407	Never use the clause signal **which** to refer to (*animals, persons, things*). 1408

b
 	
1594
	Sometimes a person runs one sentence into another with only a comma between them. Sometimes he runs them together with nothing between them. Both are equally wrong.
	
	    a. **We took our seats the show began.**
	    b. **We took our seats, the show began.**
	
	Are both *a* and *b* run-on sentences? (*Yes, No*)
	
	1595

before 1781	a. **I saw Andrew Young** *at the game in the Astrodome.* b. *At the game in the Astrodome,* **I saw Andrew Young.** Which sentence begins with an introductory word group? ——— 1782
I'd, you're 1968	**Virginia** *cannot* (_____) **study well when** *there is* (_____) **too much noise.** 1969
second 2155	**We met at the Trinity Episcopal Church** If you dropped the name **Trinity,** would you still write **Church** with a capital letter? (*Yes, No*) 2156

<u>knows</u> 93	Underline the verb with two lines: **The first chapter described the ranch.** 94
modifiers 281	The modifiers that we use with nouns and pronouns are called _____. 282
and, but, or 469	In a compound sentence, put a comma (*before, after*) the conjunction **and, but,** or **or.** 470
Yes 657	PRESENT SIMPLE PAST PAST WITH HELPER **bring** **brought** **(have) brought** Write the correct past forms of **bring:** **Peggy _____ the same kind of cookies that Leo** **had _____ last week.** 658
of, motors 845	**One** *of the motors* **was very noisy.** The prepositional phrase *of the motors* modifies the sub- ject of this sentence, which is the pronoun _____. 846
fastest 1033	**A plane is** *faster* **than a train.** **A plane is the** *fastest* **means of travel.** When we compare a plane with one other means of travel, we add _____ to the word *fast*. When we compare a plane with more than one other means of travel, we add _____ to the word *fast*. 1034 *page 187*

those 1221	Underline the correct word: **Why don't you put** (*them, those*) **stamps in your album?** 1222
persons 1408	**driver nurse editor doctor** Would it be correct to use the clause signal **which** to refer to any of the above nouns? (*Yes, No*) 1409
Yes 1595	a. **We took our seats the show began.** b. **We took our seats, the show began.** Both *a* and *b* are run-on sentences. There is no _____ to show where the first sentence ends. There is no _____ letter to show where the second sentence begins. 1596
b 1782	a. **I saw Andrew Young** *at the game in the Astrodome.* b. *At the game in the Astrodome,* **I saw Andrew Young.** One sentence has a comma; the other does not. The comma is necessary only when the sentence begins with the (*main statement, introductory word group*). 1783
can't, there's 1969	*He will* (_____) **let you know if he** *is not* (_____) **satisfied.** 1970

No
 	
2156
	Capitalize the names of *particular* clubs and organizations.
	  a. **The Schubert music club will provide the orchestra.**
	  b. **A music club will provide the orchestra.**
	In which sentence should the words **music club** be capitalized because they are part of the name of a particular club? ____
	
	2157

described 94	To find the subject and verb in a sentence, it is better to find the verb first. Let's suppose that the verb is *told*. Now ask yourself, "Who or what *told*?" The answer to this question is always the subject. **The new boy from Alaska told about his trip.** Who **told?** _____ (one word) 95
adjectives 282	The modifiers that we use with verbs are called _____. 283
before 470	Lesson **16** Unit Review [Frames 472-503]

brought, brought
 	
658
	PRESENT SIMPLE PAST PAST WITH HELPER
	  ring **rang** **(have) rung**
	  sing **sang** **(have) sung**
	  bring **brought** **(have) brought**
	Which of these three verbs behaves differently from the other two? _____
	
	659

One 846	**One** *of the motors* **was very noisy.** We have added a prepositional phrase merely to make clear what we mean by **One**. The subject of this sentence is still the word _____. 847
–er, –est 1034	Most adjectives and adverbs have three degrees (or steps) of power. The *first degree* merely states a quality—like *young, slow, clean.* Underline the adjective in the first degree: **fast faster fastest** *page 189* 1035

those 1222	In this and the following frames, underline the correct word or words, according to the rules you studied in this lesson: (*We, Us*) **boys can decorate the gym.** 1223

No
 	
1409
	The clause signal **that** can be used to refer to persons, things, or animals.
	
	      a. **I like people ... are jolly.**
	      b. **I like a room ... is cozy.**
	      c. **I like dogs ... obey promptly.**
	
	Would **that** be correct in each of these sentences? (*Yes, No*)
	1410

period capital 1596	You learned earlier how to join two sentences into a compound sentence. You merely put the conjunction (connecting word) **and, but,** or **or** between them. **We took our seats,** *and* **the show began.** The two sentences are joined by the conjunction _____. 1597
introductory word group 1783	The comma after an introductory word group helps you to read the sentence correctly. **While I was eating the cat jumped on my lap.** The reader might get the wrong meaning unless we put a comma after (*eating, cat*). 1784
He'll, isn't 1970	*She is* (_____) **very sure that Mickey** *has not* (_____) **written to him.** 1971
a 2157	Do not capitalize the word **the, and,** or any short preposition (**of, in, for, to**) when it is part of a name. **Society for the Prevention of Cruelty to Animals** How many words in this name are not capitalized? _____ 2158

boy 95	The new boy from Alaska <u>told</u> about his trip. The subject of the verb **told** is _____. 96
adverbs 283	a high mountain Because the word **high** modifies the noun **mountain,** it is an _____. 284
	Certain words answer the questions *What kind? Which one(s)? How many?* and *How much?* about nouns and pronouns. These words are called _____. 472
bring 659	Write the correct past form of each verb in parentheses: We _____ (*sing*) **songs from books that Ms. Diaz had** _____ (*bring*) **to the meeting.** 660
One 847	**One** *of the motors* **was very noisy.** The singular pronoun **One** is the subject of this sentence. In choosing our verb, should we pay any attention to the plural noun *motors*? (*Yes, No*) 848
fast 1035	The *second degree* shows that one of *two* things has *more* of this quality than the other—*younger, slower, cleaner.* Underline the adjective in the second degree: **fast faster fastest** 1036

We 1223	(*Our teacher, Our teacher she*) **goes to all the games.** 1224
Yes 1410	a. **People** *who* **are lazy find excuses.** b. **The suit** *which* **he wore needed pressing.** Could you use **that** in place of the italicized clause signal in each sentence? (*Yes, No*) 1411
and 1597	a. **We took our seats, the show began.** b. **We took our seats, and the show began.** Which is wrong because it is a run-on sentence? ____ 1598
eating 1784	Put a comma after an introductory word group—a word group that comes ahead of the main statement. a. **At the end of the game we cheered the other team.** b. **We cheered the other team at the end of the game.** Which sentence requires a comma? ____ 1785
She's, hasn't 1971	**You** *have not* **(_____) told Phyllis that** *we are* **(_____) going to the carnival.** 1972
four 2158	Here is the name of a national organization. Underline two words that should not be capitalized: **national conference of christians and jews** 2159

boy 96	**Apples from our neighbors' tree <u>fell</u> into our yard.** What **fell?** _____ (one word) 97

adjective
 	
284
	All mountains are high, but some are much higher than others.
	
	      a. **a high mountain**
	      b. **a very high mountain**
	
	Which gives you the idea of a higher mountain—*a* or *b?* ___
	
	285

adjectives 472.	Underline three adjectives in this sentence: **Good seats for this concert cost six dollars.** 473
sang, brought 660	Write the correct past form of each verb in parentheses: **The bell had** _____ (*ring*) **before Dave** _____ (*bring*) **back the report from the office.** 661
No 848	**One ... the flute.** **One of my sisters ... the flute.** Would the singular verb **plays** be correct in both sentences? (*Yes, No*) 849
faster 1036	The *third degree* shows that one of *three or more* things has the *most* of this quality—*youngest, slowest, cleanest.* Underline the adjective in the third degree: **fast faster fastest** 1037

Our teacher 1224	Grandfather fascinated (*we, us*) children with stories of Geronimo's bravery. 1225
Yes 1411	**We feed a squirrel ... comes to our door.** The *two* clause signals that would be correct in this sentence are (*who, which, that*). 1412
a 1598	Is it correct to separate two sentences by putting only a comma between them? (*Yes, No*) 1599
a 1785	**Bears can run fast although they look slow and clumsy.** Suppose that you saw a bear close to you in the woods. The more important fact for you to know is in the (*first, second*) word group. 1786
haven't, we're 1972	**You** *should not* (_____) **buy it just because** *it is* (_____) **cheap.** 1973
of, and 2159	Underline two words that should not be capitalized: **american foundation for the blind** 2160

Apples	**Apples from our neighbors' tree fell into our yard.** The subject of the verb **fell** is _____.
97	98

	a. **a high mountain** b. **a very high mountain**
b	The words after *b* give you an idea of greater height be- cause the word _____ has been added.
285	286

	Some words can be used as either nouns or adjectives, depending on the job they do in the sentence.
good, this, six	a. **I prefer** *light* **colors.** b. **The** *light* **went out.**
473	In which sentence is *light* used as an adjective? _____ 474

rung, brought	Lesson **22** Straightening Out *Lie* and *Lay*
661	[Frames 663-695]

	a. **My sisters ... the flute.** b. **One of my sisters ... the flute.**
Yes	In which sentence would the plural verb **play** be correct because the subject is plural? _____
849	850

	FIRST DEGREE	SECOND DEGREE	THIRD DEGREE
	high	high<u>er</u>	high<u>est</u>
	strong	strong<u>er</u>	strong<u>est</u>
fastest	With short words of one syllable (and sometimes two) we form the second degree by adding *–er;* the third degree		
1037	by adding _____.		1038

us 1225	**Mr. Page let** (*me and Phyllis, Phyllis and me*) **use his canoe.** 1226

which, that
 	
1412
	In this and the following frames, underline the correct clause signal.
	
	Remember: **who** and **whom**...persons
	            which ....things and animals
	            that ....persons, things, and animals
	
	     any bank (*which, who*)
	1413

No 1599	A comma is often right when one of the two word groups is *not* a sentence. *When we took our seats,* **the show began.** Is this a run-on sentence? (*Yes, No*) 1600
first 1786	a. **Bears can run fast although they look slow and clumsy.** b. **Although they look slow and clumsy bears can run fast.** Which sentence begins with an introductory word group, not with the main statement? ____ 1787
shouldn't, it's 1973	**The elevator** *will not* (_____) **start if the doors** *are* *not* (_____) **closed.** 1974
for, the 2160	**My best friend is in the** ∧ **hospital.** If you inserted the name **Lancaster** before the noun **hospital,** would you capitalize the noun **hospital?** (*Yes, No*) 2161

Apples 98	In most sentences that state a fact, the subject comes *before* the verb, not *after* it. **People often <u>complain</u> about the weather.** The subject of the verb **complain** is (*People, weather*). 99
very 286	a *very* **high mountain** The word *very* modifies the adjective **high.** It tells _____ **high** the mountain is. 287
a 474	a. **The** *glass* **broke.** b. **We used a** *glass* **pitcher.** In which sentence is *glass* used as an adjective? ____ 475
	To lie means "to rest in a flat position" or "to be in place." We say, "I *lie* in bed and read" and "The rug *lies* on the floor." Supply the missing word: **Our cat often _____ on the windowsill.** 663
a 850	Don't let a prepositional phrase that follows the subject trick you into choosing the wrong verb. Here are nine common prepositions that often start such phrases: PREPOSITIONS: **of in to at on by for from with** **The need** *for more schools* **(is, are) very great.** The subject of this sentence is (*need, schools*). 851
–est 1038	The second degree of *cheap* is _____. The third degree of *cheap* is _____. 1039

Phyllis and me 1226	(*Those, Them*) are exactly like ours. 1227
which 1413	the teacher (*which, that*) 1414
No 1600	a. I turned off the light, I went to sleep. b. Turning off the light, I went to sleep. Which is a run-on sentence? ____ 1601
b 1787	Although they look clumsy, bears can run fast. We use a comma in this sentence because it begins with the (*main statement, introductory word group*). 1788
won't, aren't 1974	Lesson **69** **Possessive Pronouns— No Apostrophes!** [Frames 1976-1997]
Yes 2161	a. My aunt is a doctor at the Hospital. b. My aunt is a doctor at the Redstone County Hospital. Which sentence is correct? ____ 2162

People 99	**The bright lights <u>blinded</u> the driver.** The subject of the verb **blinded** is (*lights, driver*). 100
how 287	**drove slowly** Because the word **slowly** modifies the verb **drove,** it is an _____. 288
b 475	Certain words answer the questions *When? Where? How? How much?* and *How often?* about the actions of verbs. These words are called _____. 476
lies 663	PRESENT SIMPLE PAST PAST WITH HELPER **lie** (in bed) **lay** **(have) lain** Is the word **laid** either one of the past forms of the verb **lie?** (*Yes, No*) 664
need 851	Underline the verb that agrees with the subject: **The need for more schools** (*is, are*) **very great.** 852
cheaper cheapest 1039	To compare one person or thing with another person or thing, we use the second degree, which ends with the letters (*–er, –est*). 1040

Those 1227	This book (*it's, is*) about Jade Snow Wong's childhood. 1228
that 1414	the mouse (*who, which*) 1415
a 1601	a. The wrappers are different. The sandwiches are all alike. b. Although the wrappers are different, the sandwiches are all alike. c. The wrappers are different, the sandwiches are all alike. Which is a run-on sentence? ____ 1602
introductory word group 1788	a. After I returned to the city my coat of tan soon faded. b. My coat of tan soon faded after I returned to the city. Which sentence requires a comma? ____ 1789
	To possess means "to own." A family may possess, or own, their own home. Pronouns that show ownership are called **possessive** pronouns. **mine yours his hers its ours theirs** Do you see an apostrophe before the final *s* in any of these possessive pronouns? (*Yes, No*) 1976
b 2162	a. You can get the book at the Emerson library. b. You can get the book at almost any library. In which sentence should **library** be capitalized? ____ 2163

lights 100	In this and the following frames, find the verb first and underline it with two lines. Then use the *Who?—What?* method to find the subject and underline it with one line. **The meeting started on time.** 101

adverb
 	
288
	The word **slowly** could mean anything from scarcely moving to perhaps fifteen or twenty miles per hour.
	
	      a. **drove slowly**
	      b. **drove very slowly.**
	
	Which gives you the idea of slower speed—*a* or *b*? ____
	
	289

adverbs 476	Underline two adverbs in this sentence: **There he waited patiently for his friend.** 477
No 664	PRESENT SIMPLE PAST PAST WITH HELPER **lie** (in bed) **lay** **(have) lain** The simple past form of **lie** is not **laid** but _____. 665
is 852	**The pictures on the wall (show, shows) the history of our country.** The subject of this sentence is (*pictures, wall*). 853
–er 1040	Underline the correct adjective: **Paul is the (*shorter, shortest*) of the two boys.** 1041

is 1228	(*We, Us*) girls must stick together in this election. 1229
which 1415	**the cashier** (*that, which*) 1416
c 1602	Beginning in the next frame, you will find a story about the adventure of a truck driver. If the sentence is correct, write *Correct* on the blank line. If the sentence is a run-on sentence, correct it like this: EXAMPLE: **The soup was too salty, nobody could eat it.** _salty. Nobody_ (*Turn to the next frame.*) 1603
a 1789	a. **As we were rowing toward shore we noticed a black cloud.** b. **We noticed a black cloud as we were rowing toward shore.** Which sentence requires a comma? ___ 1790
No 1976	To make nouns show ownership, we need to use apostrophes. *John's* **score was higher than** *Helen's* **score.** In this sentence, there are two nouns that show ownership. Are both these nouns written with apostrophes? (*Yes, No*) 1977
a 2163	In this and the following frames, copy and capitalize only the words to which capitals should be added: **When I complete high school, I plan to go to Cornell university.** 2164

meeting <u>started</u>	Continue to underline the verb with two lines and the subject with one. **Huge waves crashed noisily against the rocks.**
101	102
b	a. **drove slowly** b. **drove very slowly** The words after *b* give you the idea of slower speed because the word _____ has been added.
289	290
There, patiently	Some words can be used as either adjectives or adverbs, depending on whether they modify nouns (pronouns) or verbs. a. **The band played** *loud.* b. **Perry has a** *loud* **voice.** In which sentence is *loud* used as an adverb? ____
477	478
lay	Underline the correct verb: **Last night I** *(lay, laid)* **on the sofa and watched television.**
665	666
pictures	Underline the verb that agrees with the subject: **The pictures on the wall** *(show, shows)* **the history of our country.**
853	854
shorter	When our comparison involves three or more persons or things, we use the third degree, which ends with the letters *(–er, –est).*
1041	1042

We 1229	How much is one of (*those, them*) **apples?** 1230
that 1416	**libraries** (*who, that*) 1417
1603	**As Jo Kelly was driving her truck out Main Street, she heard a siren.** ――――――――――――― 1604
a 1790	*When they have nothing to do,* **children often quarrel.** If you moved the introductory clause to the end of the sentence, would you use a comma in this sentence? (*Yes, No*) 1791
Yes 1977	Possessive pronouns are different from nouns. They are possessive words in themselves. They show ownership without the use of apostrophes. *Yours* **was higher than** *hers.* Here we have two pronouns that show ownership. Is either pronoun written with an apostrophe? (*Yes, No*) 1978
University 2164	**The Parkman library circulates books among the patients at Auburn children's hospital.** ――――――――――――― 2165

waves <u>crashed</u> 102	An old British fort once stood on this spot. 103
very 290	drove *very* **slowly** The word *very* tells how **slowly** someone drove. The word *very*, therefore, modifies the adverb _____. 291
a 478	a. **He took a** *fast* **train.** b. **He talks** *fast*. In which sentence is *fast* used as an adverb? ____ 479
lay 666	Underline the correct verb: **Heavy clouds** (*laid, lay*) **over the airport all day.** 667
show 854	Here are two groups of words that you might make sentences about. Underline the word in each group with which the verb would need to agree: a. **My interest in rocks...** b. **The visitors from Philadelphia...** 855
−est 1042	Underline the correct modifier: **Paul is the** (*shorter, shortest*) **of the three boys.** 1043

those 1230	(*We and our neighbors, Our neighbors and we*) **cleaned up the vacant lot.** 1231
that 1417	**a dentist** (*who, which*) 1418
Correct 1604	**A moment later she looked back, a fire engine was just behind her.** _____ 1605
No 1791	**The Mississippi River became a busy waterway** *after the steamboat was invented.* If you moved the italicized clause to the beginning of the sentence, would you put a comma after it? (*Yes, No*) 1792
No 1978	You are in the habit of using apostrophes in possessive nouns. Therefore, you must make a special effort not to use apostrophes whenever you write possessive pronouns. Add *one* apostrophe to this sentence: *Bobs* **locker is right next to** *ours.* 1979
Library, Children's Hospital 2165	**We were taken by bus from our hotel to the empire state building.** _____ 2166

fort <u>stood</u> 103	Several boys climbed to the top of the tower. 104
slowly 291	a. a *very* **high mountain** b. **drove** *very* **slowly** Can the word *very* modify either an adjective or an adverb? (*Yes, No*) 292

b
 	
479
	There are a small number of special adverbs that modify other modifiers—both adjectives and adverbs.
	
	    a. **He took a** *very* **fast train.**
	    b. **He talks** *very* **fast.**
	
	In which sentence does the adverb *very* modify another adverb? ____
	
	480

lay 667	**Terry's bicycle** *lies* **on the sidewalk.** If you changed this sentence from present to past, you would need to change *lies* to _____. 668

a. interest
b. visitors
 	
855
	Underline the word in each group with which the verb would need to agree:
	
	    a. **The reason for her good grades . . .**
	    b. **My cousin with several friends . . .**
	
	856

shortest 1043	**I chose the** *smallest* **of the five puppies.** If we changed the number of puppies from **five** to **two**, we would change the adjective *smallest* to _____. 1044

Our neighbors and we 1231	The engineer took (*we, us*) girls down to see the engine room. 1232
who 1418	all animals (*who, that*) 1419
back. A 1605	Its siren was screaming, she must get out of its way. _____ 1606
Yes 1792	A comma should generally be used when a sentence begins with (*the main statement, an introductory word group*). 1793
Bob's 1979	Bob's **locker is right next to** *ours.* We do not put an apostrophe in *ours* because it is a possessive (*noun, pronoun*). 1980
Empire State Building 2166	The employees of the Globe insurance company were entertained at the Oakland golf club. _____ 2167

boys climbed 104	The car ahead of us suddenly stopped. 105

Yes
 	
292
	You have just become acquainted with a special kind of adverb. This kind of adverb can modify either an adjective or an adverb.
	
	    a. **A** *very* **heavy snow fell.**
	    b. **The snow fell** *very* **fast.**
	
	The adverb *very* modifies an adverb in sentence (*a, b*).
	
	293

b 480	Many adjectives can be changed into adverbs. The adverb form of the adjective *brave* is _____. 481
lay 668	PRESENT SIMPLE PAST PAST WITH HELPER **lie** (in bed) **lay** **(have) lain** After *have, has,* or *had,* we use the word _____. 669
a. reason b. cousin 856	Should a verb ever be made to agree with the object of a preposition that follows the subject? (*Yes, No*) 857
smaller 1044	Adding *–er* or *–est* to long words would make them very clumsy to pronounce. Therefore, instead of saying *particularer,* we say *more particular.* Instead of saying *particularest,* we say *most particular.* The second degree of the adjective *wonderful* would be (*more wonderful, wonderfuller*). 1045

us

1232

Lesson **42** Using the Right Pronouns in a Story

[Frames 1234-1256]

---

that

1419

our neighbor (*which, who*)

1420

---

screaming. She

1606

As she put on more speed, the fire engine increased its speed, too.

_____

1607

---

an introductory word group

1793

If the introductory word group is short, the comma may be omitted.

a. *During the argument,* **a crowd had gathered.**

b. *During the argument between the two drivers,* **a crowd had gathered.**

From which sentence might you omit the comma? ____

1794

---

pronoun

1980

a. **Bobs** *locker* **is right next to** *our's.*
b. **Bob's** *locker* **is right next to** *ours.*
c. **Bob's** *locker* **is right next to** *our's.*

Which sentence is correct? ____

1981

Insurance Company, Golf Club

2167

A new theater will be built right across from the Ambassador hotel.

_____

page 210

2168

car <u>stopped</u> 105	**In the morning we start for California.** 106
b 293	We are now ready to write a full definition of an adverb: An adverb is a word that is used to modify a verb or another modifier. By "another modifier," we mean either an adjective or an _____. 294
bravely 481	a. **Frank** _was_ **our guide.** b. **Frank** _hired_ **a Navajo guide.** One sentence contains an action verb; the other, a linking verb. Which sentence contains the linking verb? ____ 482
lain 669	Write the correct past form of **lie:** **The injured man must** _have_ _____ **there for an hour.** 670
No 857	**One . . . <u>is</u> loose.** This sentence is correct. If you added the prepositional phrase _of my teeth_, would you need to make the verb plural? (_Yes, No_) 858
more wonderful 1045	The third degree of the adjective _interesting_ would be (_interestingest, most interesting_). 1046

Each sentence in the following story presents a problem in the choice of pronouns. Underline the correct pronoun or pronouns in each sentence.

When my friend Pete and (*I, me*) were six years old, we were full of schemes for making money.

1234

---

who

1420

a large robin (*that, who*)

1421

Correct

1607

Soon she was doing nearly fifty, her truck could go no faster.

_____

1608

---

a

1794

a. *When we finally reached the station,* **the train had already left.**
b. *When we arrived,* **the train had already left.**

From which sentence might you omit the comma? ____

1795

---

b

1981

Add *one* apostrophe to this sentence:

We put *theirs* in *Annas* car.

1982

Hotel

2168

The Fremont high school holds its graduation exercises in the Beverly theater.

_____

2169

we <u>start</u>	The principal very often comes to our games.

---

adverb	*very* **difficult** *so* **difficult** *terribly* **difficult** *rather* **difficult** *too* **difficult** *extremely* **difficult** *slightly* **difficult** *quite* **difficult** *somewhat* **difficult** We might say that all the italicized adverbs increase or decrease the "power" of the adjective _____.

294

295

---

a	a. **We** *looked* **in every corner.** b. **The restaurant** *looked* **clean.** In which sentence is *looked* used as a linking verb? ____

482

483

---

lain	Write the correct past form of **lie:** **The old trunk** *had* _____ **in our attic for years.**

670

671

No	a. **One of my teeth** *is* **loose.** b. **One of my teeth** *are* **loose.** Which sentence is correct? ____

858

859

---

most interesting	With some adjectives and adverbs of two syllables, we can use either method: FIRST DEGREE SECOND DEGREE THIRD DEGREE happy happier happiest or: happy more happy most happy Another two-syllable word that can be handled either way is (*regular, lovely, courteous*).

1046

1047

1234 I	It was the day after Halloween, and the previous night (*we, us*) boys had covered the neighborhood very thoroughly, begging for treats. **1235**
1421 that	Lesson **49** Putting Adjective Clauses to Work [Frames 1423-1447]
1608 fifty. Her	Jo became very nervous, and she looked back again. _____ **1609**
1795 b	In this and the following frames, put a comma after each introductory word group. If the main statement of the sentence comes first, make no change. **For the youngsters with ice skates the winter was a great disappointment.** **1796**
1982 Anna's	**We put *theirs* in *Anna's* car.** We do not put an apostrophe in *theirs* because it is a possessive (*noun, pronoun*). **1983**
2169 High School, Theater	**The Redeemer lutheran church uses the parking lot of the Jordan building.** _____ **2170**

principal <u>comes</u>	**A young man in a blue suit jumped out of the car.**
107	108

difficult	*very* **neatly** *so* **neatly** *rather* **neatly** *quite* **neatly** *too* **neatly** *somewhat* **neatly** Here the italicized adverbs increase or decrease the "power" of the adverb _____.
295	296

b	Every linking verb must be completed by a (*direct object,* *subject complement*).
483	484

lain	Write the missing forms of **lie:** PRESENT SIMPLE PAST PAST WITH HELPER **lie** _____ **(have)** _____
671	672

a	Remember that **doesn't** means **does not,** and **don't** means **do not.** Underline the verb that is always singular: **doesn't don't**
859	860

lovely	a. **I have never had a** *happier* **day.** b. **I have never had a** *more happy* **day.** Are both sentences correct? (*Yes, No*)
1047	1048

we 1235	**Pete had collected as much as** (*I, me*). 1236
	We often write a sentence that states a fact about a person or thing in the previous sentence. a. **We found a robin.** b. **It couldn't fly.** Sentence *b* states a fact about the noun _____ in sentence *a*. 1423
Correct 1609	**Her pursuer was still at her heels, the driver was waving his arms wildly.** _____ 1610
skates, 1796	**Stores often have sales at the end of the year.** 1797

pronoun
 	
1983
	a. **We put** *their's* **in** *Anna's* **car.**
	    b. **We put** *theirs* **in** *Annas* **car.**
	    c. **We put** *theirs* **in** *Anna's* **car.**
	
	Which sentence is correct? ____
	
	1984

Lutheran Church, Building 2170	**The Bingham motor company donated an ambulance to our hospital.** _____ 2171

<u>man</u> <u>jumped</u> 108	**The smoke from the factory spreads over the entire neighborhood.** 109

neatly
 	
296
	Because adverbs like *very, quite, rather,* and *extremely* control the power of other modifiers, we can think of them as "power" adverbs.
	
	     a. **a** *rather* **jealous person**
	     b. **an** *extremely* **jealous person**
	
	The adverb has more power in (*a, b*). 297

subject complement 484	A subject complement always refers back to the _____ of the sentence. 485
lay, lain 672	Now let's look at the verb **lay,** with which **lie** is sometimes confused: **To lay** means "to put *something* down." **You can** *lay* **your coat on a chair.** What object do you *put down* in this sentence? _____ 673
doesn't 860	<u>One</u> ... <u>doesn't open.</u> This sentence is correct. If you added the prepositional phrase *of these windows,* would you need to make the verb plural? (*Yes, No*) 861

Yes
 	
1048
	Form the second degree of a word by adding either *–er* or the word *more,* never both.
	
	     a. **Oleo is** *cheaper* **than butter.**
	     b. **Oleo is** *more cheaper* **than butter.**
	
	Which sentence is correct because there is no duplication? ____
	1049

I 1236	Our collection of candy, cookies, and fruit was too much for (*he, him*) and (*I, me*) to eat. 1237

robin
 	
1423
	See how we can combine two such sentences.
	
	    a. **We found a robin.** b. **It couldn't fly.**
	       We found a robin *that couldn't fly.*
	
	We combined these two sentences by changing sentence *b*
	
	to an adjective _____.
	
	1424

heels. The 1610	**She didn't dare stop now, the fire truck would crash into her.** _____ 1611
No comma 1797	**When the Mesquakie Indians returned to Iowa they purchased their own land.** 1798

c
 	
1984
	a. *Judys* house is closer than *yours.*
	    b. *Petes* dog was chasing the *Neffs* cat.
	    c. *Ours* has won more games than *theirs.*
	
	Which sentence requires *no* apostrophes? ____
	
	1985

Motor Company 2171	Can you think of a name for a stamp club we are starting at the Cooke school? _____ 2172

smoke spreads 109	The last leaves on the tree finally fluttered to the ground. 110
b 297	a. a *terribly* **cold day** b. a *fairly* **cold day** The adverb has more power in (*a, b*). 298
subject 485	a. **Carmen became a** *doctor.* · b. **Carmen called a** *doctor.* In which sentence is the noun *doctor* a subject complement because it refers back to the subject? ____ 486
coat 673	**To lay** means "to put *something* down." Never use this word unless you mention the "something" that is *put down* or *moved* somewhere. **Don't** *lay* **the wet towel on the table.** Which object should you not *put down*? _____ 674
No 861	a. **One of the windows** *don't* **open.** b. **One of the windows** *doesn't* **open.** Which sentence is correct? ____ 862
a 1049	WRONG: **Oleo is** *more cheaper* **than butter.** This sentence is wrong because the comparison is duplicated by the use of both *–er* and the adverb _____. 1050

him, me

1237

"What can we do with all (*those, them*) things?" I asked Pete.

1238

---

clause

1424

Let's see how this is done:

    a. **I have a friend.**   b. **He plays the accordion.**

Sentence *b* states a fact about the noun _____ in sentence *a*.

1425

---

now. The

1611

This mad chase must end she would turn off at the next street.

_____

1612

Iowa,

1798

We could hardly hear the announcement   because everybody was chattering.

1799

---

c

1985

    a. *Judys* **house is closer than** *yours*.
    b. *Petes* **dog was chasing the** *Neffs* **cat.**
    c. *Ours* **has won more games than** *theirs*.

Which sentence requires *two* apostrophes? ____

1986

School

2172

Lesson **76** Capitals for Calendar Items and Brand Names

[Frames 2174-2196]

leaves fluttered 110	When you analyze a sentence, always look for the (*subject, verb*) first. 111
a 298	**They served a slightly tough steak.** To *increase* the power of the adjective **tough,** you would change the adverb _____. 299

a
 	
486
	A subject complement can be a noun, a pronoun, or an adjective.
	    a. **The driver was** *Carl.*
	    b. **The driver was** *he.*
	    c. **The driver was** *careful.*
	The subject complement is an adjective in sentence ____.
	487

towel 674	After you *lay* something down, it *lies* there until it is moved somewhere else. **You** *lay* **your books down, and they** _____ **there.** 675
b 862	Underline the correct verb: **One of the streets (***don't, doesn't***) run through.** 863
more 1050	Underline the correct choice: **I have never seen a (***bluer, more bluer***) sky.** 1051

page 221

those 1238	The problem of what to do with all our loot puzzled Pete as well as (*I, me*). 1239
friend 1425	a. **I have a friend.** b. **He plays the accordion.** Because sentence *b* states a fact about **friend** in sentence *a*, we can change it to an adjective clause. The adjective clause will modify the noun _____ in sentence *a*. 1426
end. She 1612	Jo made the turn on two wheels, the tires screeched. _____ 1613
No comma 1799	Although it was rare for a woman to fly in the early 1900's Bessie Coleman was a fine stunt pilot. 1800
b 1986	Remember that **its** is a possessive pronoun. Don't confuse it with **it's**, which is a shortened form of **it is**. Underline the correct word: **Don't disturb (*its, it's*) nest.** 1987

	Capitalize the names of days of the week, months, and holidays.
	
	   Wednesday February Christmas
	
	Copy and add capital letters to two words.
	
	   We will meet on the first tuesday in october.
	
	2174

verb 111	When you change a sentence from present to past time, or from past to present time, the only word that changes is the _____. 112
slightly 299	**Howard drove frightfully fast.** To *decrease* the power of the adverb **fast**, you would change the adverb _____. 300
c 487	The verb **be** is the most common linking verb. FORMS OF *BE*: **is, am, _____—was, _____, been** Underline the two forms of **be** that are missing in the above line: **do are has will were** 488
lie 675	Here are the forms of the verb **lay:** PRESENT SIMPLE PAST PAST WITH HELPER **lay** (to put) **laid** **(have) laid** The simple past form and the helper form used with *have, has,* or *had* are (*alike, different*). 676
doesn't 863	In this and the following frames, find the subject of the sentence and underline it. Then underline the verb that agrees with the subject. Pay no attention to the prepositional phrase. **The demand for tickets (*is, are*) enormous.** 864

bluer
 	
1051
	Form the third degree of a word by adding either *–est* or the word *most*, never both.
	
	    a. **Julie has the** *most latest* **record albums.**
	    b. **Julie has the** *latest* **record albums.**
	Which sentence is correct because there is no duplication? ____
	
	1052

me 1239	(*Pete he*, **He**) **thought the matter over for a few seconds.** 1240
friend 1426	Here is the sentence that we shall change to an adjective clause: **He plays the accordion.** Since our clause will modify the noun **friend,** we shall start our clause with the clause signal (*which, who*). 1427
wheels. The 1613	**She was about to breathe a sigh of relief when she noticed the fire truck still behind her.** _____ 1614
1900's, 1800	**From the top of a skyscraper** **the people and cars look like toys.** 1801
its 1987	The possessive pronoun **its**—just like **yours, hers, ours,** and **theirs**—is written without an apostrophe. Underline the correct word: (*It's, Its*) **wing must be broken.** 1988
Tuesday, October 2174	There is more than one way of referring to some holidays. **Thanksgiving** **Thanksgiving Day** **New Year** **New Year's** **New Year's Day** When the word **day** is part of the name of a holiday, do we capitalize it? (*Yes, No*) 2175

verb 112	If the verb of a sentence is *disappeared*. find the subject by asking yourself, "_____ or _____ *disappeared*?" 113
frightfully 300	When we say that adverbs can modify other modifiers, we mean that they can modify _____ and _____. 301
are, were 488	FORMS OF *BE*: is, _____, are—_____, were, been Underline the two forms of **be** that are missing in the above line: **am did can was have** 489

alike
 	
676
	PRESENT SIMPLE PAST PAST WITH HELPER
	  pay **paid** **(have) paid**
	  lay **laid** **(have) laid**
	The verb **pay** is regular because both past forms end in –*d*.
	Is the verb **lay** regular, too? (*Yes, No*)
	
	677

demand, is 864	**Only one of my parents** (*were, was*) **at home.** 865
b 1052	WRONG: **Julie has the** *most latest* **record albums.** This sentence is wrong because the comparison is duplicated by the use of both –*est* and the adverb _____. 1053

He 1240	Then Pete said, "Why don't (*we, us*) guys sell (*them, those*) things back to our neighbors?" 1241
who 1427	We put the clause signal *who* in front of the sentence and omit any unnecessary words: *who* ~~He~~ plays the accordion. We end up with the clause _____. 1428
Correct 1614	She stopped her truck, there was nothing else to do. _____ 1615
skyscraper, 1801	You are safe from the lightning when you hear the sound of the thunder. 1802
Its 1988	An apostrophe should be used in every possessive (*noun, pronoun*). 1989
Yes 2175	Copy and add capital letters to four words that should be capitalized: I remembered that labor day is always the first monday in september. 2176

Lesson 5 Verbs That Serve as Helpers

[Frames 115-146]

---

adjectives,
adverbs

301

However, most adverbs modify verbs.

When?   Where?   How?   How much?   How often?

These are questions that we can ask about verbs.

Words that answer these questions are _____.

302

---

am, was

489

a. **cooked, sold, built, spoke, opened**
b. **was, seemed, became, appeared, looked**

Which group of verbs could be used as linking verbs? ____

490

Yes

677

We ... our work aside.
We *had* **... our work aside.**

In both sentences we would use the same form of the verb

lay. This form would be _____.

678

---

one, was

865

The sharp turns in this road (*makes, make*) **it dangerous.**

866

---

most

1053

In this and the following frames, underline the word or
words that make the comparison correctly:

Which is (*more, most*) **interesting—the book or the movie?**

1054

we, those 1241	(*He, Him*) and (*I, me*) agreed to start with our neighbors, the Stokeses. 1242
who plays the accordion 1428	**I have a friend** *who plays the accordion.* We put the adjective clause right after the noun _____, which it modifies. 1429
truck. There 1615	Two fire fighters jumped off and rushed with fire extinguishers to the back of her truck. _____
No comma 1802	Tagging the corner of third base Lou Brock ran to home plate. 1803
noun 1989	POSSESSIVE PRONOUNS: **yours, hers, ours, theirs** Should these words ever be written with apostrophes? (*Yes, No*) 1990
Labor Day, Monday, September 2176	a. **Banks are closed on Washington's birthday.** b. **We are planning a party for Arlene's birthday.** In which sentence should **birthday** be capitalized because it is part of the name of a national holiday? ____

So far we have been working with one-word verbs, but with only single verbs, we often can't say what we mean.

Joe <u>can go</u>.   **Joe <u>could go</u>.**   **Joe <u>must go</u>.**

Joe <u>will go</u>.   **Joe <u>should go</u>.**   **Joe <u>might go</u>.**

Do these sentences have the same meaning? (*Yes, No*)

115

---

adverbs

One of these groups of adverbs can modify verbs; the other can modify other modifiers:

    a. **very, too, quite, rather, somewhat, extremely**
    b. **recently, truthfully, politely, stubbornly, promptly**

Which group can modify other modifiers? ____

302   303

---

b

We drove .?. the park.

Any word that would fit into the blank space in this sentence would be a *pre_____*.

490   491

---

laid

Now let's compare the forms of the verbs **lie** and **lay**:

PRESENT	SIMPLE PAST	PAST WITH HELPER
lie (in bed)	**lay**	**(have) lain**
lay (to put)	**laid**	**(have) laid**

One verb has three different forms, and the other has only two. Which verb has three different forms? _____

678   679

---

turns, make

The removal of the roots (*takes, take*) considerable time.

866   867

---

more

Of the Brontë family, Emily is the (*more, most*) famous.

1054   1055

He, I 1242	Our families and (*they, them*) were very good friends. 1243
friend 1429	Here is another pair of sentences to combine: a. **Mother bought a book.** b. **She didn't like the book.** Suppose that we want to change sentence *b* to an adjective clause that will modify the noun **book** in sentence *a*. Since this clause will modify the noun **book,** we shall start our clause with the clause signal (*who, which*). 1430
Correct 1616	**Now Jo understood everything, her truck was on fire.** _____ 1617
base, 1803	**You will find the products of American factories in every country in the world.** 1804
No 1990	In this and the following frames, underline the correct word in each italicized pair. (*Yours, Your's*) **is easier than** (*Helens, Helen's*) **recipe.** 1991

a
 	
2177
	Do *not* capitalize the names of the seasons.
	
	       spring **winter**
	       summer **fall, autumn**
	
	Fill each space with a small or capital letter, as the word requires:
	
	      Next ____uesday is the first day of ____inter.
	
	2178

These sentences have the same **main verb**, the word **go**:

    Joe can go.   **Joe could go.**   **Joe must go.**

    Joe will go.   **Joe should go.**   **Joe might go.**

Each time we change the verb before the *main verb* **go**,

the meaning of the sentence _____.

No

115

116

---

a

Underline two adverbs:

    Her older brother typewrites quite rapidly.

303

304

---

preposition

A preposition shows the *rel* _____ between
the noun or pronoun that follows it and some other word
in the sentence.

491

492

---

lie

PRESENT	SIMPLE PAST	PAST WITH HELPER
lie (in bed)	lay	(have) lain
lay (to put)	laid	(have) laid

Here is something that sometimes causes confusion:
The word **lay,** which means "to put *something* down," is

also the simple past form of the verb _____.

679

680

---

removal, takes

One of your lines (*don't, doesn't*) **rhyme well.**

867

868

---

most

We took the (*shorter, shortest*) **of the two routes.**

1055

1056

they 1243	When Mr. Stokes saw (*we, us*) boys at the door with our Halloween baskets, he looked very surprised. 1244
which 1430	We put the clause signal *which* in front of the sentence and omit any unnecessary words. *which* **She didn't like** ~~the boat~~. We end up with the clause _____. 1431
everything. Her 1617	Lesson **56** Three Words That Cause Run-ons [Frames 1619-1650]
No comma 1804	Before Buffy St. Marie went on stage she heard applause from the audience. 1805
Yours, Helen's 1991	(*Ken's, Kens*) **radio gets more stations than** (*theirs, their's*). 1992
T, w 2178	Fill in the missing letters: Our _____pring vacation comes in _____pril. 2179

changes 116	Joe **can** go. Joe **could** go. Joe **must** go. Joe **will** go. Joe **should** go. Joe **might** go. A verb that helps the main verb to express our meaning more exactly is called a **helping verb**—or just a **helper**. The shortest helper in the above sentences is the word _____. 117

quite rapidly
 	
304
	Underline two adverbs:
	
	    A very strange accident occurred recently.
	
	                                         305

relationship 492	After every preposition, we expect to find a noun or pronoun that is called its _____. 493
lie 680	**He** *lay* **on the beach for an hour.** In this sentence, *lay* does not mean "to put something down." Instead, it is the simple past form of the verb _____. 681
One, doesn't 868	**Crowds from the football game** (*jam, jams*) **the streets.** 869
shorter 1056	**Which one of these three dresses do you think is the** (*prettier, prettiest*)? 1057

us	"Are you fellows here again?" he asked Pete and (*I, me*).
1244	1245

which she didn't like	After you change a sentence to an adjective clause, be sure to put the clause right after the word it modifies. a. **A boy saw the accident.** b. *who was standing on the corner.* The adjective clause *who was standing on the corner* should be put after the noun (*boy, accident*).
1431	1432

	A run-on sentence is a collision between two sentences. In this lesson, we shall look at some of the words that cause these collisions. **I approached the colt. The colt ran away.** Does each sentence have a subject and a verb? (*Yes, No*)
	1619

stage,	**Although goats like to explore rubbish heaps** **they do not eat tin cans.**
1805	1806

Ken's, theirs	**My** (*sisters, sister's*) **violin was not in** (*its, it's*) **case.**
1992	1993

s, A	Fill in the missing letters: **Children look forward to ____hanksgiving in the ____all.**
2179	2180

can 117	Joe <u>can</u> go. Joe <u>could</u> go. Joe <u>must</u> go. Joe <u>will</u> go. Joe <u>should</u> go. Joe <u>might</u> go. The longest helper in the above sentences is the word _____. 118
very, recently 305	Underline two adverbs: **My dad always rises early.** 306
object 493	A group of words that begins with a preposition and ends with its object is called a prepositional _____. 494
lie 681	PRESENT SIMPLE PAST PAST WITH HELPER **lie** (in bed) lay (have) **lain** **lay** (to put) laid (have) **laid** Would you ever use **laid** to mean "rested in a flat posi- tion"? (*Yes, No*) 682
Crowds, jam 869	**The correction of these mistakes** (*requires, require*) **a great deal of time.** 870
prettiest 1057	**Chess is** (*more difficult, difficulter*) **than checkers.** 1058

me 1245	"You beggars did such a good job last night," Mr. Stokes went on, "that there's hardly anything left in the house for (*we, us*) folks to eat." 1246
boy 1432	a. **A boy** *who was standing on the corner* **saw the accident.** b. **A boy saw the accident** *who was standing on the corner.* Which sentence is correct? ____ 1433
Yes 1619	**I approached the colt. The colt ran away.** Now let's substitute the pronoun **It** for the subject **colt.** **I approached the colt. It ran away.** Does the second sentence still have a subject and a verb? (*Yes, No*) 1620
heaps, 1806	Lesson **63** Commas in a Series [Frames 1808-1836]
sister's, its 1993	There was (*nobodys, nobody's*) name after the "(*Your's, Yours*) truly." 1994
	Capitalize the names of particular brands of products. **Buick Kleenex Jello Lux** **We spray our roses with** (*protex, Protex*). 2181

should
 	
118
	HELPERS: **shall, will** **must, might**
	              may, can **should, would, could**
	How many helping verbs end with the same four letters?
	
	_____
	
	                      119

always, early
 	
306
	Underline two adverbs:
	
	        Very many Apaches live there.
	
	                      307

phrase
 	
494
	A prepositional phrase can do the job of either an adjective or an adverb.
	
	      a. **I sat** _near the stage._
	      b. **A seat** _near the stage_ **was vacant.**
	
	In which sentence is the phrase used as an adverb? ____
	                      495

No
 	
682
	Use the word **laid** only when you mention the "something" that is put down somewhere.
	
	      a. **I caught cold because I . . . in a draft.**
	      b. **I . . . my** _money_ **on the counter.**
	
	In which sentence would **laid** be correct? ____
	                      683

correction, requires 870	**One of the ten-dollar bills** (_were, was_) **counterfeit.** 871
more difficult 1058	**This is the** (_dangerousest, most dangerous_) **animal in the entire zoo.** 1059

us 1246	"Jimmie and (*I, me*) aren't begging," explained Pete. "We just thought that maybe we could sell you something." 1247
a 1433	a. **She served custard to the child** *that was full of lumps.* b. **She served custard** *that was full of lumps* **to the child.** In which sentence is the clause placed correctly next to the word it modifies? ____ 1434
Yes 1620	It I approached the colt. ~~The colt~~ ran away. **It ran away** is a complete sentence. It is just as clear as **The colt ran away.** You know from the previous sentence that **It** refers to the _____. 1621
	A **series** is a number of similar things in a row. For example, we speak of a series of games or a series of parties when one comes after another. In baking a cake, selecting a recipe is the first in a *s* _____ of several steps. 1808
nobody's, Yours 1994	(*Hers, Her's*) **was just as good as** (*our's, ours*). 1995
Protex 2181	**We feed our dog** (*Huskies, huskies*). 2182

three 119	HELPERS: **shall, will must, might** **may, can should, would, could** How many of these helping verbs begin with the letter **m**? _____ 120
Very, there 307	Underline two adverbs: **Aretha Franklin sings extremely well.** 308
a 495	a. **We often played football** *in the vacant lot.* b. **The boys** *in the vacant lot* **were playing football.** In which sentence is the phrase used as an adjective? ____ 496
b 683	The main point to remember is to use **lay**—never **laid**—as the simple past form of **lie** (in bed). Underline the correct verb: **The boat** (*lay, laid*) **on the beach all winter.** 684
One, was 871	Think about a sentence that has a *singular* subject followed by a prepositional phrase with a *plural* object. The verb in such a sentence should be (*singular, plural*). 872
most dangerous 1059	**I have never read a** (*more funnier, funnier*) **story.** 1060

I 1247	"Let me call Mrs. Stokes," he said. "She knows more about what we need than (*I, me*)." 1248
b 1434	**Every part is thoroughly tested** *that goes into a plane.* The italicized clause in this sentence is out of place. It should be put right after the noun _____, which it modifies. 1435

colt
 	
1621
	Be especially careful not to run two sentences together when the second sentence starts with **It**.
	
	    a. **I approached the colt, the colt ran away.**
	    b. **I approached the colt, it ran away.**
	
	Are both *a* and *b* run-on sentences? (*Yes, No*)
	
	1622

series 1808	Sentences often contain a *series* of words or word groups all doing the same job in the sentence. For example, a sentence might have a series of subjects, verbs, direct objects, subject complements, or modifiers. **My** *aunts,* *uncles,* **and** *cousins* **came to the party.** This sentence contains a series of (*subjects, objects*). 1809
Hers, ours 1995	**The** (*Watsons, Watsons'*) **car is newer than** (*theirs, their's*). 1996

Huskies
 	
2182
	Although brand names should be capitalized, the products that they identify should *not* be capitalized.
	
	  Krispie cornflakes **Walkaway shoes** **Vitex bread**
	
	    The program advertises Peerless (*tires, Tires*).
	
	2183

three 120	The three verbs that follow are often used as helpers. Notice their various forms: **be (is, am, are—was, were, been)** **have (has, had)** **do (does, did)** Which of these three verbs has the most forms? _____ 121
extremely, well 308	**Frank is . . .** *tall.* **Frank talks . . .** *fast.* To explain *how tall* Frank is or *how fast* he talks, we would need to use an (*adjective, adverb*). 309
b 496	Some words can be used as prepositions or adverbs. a. **The sun went** *down.* b. **We slid** *down* **the hill.** In which sentence is *down* used as a preposition? ____ 497
lay 684	The *–ing* forms of **lie** and **lay** are different: **lie** (in bed)—**lying** **lay** (to put)—**laying** Underline the correct verb: **The dog was (***laying, lying***) near the hot stove.** 685
singular 872	Lesson **29** When the Verb Comes First [Frames 874-902]
funnier 1060	**This was the (***longest, most longest***) trip I have ever taken.** 1061

1248	When his wife came to the door, we showed Mr. Stokes and (*she, her*) all the goodies we had for sale. 1249
part 1435	The house is nearly finished *that the Chans are building.* The italicized clause in this sentence should be put after the noun _____, which it modifies. 1436
Yes 1622	a. The plant was dry. It needed water. b. The plant was dry, it needed water. Which arrangement is correct? ____ 1623
subjects 1809	The cashier put the *pennies, nickels,* **and** *dimes* **in separate piles.** This sentence contains a series of (*subjects, direct objects*). 1810
Watsons', theirs 1996	(*Its, It's*) **color is just like** (*our's, ours*). 1997
tires 2183	a. The first prize was a Cookrite electric stove. b. The first prize was a Cookrite Electric Stove. Which sentence is correctly capitalized? ____ 2184

be 121	**be (is, am, are — was, were, been)** Forms of **be** can serve either as main verbs or as helpers to other verbs. When **is** occurs as a helper, it is followed by the *-ing* form of the main verb. a. **Pam is a painter.** b. **Pam is painting our house.** The verb **is** serves as a helper in sentence ____. 122
adverb 309	Besides modifying verbs, adverbs can also modify adjectives and other _____. 310
b 497	*Compound* means "having _____ or more parts." (How many?) 498
lying 685	Underline the correct verb: **The dishes were still (*lying, laying*) on the table.** 686
	Two <u>fish</u> <u>are</u> in the bowl. The subject of this sentence is _____, and the verb is _____. 874
longest 1061	**Bob thought that a pound of nails would be (*more heavier, heavier*) than a pound of feathers.** 1062

her 1249	Mr. Stokes and (*she, her*) looked over our collection very carefully. 1250
house 1436	In this and the following frames, combine each pair of sentences by changing the italicized sentence to an adjective clause. Write the full sentence in the blank space. **We go to a park.** *It is near our house.* _____ _____ 1437
a 1623	Don't let other pronouns, either, lead you into writing run-on sentences. **Carol knew the answer. Carol raised her hand.** Suppose that we put **She** in place of **Carol** in the second sentence. Would it still be a separate sentence? (*Yes, No*) 1624

direct objects
 	
1810
	It takes at least *three* items to make a series.
	
	    a. **My** *aunts* **and** *uncles* **came to the party.**
	    b. **My** *aunts*, *uncles*, **and** *cousins* **came to the party.**
	
	Which sentence contains a series? ____
	1811

Its, ours 1997	Lesson **70** Contraction or Possessive Pronoun? [Frames 1999-2027]
a 2184	a. **The new station sells Blue Star Gasoline.** b. **The new station sells Blue Star gasoline.** Which sentence is correctly capitalized? ____ 2185

b
 	
122
	have (has, had)
	Forms of **have**, too, can serve either as main verbs or as helpers to other verbs.
	
	    a. I have found a job. **b. I have a job.**
	
	The verb **have** serves as a helper in sentence _____.
	
	    123

adverbs 310	Adjectives can modify two kinds of words: *nouns* and *pronouns*. Adverbs can modify (*two, three*) kinds of words. 311
two 498	**We closed and locked all the windows.** This sentence has a compound (*verb, subject*). 499
lying 686	In this and the following frames, underline the correct forms of **lie** and **lay**: **Henry must (*lay, lie*) in bed for a few more days.** 687
fish, are 874	**Two fish are in the bowl.** As in most English sentences, the subject comes (*before, after*) the verb. 875
heavier 1062	Lesson **36** Avoiding the Double Negative Blunder [Frames 1064-1093]

she 1250	"(*Those, Them*) apples look very nice," Mrs. Stokes said. "I was just going to the store to buy some." 1251
We go to a park which (that) is near our house. 1437	Be sure to use **who** or **whom** to refer to persons, **which** to refer to things or animals, **that** to refer to any of these. **Lopes hit the home run.** *It won the game.* _____ _____ 1438
Yes 1624	a. **Carol knew the answer, she raised her hand.** b. **Carol knew the answer. She raised her hand.** Which arrangement is correct? ____ 1625
b 1811	**My** *aunts,* *uncles,* **and** *cousins* **came to the party.** This sentence has a series of three nouns used as subjects. How many commas are used to separate the nouns in this series? _____ 1812

	A few contractions and possessive pronouns sound just alike. Don't confuse them.
	
	         you're (*means* **you are**)
	         your (*means* **belonging to you**)
	 Use **you're** only when you can put the two words _____
	
	 _____ in its place.
	
	 1999

b 2185	In this and the following frames, copy only the words to which capitals should be added, and write them with capitals. (Some of the uses of capitals studied in the two preceding lessons are included.) **Mother's day is always the second sunday in may.** _____ 2186

a 123	**do (does, did)** a. **I did my work.** b. **I did finish my work.** The verb **did** serves as a helper in sentence ___. 124
three 311	Adverbs can modify _____, _____, and other _____. 312
verb 499	**We locked all the doors and windows.** This sentence has a compound (*direct object, subject complement*). 500
lie 687	**Don't** (*lay, lie*) **the hot pan on the table.** 688
before 875	**Two fish are in the bowl.** We can express the same fact in another way: **There are two fish in the bowl.** Do both of these sentences have the same subject and verb? (*Yes, No*) 876
	A *negative* word says *no*. A *positive* word says *yes*. Underline two negative words: **some none ever never** *page 247* 1064

Those 1251	(*Mrs. Stokes she, She*) **got her purse and gave us fifteen cents.** 1252
Lopes hit the home run which (that) won the game. 1438	**A man came to our door.** *He was a salesman.* _____ _____ (Be sure to put the clause next to the noun it modifies.) 1439

b
 	
1625
	The word **then** is an adverb that tells *when*—just like **now, soon, yesterday,** or **recently. Then** is not a conjunction like **and.** It has no power to join sentences.
	
	    a. **We played tennis,** *then* **we went swimming.**
	    b. **We played tennis,** *and* **we went swimming.**
	
	Which is a run-on sentence? ____
	1626

two 1812	**My** *aunts,* **uncles, and** *cousins* **came to the party.** Notice that commas are used *between* the items of a series. Is there a comma before the first item in this series? (*Yes, No*) 1813
you are 1999	To show ownership, use the possessive pronoun (*you're, your*). 2000
Day, Sunday, May 2186	**I spent the summer on a small island in Georgian bay.** _____ 2187

b 124	There are several ways of showing present, past, and future time. To express some of them, we must use one or more helpers before the main verb. PRESENT: a. **I talk.** b. **I am talking.** A helper is used with the main verb to show present time in (*a, b*). 125
verbs, adjectives, adverbs 312	Lesson **11** **Linking Verbs and the Subject Complement** [Frames 314-349]
direct object 500	The connecting words **and, but,** and **or,** which are used to connect compound parts, are called *con*_____. 501
lay 688	Mother (*laid, lay*) **a cold cloth on my forehead.** 689
Yes 876	a. **Two** <u>fish</u> <u>are</u> **in the bowl.** b. **There** <u>are</u> **two** <u>fish</u> **in the bowl.** In which sentence does the verb come *before* the subject? ____ 877
none, never 1064	a. **Somebody was at the door.** b. **Nobody was at the door.** Which sentence is negative? ____ 1065

She 1252	(*I and my friend, My friend and I*) **were delighted with our quick success in making a sale.** 1253
A man who (that) was a salesman came to our door. 1439	**The Bergs have a dog.** *It chases cars.* _____ _____ 1440
a 1626	a. **I put down the right answer,** *then* **I changed it.** b. **I put down the right answer.** *Then* **I changed it.** Which arrangement is correct? ____ 1627
No 1813	**My** *aunts, uncles,* **and** *cousins* **came to the party.** Is there a comma after the last item in this series? (*Yes, No*) 1814
your 2000	a. **I think ... right.** b. **You missed ... bus.** In which sentence would the words **you are** make sense? ____ 2001
Bay 2187	**On saturday afternoon, the Atlas theater will give away a victor bicycle.** _____ 2188

PAST: **I talked.   I have talked.   I had talked.**
I have been talking.   I had been talking.

In these sentences that show past time, some of the main verbs have as many as (*one, two, three*) helpers.

126

Rosa   treasurer

Do these two nouns by themselves form a sentence? (*Yes, No*)

314

When you connect two separate sentences with the conjunction **and, but,** or **or,** you make a _____ sentence.

502

Dad (*laid, lay*) **back in the chair and fell asleep.**

690

We start many sentences with the words **There is** and **There are** or **There was** and **There were.** In all such sentences, the verb comes ahead of the subject.

Underline the subject with one line and the verb with two lines:

There are some good stories in this book.

878

Underline the word that makes this sentence negative:

Nobody was at the door.

1066

My friend and I 1253	Mr. and Mrs. Stokes seemed just as pleased as (*we, us*) with the transaction. 1254
The Bergs have a dog which (that) chases cars. 1440	**I have a friend.** *Her father owns a speedboat.* (Try *whose.*) _____ _____ 1441

b
 	
1627
	A new sentence can begin with **Then**—just as it can begin with any other word that tells *when*.
	
	    The sky darkened. *Soon* **it began to rain.**
	    The sky darkened. *Later* **it began to rain.**
	    The sky darkened. *Then* **it began to rain.**
	
	Is each pair of sentences correct? (*Yes, No*) 1628

No
 	
1814
	Put commas *between* the items in a series—not before or after the series.
	
	  a. **We put the,** *pennies, nickels,* **and** *dimes* **in piles.**
	  b. **We put the** *pennies, nickels,* **and** *dimes,* **in piles.**
	  c. **We put the** *pennies, nickels,* **and** *dimes* **in piles.**
	
	Which sentence is punctuated correctly? ____
	
	1815

a 2001	a. **I think ... right.** b. **You missed ... bus.** In which sentence would the contraction **you're** be correct? ____ 2002
Saturday, Theater, Victor 2188	**St. Agnes church was very crowded on good friday.** _____ 2189

two 126	FUTURE: **I shall walk. I shall be walking.** **I shall have walked.** Is the main verb used without a helper in any one of these sentences that show future time? (*Yes, No*) 127
No 314	**Rosa . . . treasurer.** Underline the one word that you could add to turn the above words into a sentence: **good is new** 315
compound 502	a. **The little colt came to the fence and licked my hand.** b. **The little colt came to the fence and I patted its head.** In which sentence should a comma be inserted before the conjunction **and**? _____ Note to student: You are now ready for Unit Test 2. 503
lay 690	**We** (*laid, lay*) **on the beach and watched the water-skiers.** 691
are stories 878	We often start sentences, too, with the words **Here is** and **Here are**. In these sentences the verbs also come before the subjects. **Here is your pen.** Underline the subject and the verb: **Here are your sandwiches.** 879
Nobody 1066	Here is a list of negative words: **not (n't) never no one nothing** **none neither nobody nowhere** Every one of these negative words, just like the word **no**, begins with the letter _____. 1067

we	We thanked Mr. Stokes and (*she, her*) and went on our way.
1254	1255

I have a friend whose father owns a speedboat.	The heat wave is the worst one in ten years. *It started last week.*
	_____
	_____
1441	1442

Yes	a. The car slowed down. It stopped. b. The car slowed down. *Then* it stopped. Is each pair of sentences correct? (*Yes, No*)
1628	1629

c	We can also have a series of verbs or modifiers in a sentence. a. **Africa's** *dark, moist,* **and** *tangled* **forests are full of animal life.** b. **Jerry** *dressed, ate* **his breakfast, and** *hurried* **to school.** Which sentence contains a series of verbs? ____
1815	1816

a	Underline the correct word: **You missed** (*you're, your*) **bus.**
2002	2003

Church, Good Friday	**Have you seen the christmas display at the Whitman library?** _____
2189	2190

No 127	See what usually happens when we change a sentence from a statement to a question: STATEMENT: **Ellen can swim.** QUESTION: **Can Ellen swim?** The subject comes between the verb and its helper in the (*statement, question*). 128
is 315	**Rosa is treasurer.** We have now turned these words into a sentence by adding the verb _is_. 316
b 503	UNIT 3: **GETTING YOUR VERB FORMS RIGHT** Lesson **17** See, Do, and Go |Frames 505-538|
lay 691	**Dr. Diaz remembered where she had (*laid, lain*) her notes.** 692
<u>are sandwiches</u> 879	In most of our sentences, we state the subject first. Then we select a _____ that agrees with it in number. 880
n 1067	a. **none** **never** **nobody** **nowhere** **nothing** b. **some** **ever** **somebody** **somewhere** **something** Which list of words is negative? ____ 1068

her

1255

Do you wonder that the neighbors predicted successful business careers for Pete and (*I, me*)?

1256

The heat wave which (that) started last week is the worst one in ten years.

1442

We took a narrow road. *It had many turns.*

_____

_____

1443

Yes

1629

Rita decided to write a poem. ∧ She changed her mind.

If we added the adverb **Then** at the point marked by the caret (∧), would we still have two separate sentences? (*Yes, No*)

1630

---

b

1816

To be a series, there must be at least (*two, three*) items.

1817

---

your

2003

Here are two more words that should not be confused:

    they're (means **they are**)
    their (means **belonging to them**)

Use **they're** only when you can put the two words _____

_____ in its place.

2004

Christmas, Library

2190

The Rex hardware company is giving away free samples of glasscote enamel this week.

_____

2191

question

a. **Ross lives on a farm.**
b. **Does Ross live on a farm?**

In which sentence does the subject come between the

verb and its helper—*a* or *b*? _____

128   129

To *link* means "to connect." We might, for example, link
two chains together.

Rosa is treasurer.

is

In this little sentence, the verb **is** links the noun **treasurer**

to the subject _____.

316   317

Most verbs show by their endings whether they mean
present or past time.

a. I *walk* **to school every day.**
b. I *walked* **to school every day.**

In which sentence does the verb show past time? _____

505

---

laid   **The dog must have** (*laid, lain*) **down in a mud puddle.**

692   693

However, in sentences that begin with words like **There is**
and **Here are**, the verb comes first. Therefore, before se-
verb   lecting your verb, you must look ahead to see whether a

_____ or _____ subject is coming.

880   881

---

a   Any verb that ends in **n't** is negative because **n't** means

_____.

1068   *page 257*   1069

Lesson 43 Unit Review

We took a narrow road which (that) had many turns.

1443

We parked next to a fireplug. *Nobody had noticed it.*

_____

_____

1444

Yes

1630

The word **therefore** also causes many run-on sentences. **Therefore** is an adverb that tells *why*. It is not a conjunction like **and**. It has no power to join sentences.

    a. **My line broke,** *and* **the fish got away.**
    b. **My line broke,** *therefore* **the fish got away.**

Which is a run-on sentence? _____

1631

---

three

1817

a. **We talked, and joked together for two hours.**
b. **We talked, joked, and laughed together for two hours.**

One sentence does not contain a series of three items. From which sentence should the comma or commas be dropped? _____

1818

---

they are

2004

        a. **... car broke down.**
        b. **... coming over later.**

In which sentence would the two words **They are** make sense? _____

2005

Hardware Company, Glasscote

2191

We celebrate thanksgiving on the fourth thursday in november.

_____

2192

In the following question, underline the subject with one line, the main verb and its helper with two lines:

Must you study tonight?

Rosa is treasurer.

Any verb that links a word that follows it to the subject of the sentence is called a **linking verb**.

Underline the linking verb:

The woman was a detective.

PRESENT: I *walk*
PAST: I *walked*

To change the verb *walk* from present to past, we merely

add the letters _____.

We had (*laid, lain*) away all the gifts until Christmas.

There (was, were) only three boys in the class.

The subject that follows the verb in this sentence is the

noun _____.

---

a. **does**   **could**   **have**   **was**   **did**
b. **doesn't**   **couldn't**   **haven't**   **wasn't**   **didn't**

Which list of verbs is negative? ____

a. I, he, she, we, they
b. me, him, her, us, them

Which group of words would you use for the subjects of sentences? ____

1258

We parked next to a fireplug which (that) nobody had noticed.

1444

Friends gave us advice. *They had been to Canada.*

_____

_____

1445

---

b

a. **I had read the book.** *Therefore* **I wanted to see the movie.**
b. **I had read the book,** *therefore* **I wanted to see the movie.**

Which arrangement is correct? ____

1631

1632

---

a

a. **We were surrounded by a mountain of bundles, bags, and valises.**
b. **We were surrounded by a mountain of bundles, and bags.**

From which sentence should the comma or commas be dropped? ____

1818

1819

---

b

a. **... car broke down.**
b. **... coming over later.**

In which sentence would the contraction **They're** be correct? ____

2005

2006

Thanksgiving, Thursday, November

2192

I plan to enter Norris high school in the fall.

_____

2193

<u>Must</u> <u>you</u> <u>study</u> tonight? 130	In this question, underline the subject with one line, the main verb and its helper with two lines: **Can this parrot talk?** 131
was 318	**The woman was a detective.** The linking verb **was** shows that the **detective** and the **woman** are (*the same, different*) person(s). 319
–ed 506	Underline the two verbs that show past time: **appear laughed open smiled** 507
laid 694	**My wallet was still (*lying, laying*) on the sidewalk.** 695
boys 882	**There (was, were) only three boys in the class.** Because the subject of this sentence is the plural noun **boys,** we would choose the plural verb _____. 883
b 1070	It takes only one negative word to make a sentence negative. **These roses don't have thorns.** The word that makes this sentence negative is _____. 1071

When a pronoun follows the word **than** or **as,** don't select your pronoun until you think of the missing word or words.

a. **The problem puzzled Jack more than** (*it puzzled*) *me.*
b. **Jack understood the problem no better than** *me* (*did*).

In which sentence is the object form *me* correct? ____

1259

Friends who (that) had been to Canada gave us advice.

1445

The speaker told a story. *We thought it was very funny.*

_____

_____

1446

---

a

The ice had melted. ∧ **We couldn't skate.**

If we added the adverb **Therefore** at the point marked by the caret (∧), would we still have two separate sentences? (*Yes, No*)

1632

1633

---

b

We generally use the conjunction **and** or **or** to connect the last two items in a series.

Our team practices on Monday, Wednesday, and Friday of each week.

The last two items in this series are connected by the conjunction _____.

1819

1820

---

b

Underline the correct word:

(*Their, They're*) **car broke down.**

2006

2007

High School

Several stores on Drummond avenue sell mohawk sweaters.

_____

2193

2194

Can this parrot talk?	Before doing the next frames, take another look at these helping verbs, which have no other forms:
	
	     shall, will must, might
	     may, can should, would, could
	
	How many of these helpers have exactly five letters? _____

131	132

the same	**The building was a hospital.** The noun **hospital** refers to the same thing as the subject _____.
319	320

laughed, smiled	PRESENT: **chase wave smile taste** PAST: **chased waved smiled tasted** The present forms of these verbs already end in _e_. To change these verbs to the past, we do not need to add _–ed_ but only ____.
507	508

lying	Lesson **23** *Sit* and *Set*;
	              Rise and *Raise*
	
	                            [Frames 697-725]

695	

were	a. **There ... a big tree in our yard.** b. **There ... several big trees in our yard.** In which sentence would it be wrong to use the singular verb **is?** ____
883	884

don't	**These roses have no thorns.** The word that makes this sentence negative is _____.
1071	1072

When you use pronouns in pairs, use the same pronouns that you would if you used them one at a time.

He **repaired the bike.**   *I* **repaired the bike.**

Now let's put these two sentences together:

_____ **and** ____ **repaired the bike.**

1260

The crowd cheered Nina. *Her hit won the game.* (Try *whose*.)

_____

_____

1447

Can the pronoun **it** or the adverb **then** or **therefore** start a new sentence? (*Yes, No*)

1634

Do not leave money, jewelry, or other valuables in your desk.

The last two items in this series are connected by the conjunction _____.

1821

Here are two more words to straighten out in your mind:

who's (means who is *or* who has)
whose (means belonging to whom)

Do not use the contraction **who's** unless you can fit in the two words _____ or the two words _____.

2008

We got our new ford right after easter and drove to the Smoky mountains.

_____

2195

Here, once again, are the three verbs that can be used as either helpers or as main verbs:

be (is, am, are — was, were, been)
have (has, had)   do (does, did)

The verbs **was** and **been** are forms of the verb _____.

132   133

---

building

Rosa is . .?. .

This sentence must be completed. Any word that completes it might be called a _completer_. The grammar name for _completer_ is **complement**.

The first _____ letters of the words _completer_ and _complement_ are the same. (How many?)

320   321

–d

a. **We** _washed_ **the car.**
b. **We** _have washed_ **the car.**

Both these sentences show past time.

In which sentence does the verb consist of two words? _____

508   509

To sit means "to take a sitting position" or "to be in place."

We say, "Don _sits_ in the front row" and "The dictionaries _sit_ on the top shelf."

Supply the missing verb:

The patients _____ and wait for the doctor.

697

---

b

a. **There ... several telephones in the office.**
b. **There ... a telephone in the office.**

Which sentence requires the plural verb **are?** _____

884   885

---

no

These roses don't have thorns.
These roses have no thorns.

How many negative words does each of these sentences have? _____

1072   1073

When you use a pronoun with a noun, use the same pronoun that you would if you used the pronoun alone.

Del waited for *Bob*.   **Del waited for** *me*.

Del waited for Bob and _____.

1261

Lesson **50** Using *–ing* Word Groups

[Frames 1449-1471]

The words **it, then,** and **therefore** do not always start new sentences. They can come, too, in the middle of sentences.

If you tease the dog, *it* **might bite you.**
If you can't be a good loser, *then* **you had better not play.**
New drivers, *therefore*, **should drive slowly.**

Are these run-on sentences? (*Yes, No*)

1635

When all the items in a series are connected by the conjunction **and** or **or**, do not use any commas at all.

a. **The leaves turn** *red* **and** *brown* **and** *yellow* **in the autumn.**
b. **The leaves turn** *red brown* **and** *yellow* **in the autumn.**

Which sentence does *not* require any commas? _____ 1822

. . . paper did you correct?

Would the words **Who is** (or the words **Who has**) make sense in this sentence? (*Yes, No*)

2009

The Belleville voters' club will hold its september meeting in our school auditorium.

_____

2196

be

133

In this and the following frames, the main verb is printed in italics, and the first letter of one or more helping verbs is given. Complete the spelling of each helping verb.

I _w_____ *watching* **the steam shovel.**

134

---

six

321

Rosa is *treasurer.*

Here the *complement* is the noun _____.

The complement **treasurer** refers to the same person as the subject _____.

322

---

b

509

We *have washed* **the car.**

In this sentence the main verb *washed* is used with the helping verb _____.

510

---

sit

697

PRESENT   SIMPLE PAST   PAST WITH HELPER
sit (on a chair)   **sat**   **(have) sat**

Is the word **set** either one of the past forms of the verb **sit**? (*Yes, No*)

698

---

a

885

Underline the verb that agrees with the subject:

Here (*is, are*) the tickets to the game.

886

---

one

1073

Using two negative words to make a single negative statement is a bad mistake in English. This mistake is called a **double negative.**

     WRONG: **These roses** *don't* **have** *no* **thorns.**

To correct this sentence, you would need to omit either the word _____ or _____.

page 267

1074

me

1261

In this and the following frames, underline the correct word or words in each sentence:

(*He, Him*) and (*I, me*) **learned this duet last summer.**

1262

Eileen has several hobbies. *They keep her busy.*
Eileen has several hobbies *that keep her busy.*

We combined these two sentences by changing the italicized sentence to an _____ clause.

1449

No

1635

Do not capitalize **it, then,** or **therefore** unless the word group it follows is a complete sentence.

      a. **When I petted the cat,** *it* **scratched me.**
      b. **I petted the cat,** *it* **scratched me.**

Put a period after **cat,** and write *it* with a capital letter in (*a, b*).

1636

---

a

1822

The leaves turn *red* **and** *brown* **and** *yellow* **in the autumn.**

This sentence requires no commas because all the items in the series are connected by the conjunction _____.

1823

No

2009

Underline the correct word:

      (*Who's, Whose*) **paper did you correct?**

2010

Voters' Club, September

2196

Lesson **77** Capitals for Titles and Names

[Frames 2198-2228]

was 134	The key *s*_____ *fit* this lock. 135
treasurer Rosa 322	Because the complement we are studying refers back to the subject, it is called a **subject complement**. **These books are dictionaries.** The noun **books** is the subject, but the noun **dictionaries** is the *subject* _____. 323
have 510	**Bob** *has washed* **the car.** In this sentence the main verb *washed* is used with the helping verb _____. 511
No 698	PRESENT SIMPLE PAST PAST WITH HELPER **sit** (on a chair) **sat** **(have) sat** The simple past form and the helper form used with **have, has,** and **had** are (*alike, different*). 699
are 886	**There's** means **There is,** and **Here's** means **Here is.** The words **There's** and **Here's** should be used only before (*plural, singular*) subjects. 887
don't, no 1074	When you switch off a light, the light goes out. There is no use in pressing the switch again. In the same way, when you use one negative word, your sentence becomes negative, and adding a second negative word is useless. WRONG: **I didn't eat no breakfast this morning.** The two negative words are _____ and ____. 1075

He, I

Have I ever told you what nearly happened to (*she, her*) and (*I, me*)?

---

adjective

In this lesson we will learn how to combine sentences by using another device, the –*ing* word group.

a. **José walked down the aisle.**
b. *He looked for his friends.*

Sentence *b* states a fact about (*José, aisle*) in sentence *a*.

---

b

---

a. **Jan used the racket,** *then* **she tried to return it.**
b. **If Jan uses the racket,** *then* **she can't return it.**

Only one of these is a run-on sentence.

Put a period after **racket,** and write *then* with a capital letter in (*a, b*).

---

and

---

a. **We cannot** *see, smell,* **or** *taste* **pure air.**
b. **We cannot** *see,* **or** *smell,* **or** *taste* **pure air.**

From which sentence should the commas be dropped? ___

Whose

... the girl in the front seat?

Would the words **Who is** make sense in this sentence? (*Yes, No*)

A word that shows a person's profession, rank, or office is called a **title.**

doctor   professor   captain   mayor   judge

These nouns can be used as _____.

should 135	It _h_____ _b_____ _raining_ **all day.** 136
complement 323	**These books are dictionaries.** The _subject_ of a sentence usually comes before the verb. The _subject complement_ usually comes _____ the verb. 324
has 511	**Someone** _had washed_ **the car.** In this sentence the main verb _washed_ is used with the helping verb _____. 512
alike 699	a. **We . . . in the balcony.** b. **We** _had_ **. . . in the library.** In both sentences we would use the same form of the verb **sit.** This form would be _____. 700
singular 887	a. **Here are some stories by Virginia Driving Hawk Sneve.** b. **Here's some stories by Virginia Driving Hawk Sneve.** Which sentence is correct? ____ 888
didn't, no 1075	a. **I ate no breakfast this morning.** b. **I didn't eat breakfast this morning.** c. **I didn't eat no breakfast this morning.** Which sentence is wrong because it contains a double negative? ____ 1076

her, me 1263	The Changs and (*they, them*) promised to buy tickets from me. 1264
José 1450	a. **José walked down the aisle.** b. *He looked for his friends.* **José walked down the aisle,** *looking for his friends.* We changed sentence *b* to a word group that begins with a word that ends in *–ing*. This word is _____. 1451
a 1637	a. **Some of the people,** *therefore,* **had to stand.** b. **There weren't enough seats for all the people,** *therefore* **some of them had to stand.** Only one of these is a run-on sentence. Put a period after **people,** and write *therefore* with a capital letter in (*a, b*). 1638
b 1824	**We cannot** *see* **or** *smell* **or** *taste* **pure air.** This sentence requires no commas because all the items in the series are connected by _____. 1825
Yes 2011	Underline the correct word: (*Who's, Whose*) **the girl in the front seat?** 2012

titles
 	
2198
	Capitalize titles when they are used with personal names; for example, **Professor Dow, Captain Marsh, Judge Ross.**
	      a. **The boys admired their** *coach.*
	      b. **The boys admired** *coach* **Brady.**
	In which sentence should *coach* be capitalized because it is part of a person's name? ____
	
	2199

has (had) been 136	Ralph m_____ h_____ *taken* **the wrong road.** 137

after 324	Adjectives, as well as nouns, can be used as subject complements.
	    a. **Rosa is** *treasurer.*
	    b. **Rosa is** *capable.*
	In which sentence is the subject complement not a noun, but an adjective? ____ 325

had 512	Most verbs show past time in these two ways: 1. By the simple past form that ends in *–ed.* 2. By the same simple past form combined with *have, has,* or *had,* which are called _____ *ing* verbs. 513
sat 700	The verb **sit** must not be confused with the verb **set.** **To set** means "to put or to place *something.*" **We** *set* **the chairs around the desk.** What objects are put or placed somewhere in this sentence? _____ 701
a 888	a. **There's the names of our members.** b. **There are the names of our members.** Which sentence is correct? ____ 889
c 1076	a. **Chuck couldn't get along with anybody.** b. **Chuck couldn't get along with nobody.** Which sentence is wrong because it contains a double negative? ____ 1077

they 1264	Mr. Krantz appointed (*he, him*) and (*I, me*) as class representatives. 1265
looking 1451	*looking for his friends* We call this an –*ing* word group. It begins with the word *looking*, which ends with the three letters _____. 1452
b 1638	In this and in each of the following frames, you will find a sentence. If the sentence is correct, write *Correct* on the blank line. If the sentence is a run-on sentence, correct it like this: EXAMPLE: **We rang the bell, then we knocked on the door.** *bell. Then* (*Turn to the next frame.*) 1639
or (*or* conjunctions) 1825	In this and the following frames, add commas wherever the sentence contains a series. If a sentence does not contain a series, make no change. Remember that it takes *three* items to make a series. **Only Alaska Texas and California are larger than Montana.** 1826
Who's 2012	It's and its are the two words most often confused. it's (means **it is** *or* **it has**) its (means **belonging to it**) In the contraction **it's**, the apostrophe stands for the missing letter ____ or for the missing letters _____. 2013
b 2199	a. **A meeting was called by** *mayor* **Gibson.** b. **Our town will soon elect a new** *mayor.* In which sentence should *mayor* be capitalized because it is part of a person's name? ____ 2200

must (might, may) have 137	Juan *w*_____ *read* **the book as soon as he** *c*_____ *get* **it.** 138
b 325	Rosa is *capable.* The adjective *capable* modifies the subject of the sentence, which is _____. 326
helping 513	I ... *locked* **the door.** If you added the helper *have* to the verb in this sentence, would you need to change the verb *locked*? (*Yes, No*) 514
chairs 701	After you **set** something down, it **sits** there until you move it somewhere else. We **set** the dog's dinner on the floor, and it _____ there until he eats it. 702
b 889	When we change **There is** or **There are** to **Is there** or **Are there**, the sentence becomes a question. In such a question, the verb still comes before the subject. **Are there any nuts in this ice cream?** The verb **Are** agrees with the plural subject _____. 890
b 1077	Underline the correct word: **My dad never eats** (*no, any*) **onions.** 1078

him, me 1265	**The Akiras and** (*we, us*) **shop at the same market.** 1266
–ing 1452	Compare an –*ing* word group with a clause. CLAUSE: <u>*who*</u> <u>*was*</u> <u>*looking*</u> *for his friends* –*ING* WORD GROUP: *looking for his friends* Does an –*ing* word group, like a clause, have a subject and a verb? (*Yes, No*) 1453
	An empty bottle is not really empty, it is actually filled with air. _____ 1640
Alaska, Texas, 1826	**Cleaners are not responsible for ornaments belts or buckles that are not removed from suits and dresses.** 1827
i ha 2013	Don't use **it's** unless the two words **it is** or the two words **it has** would fit in. a. ... a rainy day. b. ... meal is ready. In which sentence would **It is** make sense? ____ 2014
a 2200	**The** *lieutenant* **was praised by** *major* **Lozano.** The word that should be capitalized is (*lieutenant, major*). 2201

will, can 138	Yes, I _d_____ turn_ **off the alarm this morning.** 139
Rosa 326	a. **This book is** _heavy._ b. **This book is** _a dictionary._ In which sentence is the subject complement an adjective? ___ 327
No 514	**Roy** _has corrected_ **his test.** If you dropped the helper _has_ in the above sentence, would you need to change the verb _corrected_? (Yes, No) 515
sits 702	Here are the forms of the verb **set:** PRESENT SIMPLE PAST PAST WITH HELPER **set** (to put) **set** **(have) set** This verb is different from all the other verbs we have studied because it has only _____ form. (How many?) 703
nuts 890	a. **Is there a seat for me?** b. **Are there a seat for me?** Which sentence is correct? ___ 891
any 1078	Most negative words begin with _n._ However, here are two negative words that do not begin with _n:_ **hardly, scarcely.** **I could hardly see the sign.** The word that makes this sentence negative is _____. 1079

we 1266	We couldn't find the Salazars or (*they, them*) anywhere in the park. 1267
No 1453	Let's see how we change a sentence to an –*ing* word group: <u>He</u> <u>looked</u> for his friends. ↓ *looking* for his friends We drop the subject of the sentence, **He**. Then we change the verb **looked** to _____. 1454
empty. It 1640	After you play this game a few times, you tire of it. _____ 1641
ornaments, belts, 1827	One should always keep a pad and pencil near the telephone. 1828
a 2014	Underline the correct word: (*It's, Its*) **a rainy day.** 2015
Major 2201	People were pleased that *superintendent* **Baird promoted the brave** *officer*. The word that should be capitalized is (*superintendent, officer*). 2202

did 139	Underline the complete verb in each sentence. Remember that the complete verb includes all helpers that may be present. **Perry could eat an entire pie.** 140
a 327	A linking verb is usually followed by a subject complement. The most common linking verb is **be.** Memorize its various forms for the frames that follow: **FORMS OF** *BE:* **is, am, are—was, were, been** After each of the above verbs we may expect to find a _____ *complement.* 328
No 515	**Mother . . . all day.** **Mother** *has* **. . . all day.** Would the verb *worked* be correct in both the above sentences? (*Yes, No*) 516
one 703	PRESENT: **I . . . the table for breakfast every morning.** SIMPLE PAST: **I . . . the table for dinner last night.** PAST WITH HELPER: **I** *have* **. . . the table for three.** Would the verb **set** be correct in all three of these sentences? (*Yes, No*) 704
a 891	a. **Is there any stamps in that drawer?** b. **Are there any stamps in that drawer?** Which sentence is correct? ____ 892
hardly 1079	a. **I could hardly see the sign.** b. **I couldn't hardly see the sign.** Which sentence is wrong because it contains a double negative? ____ 1080

them 1267	**Peter or** (*she, her*) **will serve as secretary.** 1268
looking 1454	**José walked down the aisle,** *looking for his friends.* The *–ing* word group *looking for his friends* modifies the noun (*José, aisle*). 1455
Correct 1641	**I got my haircut, then I discovered that I had left my money at home.** _____ 1642
No commas 1828	**The high winds damaged houses barns trees and power lines throughout the state.** 1829
It's 2015	**... meal is ready.** In this sentence, would the two words **It is** (or the two words **It has**) make sense? (*Yes, No*) 2016

Superintendent
 	
2202
	Also capitalize words that show family relationship when they are used *with* personal names; for example, **Uncle Don, Grandmother Harris.**
	
	    a. **I received a gift from my** *aunt.*
	    b. **I received a gift from my** *aunt* **Betty.**
	
	In which sentence should *aunt* be capitalized? _____ 2203

could eat 140	**Have you heard the news?** 141
subject 328	Fill in the two missing forms of the linking verb *be:* **FORMS OF** *BE:* **is, am,** _____**—was, were,** _____. 329

Yes
 	
516
	Verbs like **walk, lock, close,** and **save** are called **regular verbs** because we form their past by adding *–d* or *–ed.*
	
	    a. **play—played**
	    b. **write—wrote**
	    c. **march—marched**
	
	Which one of the above verbs is not regular? ____
	
	517

Yes 704	Let's compare this pair of similar verbs: PRESENT SIMPLE PAST PAST WITH HELPER **sit** (on a chair) **sat** **(have) sat** **set** (to put) **set** **(have) set** Would you ever use **set** to mean "to take a sitting position" or "to be in place"? (*Yes, No*) 705
b 892	In question sentences that begin with **Where** or **How much,** the verb also comes ahead of the subject. Underline the subject with one line and the verb with two lines: **Where** (*was, were*) **the keys?** 893
b 1080	**We scarcely had time to eat.** The word that makes this sentence negative is _____. 1081

she

1268

There was no room for the Linds and (*we*, *us*) in their car.

1269

José

1455

José walked down the aisle, *looking for his friends.*

This is a good sentence.

Must an *–ing* word group be next to the word it modifies? (*Yes, No*)

1456

---

haircut. Then ·

1642

Sandy has moved away, therefore I seldom see him.

_____

1643

---

houses, barns, trees,

1829

My mother never irons sheets or towels or pillow cases.

1830

No

2016

Underline the correct word:

(*It's*, *Its*) meal is ready.

2017

---

b

2203

---

a. **This tree was planted by my** *grandfather.*
b. **This tree was planted by** *grandfather* **Resnick.**

In which sentence should *grandfather* be capitalized? ___

2204

Have, heard 141	**Your parents might be expecting you early.** 142
are, been 329	Fill in the two missing forms: **FORMS OF** *BE:* **is, _____, are—was, _____, been.** 330
b 517	SIMPLE PAST PAST WITH HELPER **played** **(have) played** **worked** **(has) worked** **marched** **(had) marched** These are all regular verbs. Do we use the same form with or without the helper **have, has,** or **had?** (*Yes, No*) 518

No
 	
705
	Use the verb **set** only when you mention the "something" that is put or placed somewhere.
	
	    a. I . . . my package on the next seat.
	    b. I . . . in the same seat all semester.
	
	In which sentence would **set** be correct? ____
	
	706

<u>were keys</u> 893	Underline the subject with one line and the verb with two lines: **How much** (*is, are*) **those notebooks?** 894
scarcely 1081	a. **We didn't scarcely have time to eat.** b. **We scarcely had time to eat.** Which sentence is wrong because it contains a double negative? ____ 1082

us 1269	Give the ticket to Rex because he likes hockey more than (*I, me*). 1270
No 1456	José walked down the aisle, *looking for his friends.* *Looking for his friends,* José walked down the aisle. Can an *–ing* word group be moved from one position to another? (*Yes, No*) 1457
away. Therefore 1643	If there were one tack on the Sahara Desert, Pete would probably step on it. _____ 1644
No commas 1830	The train rumbled to a stop backed up a few yards and stopped again. 1831
Its 2017	To show ownership, use the word (*it's, its*). 2018
b 2204	One of my *cousins* arrived with *uncle* Perry. The word that should be capitalized is (*cousins, uncle*). 2205

might be expecting 142	**Must we wait for Don?** 143
am, were 330	Fill in the two missing forms: FORMS OF *BE:* _____, am, are—_____, were, been 331

Yes
 	
518
	To make some verbs show past time, we do not add –*d* or –*ed*. Instead, we must change the spelling of the word itself.
	
	      PRESENT: I *see* my cousins every day.
	      SIMPLE PAST: I *saw* my cousins last week.
	
	The simple past form of *see* is _____.
	
	519

a 706	In this and the following frames, underline the correct forms of **sit** and **set:** **I will** (*sit, set*) **wherever you** (*sit, set*) **the chair.** 707
<u>are</u> notebooks 894	In this and the following frames, underline the verb or words that agree with the subject. In each sentence you will find the verb ahead of the subject. **There** (*was, were*) **several books by Maya Angelou on the shelf.** 895
a 1082	In this and the following frames, underline the correct word. To make good sense in several of the sentences you will need to choose a negative word, but remember to avoid double negatives. **I couldn't find my report card** (*anywhere, nowhere*). 1083

I 1270	The dog's constant barking annoyed our neighbors as much as (*we, us*). 1271
Yes 1457	a. **We stood at the window.** b. *We* <u>*watched*</u> *the parade.* **We stood at the window,** *watching the parade.* To change sentence *b* to an *–ing* word group, we drop the subject *We* and change the verb *watched* to _____. 1458
Correct 1644	An elephant is unable to jump, it can't get its four feet off the ground at the same time. _____ 1645
stop, yards, 1831	Wind rain ice rivers and streams are constantly changing the earth's surface. 1832
its 2018	a. you're they're who's it's b. your their whose its Which group contains words that you can use to take the place of a pronoun and its verb? ____ 2019

Uncle
 	
2205
	When **Mother, Father, Dad,** and so forth, are used as personal names, they are often capitalized.
	    Is *Mother* **calling me?** **What did** *Father* **say?**
	In the sentence below, which italicized word is used in place of a personal name? _____
	    I introduced *Father* **to Nancy's** *mother.*
	
	2206

Must, wait 143	**Uncle Ernie must have missed the train.** 144

is, was
 	
331
	Other verbs can be used as linking verbs. Some are
	    seem **feel** **become**
	    look **appear** **get** (when it means **become**)
	           The children ... tired.
	Would each of these verbs fit into the above sentence? (*Yes, No*)
	
	332

saw 519	SIMPLE PAST: I *saw* **that movie.** PAST WITH HELPER: I *have seen* **that movie.** Do we use the same form of the verb after the helper *have* that we use for the simple past? (*Yes, No*) 520
sit, set 707	(*Sit, Set*) **your work aside and** (*sit, set*) **down for a rest.** 708
were 895	**Here** (*are, is*) **the paints for the posters.** 896
anywhere 1083	**Dick** (*hasn't, has*) **never ridden a horse.** 1084

us 1271	I can't print as neatly as (*he, him*). 1272
watching 1458	Often we can change the first of two sentences to an –*ing* word group. We do this in the same way: a. *We stood at the window.* b. **We watched the parade.** ↓ _____ *at the window,* **we watched the parade.** 1459
jump. It 1645	If you eat a good breakfast, then you won't get hungry before lunch time. _____ 1646
Wind, rain, ice, rivers, 1832	Evert and Goolagong and Wade are all tennis players. 1833
a 2019	In this and the following frames, underline the correct word in each pair. Choose the contraction with an apostrophe only when you can fit two words in its place. **I'll get** (*your, you're*) **lunch if** (*your, you're*) **hungry.** 2020
Father 2206	When **mother, father, dad,** and so forth, are used merely to show family relationship, do not capitalize them. *Dad,* **may Jim stay if his** *mother* **says it's all right?** In the sentence above, which italicized word is used to show family relationship? _____ 2207

must have missed 144	I shall be flying to New York at this time tomorrow. 145
Yes 332	The children *seem* tired. The children *appear* tired. The children *look* tired. The children *become* tired. The children *feel* tired. The children *get* tired. In each of these sentences with linking verbs, the adjective **tired** refers back to the subject _____. 333
No 520	PRESENT SIMPLE PAST PAST WITH HELPER see saw (have) seen We say, "I *saw* that movie," but we say, "I *have* _____ that movie." 521
Set, sit 708	The cat (*sat, set*) waiting for me to (*sit, set*) down its meal. 709
are 896	There (*is, are*) only one thing wrong with our plans. 897
has 1084	The police searched the car very thoroughly, but they found (*something, nothing*). 1085

he	This color suits you better than (*I, me*).
1272	1273
Standing	**I heard my name.** Change the above sentence to an *–ing* word group: _____
1459	1460
Correct	**Planets give off no light of their own, they merely reflect the light of the sun.** _____
1646	1647
No commas	**Shells tobacco furs and stone are among the many things that have been used for money.**
1833	1834
your, you're	(*Their, They're*) **ripe when** (*their, they're*) **skin is speckled.**
2020	2021
mother	When a word such as **mother, father,** or **dad** is used only to show family relationship, it generally follows **a, an, the,** or a possessive word such as **my, his, their,** or **Don's.** **The** *mother* **of one of the boys asked my** *dad* **to help.** Should the italicized words be capitalized? (*Yes, No*)
2207	2208

shall be flying 145	**You should have been changing your clothes.** 146
children 333	In the lesson on adjectives that we studied earlier, all the adjectives came *before* the nouns they modified. However, adjectives that are used as subject complements come (*before, after*) the nouns they modify. 334
seen 521	We say, "Cynthia *saw* her grade," but we say, "Cynthia *has* _____ her grade." 522
sat, set 709	**If Mel had (*sat, set*) where he should have (*sat, set*), he would not have been marked absent.** 710
is 897	**Where (*are, is*) my box of tools?** 898
nothing 1085	**The driver didn't see (*any, no*) train coming.** 1086

me 1273	Sandra's parents are not as musical as (*she, her*). 1274
Hearing my name 1460	Miss Whitewater ran for office. Change the above sentence to an *–ing* word group: _____ 1461
own. They 1647	Floyd wanted a dollar for the stamp, then he lowered the price to fifty cents. _____ 1648
Shells, tobacco, furs, 1834	A bee is not likely to sting unless it is touched stepped on or molested in some way. 1835
They're, their 2021	(*Whose, Who's*) brother is the boy (*whose, who's*) leading the band? 2022
No 2208	a. A Father has many responsibilities. b. I realize that Father has many responsibilities. In which sentence should **Father** not be capitalized because it is used only to show family relationship? _____ 2209

should have been changing 146	
after 334	a. **The ride seemed** *long*. b. **We took a** *long* **ride.** The adjective *long* is used as a subject complement in sentence ____. 335
seen 522	**We** *have seen* **many beautiful birds.** If you dropped the helper *have*, you would need to change the verb *seen* to _____. 523
sat, sat 710	The verbs **rise** and **raise** sometimes cause trouble, too. **To rise** means "to go up" or "to get up." We say, "The fans *rise* from their seats" and "The smoke *rises*." Supply the missing verb: **The river _____ every spring.** 711
is 898	(*There are, There's*) **no spoons for the ice cream.** 899
any 1086	**There are many deer in these woods, but we boys didn't see** (*none, any*). 1087

she 1274	We eat our dinner earlier than (*they, them*). 1275
Running for office 1461	In this and the following frames, combine each pair of sentences by changing the italicized sentence to an –*ing* word group. Write the –*ing* word group in the blank space. **Kip got off the bus.** *He forgot his books.* **Kip got off the bus,** _____. 1462
stamp. Then 1648	**The flowers are not real, they are made entirely of glass.** _____ 1649
touched, on, 1835	**Alligators and crocodiles cannot breathe or swallow food under water.** 1836
Whose, who's 2022	(*It's, Its*) **not the same color as** (*its, it's*) **mother.** 2023
a 2209	a. **I often helped Grandfather take care of his garden.** b. **Dan helped his Grandfather take care of his garden.** In which sentence should **Grandfather** not be capitalized because it is used to show family relationship? ____ 2210

Up to this point, all the sentences we have analyzed were built on a two-part framework: a *subject* and a _____.

148

---

a

335

a. **She wore a** *beautiful* **ring.**
b. **The ring looked** *beautiful.*

The adjective *beautiful* is used as a subject complement in sentence ____.

336

---

saw

523

Now we shall look at the three forms of another verb:

PRESENT	SIMPLE PAST	PAST WITH HELPER
do	**did**	**(have) done**

We say, "I *did* the dishes," but we say, "I *have* _____ the dishes."

524

---

rises

711

PRESENT	SIMPLE PAST	PAST WITH HELPER
rise (go up)	**rose**	**(have) risen**

We say, "A strong wind *rose*," but we say, "A strong wind had _____."

712

There are

899

How much (*is, are*) **those coats in the window?**

900

---

any

1087

It must be a poor movie because I met (*nobody, anybody*) **who liked it.**

1088

they 1275	The teacher calls on Clark oftener than (*she, her*). 1276
forgetting his books. 1462	*I read over my theme.* **I found several errors.** ————————————————————, **I found several errors.** 1463
real. They 1649	**The manager didn't know Dad, therefore he wouldn't cash his check.** ———————————————— 1650
No commas 1836	Lesson **64** Commas for Interrupters [Frames 1838-1864]
It's, its 2023	(*Whose, Who's*) **going in** (*their, they're*) **car?** 2024
b 2210	**My** *mother* **and** *aunt* **Martha called on Cathy's** *grandmother*. Only one of the italicized words in this sentence should be capitalized. It is the word ————. 2211

verb 148	**The rain stopped.** In this sentence, the action verb **stopped** completes the meaning of the sentence. We feel satisfied because something sensible has been said about the subject _____. 149
b 336	It is easy to tell a subject complement from a direct object. A sentence with a direct object always has an action verb. The action passes from the subject to the direct object. **Rosa closed the door.** In this sentence, **Rosa** did something to the _____. 337
done 524	We say, "Sally *did* the writing," but we say, "Sally *has* _____ the writing." 525
risen 712	Write the correct past forms of **rise:** **The campers** _____ **after the sun** *had* _____. 713
are 900	(*Where are, Where's*) **my other shoes?** 901
nobody 1088	**Dad wouldn't take** (*anything, nothing*) **for his bad cough.** 1089

her 1276	(*Mrs. Ming, Mrs. Ming she*) **bakes wonderful pies.** 1277
Reading over my theme, 1463	**Chuck swung at the ball.** *He missed it by a foot.* **Chuck swung at the ball,** _____. 1464
Dad. Therefore 1650	Lesson **57** Spotting Sentence Errors [Frames 1652-1671]
	We sometimes interrupt a sentence to put in one or more words for clearness or emphasis. These words are less important than the rest of the sentence. **The snow,** *however,* **soon melted.** Which word could you omit without changing the meaning of this sentence? _____ 1838
Who's, their 2024	(*Your, You're*) **stepping on** (*its, it's*) **tail.** 2025
Aunt 2211	Capitalize the first word and all important words in titles of books, stories, poems, plays, and so forth. *The Red Pony*　　　　　"The Song of Hiawatha" *When the Legends Die*　　"The Last Leaf" Write only the capital letters you would use in writing this title: *the blazed trail.* _____ 2212

rain 149	**The rain stopped the game.** Here the subject and verb alone do not tell the whole story. In this sentence we are told *what* the rain **stopped.** The meaning of this sentence is not completed until we get to the noun _____. 150
door 337	Now let's look at a sentence with a subject complement: **Rosa is treasurer.** Did **Rosa** do something to the **treasurer?** (*Yes, No*) 338
done 525	**Vera *had done* every problem.** If you dropped the helper *had,* you would need to change the verb *done* to _____. 526
rose, risen 713	**To raise** means "to lift *something* up." **We *raised* the windows to let in some air.** What is the "something" that we raised? _____ 714
Where are 901	(*Here are, Here's*) **the names of our members.** 902
anything 1089	**My throat was so sore that I** (*couldn't, could*) **hardly swallow.** 1090

Mrs. Ming 1277	(*I and my friend, My friend and I*) **had just gone in swimming.** 1278
missing it by a foot. 1464	*We walked along the shore.* **We picked up interesting shells.** ————————————————————————**, we picked up interesting shells.** 1465

	In this and the following frames, one of the two items is wrong because it is a run-on sentence or because it contains a fragment. Write the letter of the *correct* item.
	
	    a. **We climbed the tower. And looked at the scenery.**
	    b. **We climbed the tower and looked at the scenery.**
	
	———
	                       1652

however
 	
1838
	The snow, *however*, **soon melted.**
	Words like *however* are called **interrupters** because they break into and interrupt the sentence. If you omit an interrupter, you do not change the meaning of a sentence.
	Underline the two-word interrupter in this sentence:
	    Nancy, of course, was surprised.
	                       1839

You're, its 2025	(*Its, It's*) **color shows that** (*its, it's*) **ripe.** 2026

T B T
 	
2212
	a. *The Bottle Imp*
	    b. *the Bottle Imp*
	    c. *The bottle imp*
	
	Which story title is correctly capitalized? ——
	
	2213

game 150	a. **The rain stopped.** b. **The rain stopped the game.** In which sentence does the action start with the **rain** and pass over to something else? ____ 151
No 338	a. **Rosa is treasurer.** b. **Rosa is capable.** In each of these sentences, the subject complement *refers back* to the subject _____. 339
did 526	Here are the three forms of our third verb: PRESENT SIMPLE PAST PAST WITH HELPER **go** **went** **(have) gone** Write the correct forms of **go**: **Matthew Henson** _____ **where few others** *have* _____. 527
windows 714	**To raise** means "to lift *something* up." Never use the verb **raise** unless you mention the "something" that is lifted. **The passing cars** *raise* **much dust.** What is the "something" that the passing cars raise? _____ 715
Here are 902	Lesson **30** Subject-Verb Agreement in a Story [Frames 904-915]
could 1090	**Virginia left the store without buying because** (*either, neither*) **of the two dresses she liked fitted her.** 1091

My friend and I 1278	(*Those, Them*) are the only ones I like. 1279
Walking along the shore, 1465	**Earl was on a ladder.** *He was washing a window.* **Earl was on a ladder,** _____. 1466

b
 	
1652
	Continue to write the letter of the correct item:
	
	    a. **Clyde was out of breath, he had been running.**
	    b. **Clyde was out of breath. He had been running.**
	
	_____
	
	1653

of course 1839	**Nancy,** *of course,* **was surprised.** **Nancy was surprised.** Does omitting the interrupter *of course* change the meaning of this sentence? (*Yes, No*) 1840
Its, it's 2026	(*Their, They're*) **not sure** (*who's, whose*) **fingerprints they are.** 2027
a 2213	Unless they are the first word in a title, do not capitalize: SPECIAL ADJECTIVES: **a, an, the** CONJUNCTIONS: **and, but, or** SHORT PREPOSITIONS: **of, in, to, for, with,** and so forth Underline the words you would capitalize in the following title: **"the hunting of the snark."** 2214

b 151	The rain stopped the game. The **rain** performs the action, and the _____ receives the action. 152
Rosa 339	a. b. One arrow goes from left to right. The other goes from right to left. Which arrow would represent a sentence with a subject complement? ____ 340
went, gone 527	Write the correct past forms of **go**: I _____ **to find out where Steve** _had_ _____. 528
dust 715	When you **raise** the flag, the flag **rises.** The flag **rises** because you _____ it. 716
	Each sentence of the incident that follows presents a problem in subject-verb agreement. Underline the verb that agrees with its subject. **There** (_is, are_) **several very young children on our block.** 904
neither 1091	**We** (_could, couldn't_) **hardly wait to hear the Diana Ross concert.** 1092

Those 1279	**Could you do** (*them, those*) **problems for today?** 1280
washing a window. 1466	*Dad backed his car.* **He struck a post.** _____, **Dad struck a post.** 1467
b —— 1653	a. **My dad has been an engineer for almost twenty years.** b. **My dad has been an engineer. For almost twenty years.** 1654
No 1840	**Nancy,** *of course,* **was surprised.** In speaking this sentence, you drop your voice when you say *of course* and pause before and after this expression. In writing, you show these pauses by using _____. 1841
They're, whose 2027	Lesson **71** How to Punctuate Quotations [Frames 2029-2055]
"The Hunting . . . Snark" 2214	Copy and capitalize this title: **"turkey in the straw"** _____ 2215

game 152	The <u>driver</u> <u>stopped</u> the car. Here the **driver** performs the action, and the _____ receives the action. 153

b
 	
340
	In this and the following frames, one sentence contains a direct object and the other a subject complement.
	
	      a. **The teacher praised the** *winner.*
	      b. **My best friend was the** *winner.*
	
	Which sentence contains a subject complement? ____
	341

went, gone 528	**All the lights** *went* **out.** If you added the helper *have* to the verb, you would need to change *went* to _____. 529

raise
 	
716
	Here are the forms of the verb **raise:**
	
	  PRESENT SIMPLE PAST PAST WITH HELPER
	  raise (to lift) **raised** **(have) raised**
	The simple past form and the form we use with *have, has,*
	or *had* are (*alike, different*).
	717

are 904	**One of these children** (*has, have*) **a very annoying habit.** 905
could 1092	**Arthur wouldn't discuss his plans with** (*nobody, anybody*). 1093

those 1280	**Mr. Osgood asked** (*we, us*) **boys to give his car a push.** 1281
Backing his car, 1467	**I sat on the dock.** *I dangled my legs over the edge.* **I sat on the dock,** _____ _____. 1468
a 1654	a. **The sky was cloudy, therefore the eclipse was not visible.** b. **The sky was cloudy. Therefore the eclipse was not visible.** ____ 1655

commas
 	
1841
	The commas around an interrupter help your reader to keep his mind on the main idea of the sentence.
	
	    a. **Marta went by the way to Washington.**
	    b. **Marta went, by the way, to Washington.**
	
	In which sentence is it easier to follow the main idea? ____
	
	1842

	To quote means "to repeat someone's words." Around the dinner table, you might quote, or repeat, what a friend, a teacher, or the newspaper said. The repeated words are called a **quotation.** To quote a person means to _____ what he said. 2029
"Turkey in the Straw" 2215	Copy and capitalize this title: **"the house on the hill"** _____ 2216

car 153	**The police stopped the fight.** Here the _____ perform the action, and the _____ receives the action. 154
b 341	a. **The strawberries look** *ripe*. b. **The sparks started a** *fire*. Which sentence contains a subject complement? ____ 342

gone
 	
 529
	Verbs like **see, do,** and **go** are called **irregular verbs** because they do not follow the *–ed* pattern of most verbs.
	
	     a. take write drive speak
	     b. bake travel change wait
	
	 Which group consists of irregular verbs? ____
	
	 530

alike 717	Now let's compare the two verbs: PRESENT SIMPLE PAST PAST WITH HELPER **rise** (to go up) **rose** **(have) risen** **raise** (to lift) **raised** **(have) raised** Which verb is regular? _____ 718
has 905	**Little Bobby Klieg** (*don't, doesn't*) **know that he should not take things that do not belong to him.** 906
anybody 1093	Lesson **37** Unit Review *page 307* [Frames 1095-1115]

us 1281	(*We*, *Us*) **girls qualified for all the final races.** 1282
dangling my legs over the edge. 1468	*He picked up his bat.* **He walked to the plate.** ———————————————**, he walked to the plate.** 1469
b 1655	a. **There was one good feature about the movie. It finally ended.** b. **There was one good feature about the movie, it finally ended.** ——— 1656
b 1842	Here are some common interrupters that should be fenced off by commas from the rest of the sentence: **however for example I suppose** **of course on the whole if possible** Punctuate this sentence: **The sandwiches for example cost twenty cents.** 1843
repeat (tell) 2029	When you repeat what a person said directly *in his own words,* you are making a **direct quotation.** a. **The teacher said, "Your work has improved."** b. **The teacher said that my work has improved.** In which sentence do you find the *actual* words that the teacher used? ____ 2030
"The House on the Hill" 2216	Capitalize, too, the titles of movies, works of art, pieces of music, and so forth. **"A Raisin in the Sun"** **"St. Louis Blues"** **"Woman with Chrysanthemums"** **"Home on the Range"** Write only the capital letters you would use in writing this movie title: **"the legend of lobo."** —————— 2217

police, fight 154	Any word that receives the action of the verb is called a **direct object**. It is called a *direct* object because it receives the action of the verb *directly* from the subject. **The <u>rain</u> <u>stopped</u> the game.** The direct object of the action verb **stopped** is the noun _____.　　　　　　　　　　　　　155
a 342	a. **The lifeguard rescued the** *swimmer.* b. **Jane is an excellent** *swimmer.* Which sentence contains a subject complement? ____ 　　　　　　　　　　　　　343
a 530	a. **saw　　did　　went** b. **seen　　done　　gone** Which group of verbs would you use to show simple past time when the helping verb **have, has,** or **had** is *not* present? ____ 　　　　　　　　　　　　　531
raise 718	Use the verb **raise** only when you mention the "something" that is lifted up. a. **The price of our paper ... this year.** b. **We ... the price of our paper this year.** In which sentence would **raised** be correct? ____　719
doesn't 906	**Any article, like a book or a sweater, often (***disappears, disappear***) if it is left on the porch.** 　　　　　　　　　　　　　907
	Underline the correct word or words in each frame: **Everything Linda does, she does (***perfect, perfectly***).** 　　　　　　　　　　　　　1095

We 1282	**Why don't you let** (*we, us*) **fellows help you?** 1283
Picking up his bat, 1469	**Shep came to the door.** *He was wagging his tail.* **Shep came to the door, _____.** 1470
a 1656	a. **A deer nudged the hunter, who had fallen asleep on a log.** b. **A deer nudged the hunter. Who had fallen asleep on a log.** ____ 1657
sandwiches, example, 1843	INTERRUPTERS: **however for example I suppose** **of course on the whole if possible** Punctuate this sentence: **Earl I suppose took all the credit.** 1844
a 2030	When you repeat what a person said indirectly in *your* words, not his words, you are making an **indirect quotation.** a. **The teacher said, "Your work has improved."** b. **The teacher said that my work has improved.** In which sentence is the teacher's remark repeated in *someone else's* words? ____ 2031
T L L 2217	a. **"On top of old Smoky"** b. **"On Top Of Old Smoky"** c. **"On Top of Old Smoky"** Which song title is capitalized correctly? ____ 2218

game

155

1 2 3
The rain stopped the *game.*

In this sentence, the subject and verb alone do not express the complete idea. The meaning is not completed until we add the direct object *game.*
We say, therefore, that this sentence has a (*two-part, three-part*) framework.

156

---

b

343

Find the subject, verb, and subject complement in each sentence and write them in the proper blanks:

The first boat was probably a log.

S   V   SC

_____ _____ _____
344

---

a

531

a. I *done* my work.   We *seen* the accident.
b. I *did* my work.   We *saw* the accident.

Which pair of sentences is correct? ____

532

---

b

719

a. **Many pupils ... their hands when the teacher asked for volunteers.**
b. **Many pupils' hands ... when the teacher asked for volunteers.**

In which sentence would **raised** be correct? ____
720

---

disappears

907

When a garden tool or an article of clothing (*is, are***) missing, one immediately thinks of little Bobby.**

908

---

perfectly

1095

Skippy barked (*angry, angrily***) at his reflection in the mirror.**

1096

us	(*We, Us*) **citizens must not fail to vote.**
	Note to student:
	You are now ready for Unit Test 6, to be followed by the Halfway Test.
1283	1284

wagging his tail.	*Maxine excused herself politely.* **She went to her room.**
	_____, Maxine went to her room.
1470	1471

a	a. **We visited Diamond Grove. The home of George Washington Carver.**
	b. **We visited Diamond Grove, the home of George Washington Carver.**
1657	___ 1658

Earl, suppose,	When an interrupter comes at the beginning or end of a sentence, only one comma is needed to set it off.
	a. *However* **the rain didn't stop the game.**
	b. **The rain** *however* **didn't stop the game.**
	Which sentence requires only one comma? ____
1844	1845

b	A quotation that repeats a person's exact words is called (*a direct, an indirect*) quotation.
2031	2032

c	In this and the following frames, copy only the words to which capitals should be added, and write them with capitals. (Several uses of capitals from the preceding lessons are included.)
	It was officer Schultz who ticketed the judge's car.
2218	2219

Anita painted the cabinet.

Anita got a bucket of paint and a brush and performed an action. She painted something—the **cabinet.**
In this sentence, as in the previous ones, the direct object

(cabinet) _____ the action of the verb.

157

---

three-part

S   V   SC
boat was log

344

This mattress feels too soft.

S	V	SC
_____	_____	_____

345

---

b

Write the correct past forms of **see:**

The shoplifter _____ **that the store detective** _had_ _____ **him.**

532 / 533

---

a

In this and the following frames, underline the correct verb:

The audience (_rose, raised_) **and applauded the orchestra.**

720 / 721

---

is

Every now and then, one of the neighbors (_come, comes_) **to the door to inquire for a lost article.**

908 / 909

---

angrily

Our argument now seems rather (_foolish, foolishly_) **to both of us.**

1096 / 1097

We

1284

Lesson **44** Meet the Adverb Clause

[Frames 1286-1316]

Excusing herself
politely,

1471

Lesson **51** Using Appositives to Combine Sentences

[Frames 1473-1500]

---

b

1658

a. **Mr. Wetherby makes appointments. Then he forgets to keep them.**
b. **Mr. Wetherby makes appointments, then he forgets to keep them.**

———

1659

---

a

1845

Here are other expressions often used as interrupters:

after all	**to tell the truth**
it seems	**on the other hand**
by the way	**as a matter of fact**

Punctuate this sentence:

The other driver it seems didn't see the light.

1846

---

a direct

2032

a. **The teacher said, "Your work has improved."**
b. **The teacher said that my work has improved.**

Only one of these sentences repeats the exact words of the teacher.

Which sentence contains a *direct* quotation? ____

2033

Officer

2219

Have you heard that umpire Ashford will be at home plate in friday's game?

_____

2220

receives 157	Instead of receiving the action, the direct object sometimes shows the *result* of an action. **Anita <u>built</u> a cabinet.** In this sentence, **Anita** didn't do something to a cabinet that was already there. Rather, the *result of her action* was a _____. 158
S V mattress feels SC soft 345	**His sister became a very good lawyer.** S V SC _____ _____ _____ 346
saw, seen 533	Write the correct past forms of **see:** **If John** *had* _____ **the accident that I** _____**, he would drive more carefully.** 534
rose 721	**I** (*rose, raised*) **the cover and peeked into the box.** 722
comes 909	**Sometimes Mr. and Mrs. Klieg** (*recognizes, recognize*) **an article and take it back to its owner.** 910
foolish 1097	**The kitchen sink was leaking** (*bad, badly*). 1098

I awoke *early*.

The word *early* is an adverb because it modifies the verb **awoke**.

The adverb **early** answers the question (*When? Where? How?*).

1286

Ritzi eats too much.

Do you know whether **Ritzi** is a boy, a girl, a dog, or an elephant? (*Yes, No*)

1473

---

a

1659

---

a. This machine weighs the eggs. And sorts them according to size.
b. This machine weighs the eggs and sorts them according to size.

_____

1660

---

driver, seems,

1846

INTERRUPTERS: after all   to tell the truth
               it seems   on the other hand
               by the way   as a matter of fact

Punctuate this sentence:

My father on the other hand is very patient.

1847

---

a

2033

---

a. Tommy said that he wouldn't eat spinach.
b. Tommy said, "I won't eat spinach."

Which sentence contains a *direct* quotation? _____

2034

Umpire, Friday's

2220

Our pastor introduced professor Mary Arkwright of Fisk university.

_____

2221

<table>
<tr>
<td>cabinet

158</td>
<td>Now we are ready to complete our definition of the direct object:

A **direct object** receives the action of the verb or shows the _____ of this action.

159</td>
</tr>
<tr>
<td>S   V
sister became
     SC
    lawyer

346</td>
<td>**The owner of the other car got angry.**

S   V   SC
_____ _____ _____

347</td>
</tr>
<tr>
<td>seen, saw

534</td>
<td>Write the correct past forms of **do:**

Dr. Robbins _____ what most doctors would *have* **_____.**

535</td>
</tr>
<tr>
<td>raised

722</td>
<td>**Traffic deaths have** (*raised, risen*) **greatly in recent years.**

723</td>
</tr>
<tr>
<td>recognize

910</td>
<td>**However, there** (*are, is*) **always many unclaimed articles in their garage.**

911</td>
</tr>
<tr>
<td>badly

1098</td>
<td>**The growth of these trees is very** (*rapid, rapidly*).

1099</td>
</tr>
</table>

When? 1286	a. **I awoke** *early.* b. **I awoke** *when the alarm rang.* In sentence *a,* the adverb *early* answers the question *When?* In sentence *b,* a group of words answers the question *When?* These words are _____. 1287
No 1473	**Ritzi,** *our* <u>*cat*</u>**, eats too much.** Now you know that **Ritzi** is a cat. The noun *cat* explains the noun _____. 1474
b 1660	a. **Some plants grow best in the sun, others do better in the shade.** b. **Some plants grow best in the sun. Others do better in the shade.** ____ 1661
father, hand, 1847	If a group of words cannot be omitted from a sentence, it is not an interrupter. a. **I was shocked** *by the way* **he drove.** b. **He drove** *by the way* **very recklessly.** *By the way* is an interrupter in only one of these sentences. Which sentence requires commas? ____ 1848
b 2034	a. **Tommy said that he wouldn't eat spinach.** b. **Tommy said, "I won't eat spinach."** Quotation marks ("—") are used only around the (*direct, indirect*) quotation. 2035
Professor, University 2221	**For my birthday this spring Ralph's aunt gave me a copy of** *the way to rainy mountain* **by N. Scott Momaday.** _____ 2222

result 159	The usual position of a **direct object** is (*before, after*) the action verb. 160
S V SC owner got angry 347	A subject complement always refers back to the _____ of the sentence. 348
did, done 535	Write the correct past forms of **do**: I _____ the same problem that Sue *had* _____. 536
risen 723	**You must have (*risen, rose*) early to catch all those fish.** 724
are 911	**Bobby's mother and father (*tries, try*) to explain to him that he must not bring home other people's belongings.** 912
rapid 1099	**Brush your teeth (*good, well*) after eating sweets.** 1100

a. I awoke *early.*
b. I awoke *when the alarm rang.*

The word group *when the alarm rang* in sentence *b* does the same job that the adverb _____ does in sentence *a.*

1288

---

a. **Pete has just started school.**
b. **Pete,** *my youngest brother,* **has just started school.**

Which sentence is clearer? ____

1475

---

a. **The strike was finally settled. We went back to work.**
b. **The strike was finally settled, we went back to work.**

____

1662

We sometimes start a sentence with the word **Yes, No, Well,** or **Why.** Put a comma after one of these words when it is not a necessary part of the sentence.

a. *No* **the Lunas are not planning to move.**
b. *No* **money is needed for this hobby.**

From which sentence could *No* be omitted? ____

1849

Let's see how a direct quotation is punctuated:

The teacher said, "Your work has improved."

The two pairs of quotation marks ("—") go around (*the entire sentence, only the quoted words*).

2036

My father is younger than uncle Bert.

_____

2223

after	Here is how to tell when a sentence has a direct object: If, for example, the verb is the word *returned*, ask yourself, "Returned *what*?" or "Returned *whom*?" If you see a word that answers this question, it is a *direct object*. **The wind rattled the windows of the old house.** "Rattled *what*?" _____ (one word)
160	161
subject	Can both nouns and adjectives serve as subject comple-ments? (*Yes, No*)
348	349
did, done	Write the correct past forms of **go**: **Dick** _____ **downstairs to see if the company** *had* _____ .
536	537
risen	a. **lie** **sit** **rise** b. **lay** **set** **raise** Which group of words would you use to show that you are changing the position of something? ___
724	725
try	**A scolding or a spanking (*seems, seem*) to do no good.**
912	913
well	**I couldn't see (*good, well*) in the darkness.**
1100	1101

early 1288	**I awoke** *when the* <u>alarm</u> <u>rang</u>. Look at just the italicized word group. It has both a subject and a verb. The subject is *alarm*, and the verb is _____. 1289
b 1475	a. **Pete has just started school.** b. **Pete,** *my youngest* <u>brother</u>, **has just started school.** Sentence *b* is clearer because the noun _____ explains who **Pete** is. 1476
a 1662	a. **Astronomers can tell what each star is made of. By its color.** b. **Astronomers can tell what each star is made of by its color.** _____ 1663
a 1849	a. *No* **the Lunas are not planning to move.** b. *No* **money is needed for this hobby.** In which sentence would you put a comma after *No*? ____ 1850
only the quoted words 2036	The **he said** (or similar expression) can be put either before or after the quotation. 　　a. *The teacher said,* **"Your work has improved."** 　　b. **"Your work has improved,"** *said the teacher.* The **he said** expression comes after the quotation in sentence ____. 2037
Uncle 2223	**The principal of Leland Junior high school got captain Baker to speak to the graduating class.** _____ 2224

windows 161	The wind rattled the windows of the old house. The noun **windows** is a *direct* _____. 162
Yes 349	Lesson **12** **Prepositions Show Relationships** [Frames 351-376]
went, gone 537	Write the correct past forms of **go:** **You should** *have* _____ **where Sandy** _____. 538
b 725	Lesson **24** **Supplying the Right Verb Forms** [Frames 727-750]
seems 913	Recently, Mrs. Klieg got a good idea. On her gate she now posts a sign which says, "The following articles (*was, were*) recently brought home by Bobby. Do any of them belong to you?" 914
well 1101	Gloria's work in math was always (*good, well*). 1102

rang 1289	*when the <u>alarm</u> <u>rang</u>* Although this word group has a subject and a verb, can it stand by itself as a complete sentence? (*Yes, No*) 1290
brother 1476	**Pete,** *my youngest <u>brother</u>*, **has just started school.** A noun (or pronoun) set *after* another noun (or pronoun) to explain it is called an **appositive.** In the above sentence, the word used as an appositive is the noun _____. 1477
b 1663	a. **Arlene lost my address, therefore she didn't write me.** b. **Arlene lost my address. Therefore she didn't write me.** ____ 1664
a 1850	a. *Why* **won't the car start?** b. *Why* **the car was hardly moving at all.** In which sentence could you omit *Why* without changing the meaning? ____ 1851
b 2037	a. *The teacher said,* **"Your work has improved."** b. **"Your work has improved,"** *said the teacher.* In both sentences, the quotation is separated from the rest of the sentence by a (*period, comma*). 2038
High School, Captain 2224	**A book that has been translated into russian, japanese, and numerous other foreign languages is Mark Twain's** *the Adventures of Tom Sawyer.* _____ 2225

object 162	**The <u>police</u> soon <u>found</u> the lost child.** "Found *whom?*" _____ (one word) 163
	bee table These nouns give you the picture of two separate, unrelated things. For all you know, could the **table** be in Chicago and the **bee** in China? (*Yes, No*)
gone, went 538	Lesson **18** *Come, Run, and Give* [Frames 540-566]
	In this story of a true experience, write the correct past form of each verb in parentheses. **One evening when Grandfather Brooks _____ (*come*) over to see them, Mr. and Mrs. Doty asked him if he would baby-sit with their six-month-old daughter while they went to a movie.** 727
were 914	**It is not unusual to see a person stop to read the list and exclaim, "(*Here's, Here are*) my lost gloves at last!"** 915
good 1102	**Our church looks (*nice, nicely*) at Christmas time.** *page 325* 1103

No 1290	*when the <u>alarm</u> <u>rang</u>* A word group that has a subject and a verb but cannot stand by itself is called a **clause**. Do both a sentence and a clause have a subject and a verb? (*Yes, No*) 1291
brother 1477	**Pete,** *my youngest <u>brother</u>,* **has just started school.** An appositive usually has words that modify it. The two words that modify the appositive *brother* are ____ and _____. 1478
b 1664	a. **Phil stood in line, hoping to get a ticket.** b. **Phil stood in line. Hoping to get a ticket.** ____ 1665
b 1851	a. *Why* **won't the car start?** b. *Why* **the car was hardly moving at all.** In which sentence would you put a comma after *Why*? ____ 1852
comma 2038	Add the missing comma: **The coach said "Stand closer to the plate."** 2039
Russian, Japanese, The 2225	**Both my mother and aunt Shirley belong to the Ellington music club.** _____ 2226

child 163	**The <u>police</u> soon <u>found</u> the lost child.** The noun **child** is a _____ _____. 164
Yes 351	**bee .?. table** If there is a relationship between these two things, there is no word to tell you what it is. Underline three words that you could put between **bee** and **table** to show what their relationship might be: **on can near big over soon** 352
	In this lesson we study three more little verbs that we use many times each day: **come, run,** and **give.** To show simple past time, do we add *–d* or *–ed* to these verbs? (*Yes, No*) 540
came 727	**Grandfather Brooks _____ (*see*) that they were eager to go; so he consented to stay.** 728
Here are 915	Lesson **31** Unit Review [Frames 917-945]
nice 1103	**Jimmy looked (*sad, sadly*) at his broken balloon.** 1104

Yes 1291	Both a sentence and a clause have a subject and a verb. The important difference between them is that a clause (*can, cannot*) stand by itself. 1292
my, youngest 1478	**Pete,** *my youngest* <u>*brother*</u>**, has just started school.** An appositive with its modifying words is set off from the rest of the sentence by _____. 1479
a 1665	a. **Although our school is large. The students are very friendly.** b. **Although our school is large, the students are very friendly.** _____ 1666
b 1852	Punctuate this sentence: **Well we can't expect to win every game.** 1853
said, 2039	Add the missing comma: **"Stand closer to the plate" said the coach.** 2040
Aunt, Music Club 2226	**Do you know that grandfather Reese was once the football coach at Ridley college?** _____ 2227

direct object
 	
164
	If the sentence has no word that answers a question like "Returned *what?*" or "Found *whom?*" the sentence has no direct object.
	
	    a. **Frank returned** very soon.
	    b. **Frank returned** my book.
	
	Which sentence answers "Returned *what?*" ____ 165

on, near, over
 	
352
	bee .?. table
	
	Underline three other words that you could put between **bee** and **table** to show what their relationship might be:
	
	   did **by** **under** **is** **beside** **must**
	
	    353

No
 	
540
	PRESENT SIMPLE PAST PAST WITH HELPER
	
	  come **came** **(have) come**
	  run **ran** **(have) run**
	  give **gave** **(have) given**
	
	These three verbs are (*regular, irregular*). 541

saw 728	**Soon after they had _____ (*go*), the baby _____ (*begin*) to cry.** 729
917	Use the verb **don't** only where you can substitute the words (*do not, does not*). 917
sadly 1104	**Onions taste (*different, differently*) when they're cooked.** 1105

cannot 1292	**I awoke** *when the alarm rang.* A clause that does the work of an adverb is called an **adverb clause.** The clause *when the alarm rang* is therefore an _____ *clause.* 1293
commas 1479	Here is the appositive with its modifiers by itself: *my youngest brother* Does an appositive, like a clause, have both a subject and a verb? (*Yes, No*) 1480
b 1666	a. **A cat seldom gives up a bad habit that it is allowed to form.** b. **A cat seldom gives up a bad habit. That it is allowed to form.** _____ 1667
Well, 1853	Punctuate this sentence: **Yes I did wipe my feet on the mat.** 1854
plate, 2040	Look at the three places where a comma or period and quotation marks come together in these sentences: a. **The coach said, "Stand closer to the plate."** b. **"Stand closer to the plate," said the coach.** The period and the comma always come (*before, after*) the quotation marks. 2041
Grandfather, College 2227	**My uncle sang "a visit from St. Nicholas" for the children at the Parkside hospital just before christmas.** _____ 2228

b 165	a. **<u>Frank</u> <u>returned</u> very soon.** b. **<u>Frank</u> <u>returned</u> my book.** Which sentence contains a direct object?___ 166
by, under, beside 353	**bee** *on* **table** **bee** *by* **table** **bee** *near* **table** **bee** *under* **table** **bee** *over* **table** **bee** *beside* **table** By using different words, we change the *re*_____ between **bee** and **table**. 354
irregular 541	PRESENT SIMPLE PAST PAST WITH HELPER **come** **came** **(have) come** The simple past form of **come** is _____. 542
gone, began 729	**He _____ (give) the baby her bottle of milk, which she** **_____ (drink) very hungrily.** 730
do not 917	Suppose that a sentence has a singular subject. If this singular subject is followed by a prepositional phrase with a plural object, the verb should be (*singular, plural*). 918
different 1105	**I felt the edge of the knife very (*cautious, cautiously*).** 1106

adverb
 	
1293
	Adverb clauses, just like adverbs, can answer other questions about verbs, too.
	
	    a. **We stopped** *there.*
	    b. **We stopped** *where the road turns.*
	
	Both the adverb *there* in *a* and the adverb clause in *b* answer the question (*When? Where? How?*). 1294

No 1480	An appositive can come at the end of a sentence as well as in the middle. **The Eiffel Tower in Paris was built by Alexandre Eiffel,** *a French engineer.* The appositive that explains who **Alexandre Eiffel** was is the noun _____. 1481
a 1667	a. **Harold offered to do the job. Then he tried to get out of doing it.** b. **Harold offered to do the job, then he tried to get out of doing it.** ____ 1668
Yes, 1854	In this and the following frames, add the necessary commas. The number after each sentence shows how many commas are needed. **Our next meeting by the way is on Tuesday. (2)** 1855
before 2041	Take a long, hard look at these punctuation marks, and make a mental picture of them: ,"____." When a comma or period and quotation marks come together, always put the comma or period (*first, last*). 2042
"A Visit …" **Hospital,** **Christmas** 2228	Lesson **78** Unit Review *page 332* [Frames 2230-2249]

b 166	**Frank <u>returned</u> very soon.** **Frank** himself returned. He didn't return something else, like a book or a bicycle or money. Does this sentence contain a direct object? (*Yes, No*). 167
relationship 354	Now instead of having two nouns, we shall have a verb and a noun. **skated park** Do you see any word that shows you the relationship between the verb **skated** and the noun **park?** (*Yes, No*) 355
came 542	Write the simple past form of **come:** **Your letter _____ yesterday.** 543
gave, drank 730	**After the baby had _____ (*fall*) asleep, Grandfather Brooks went downstairs to read the paper.** 731
singular 918	In a sentence that begins with **There is, There are, Here is,** or **Here are,** look for the subject (*before, after*) the verb. 919
cautiously 1106	**Which lives (*longer, longest*)—a dog or a cat?** 1107

Where? 1294	a. **The man greeted us** *warmly.* b. **The man greeted us** *as though he knew us.* Both the adverb *warmly* in sentence *a* and the adverb clause in sentence *b* answer the question (*When? Where? How?*). 1295
engineer 1481	An appositive always comes *after* (not before) the word it explains. a. **Donna Gold, our** *chairperson,* **was absent.** b. **Our** *chairperson,* **Donna Gold, was absent.** In which sentence is the noun *chairperson* an appositive? _____ 1482
a 1668	a. **We didn't buy the car, it had been in a bad accident.** b. **We didn't buy the car. It had been in a bad accident.** _____ 1669
meeting, way, 1855	**Aluminum for example is a very soft metal. (2)** 1856
first 2042	Add the missing punctuation: **The teacher said _____ Your work has improved _____** 2043
	In this and the following frames, copy only the words to which capitals should be added, and write them with capitals: **Perla works for the Davis drug company every saturday afternoon.** 2230

a. **Gloria studied her math.**
b. **Gloria studied in school.**

Which sentence contains a direct object? ___

The direct object is the noun _____ .

---

skated .?. park

Underline three words that you could put between **skated** and **park** to show their relationship:

in   again   through   large   around   new

PRESENT   SIMPLE PAST   PAST WITH HELPER

come   came   (have) come

Write the two different past forms of **come:**

A storm _____ up before the children had _____ **home from the park.**

An hour later the baby _____ (*begin***) to cry again.**

The words **There's, Here's,** and **Where's** should be used only when they are followed by (*singular, plural*) subjects.

Is it (*cheaper, cheapest***) to travel by bus, train, or plane?**

How?
 	
1295
	No single adverb can answer the question *Why?* An adverb clause, however, can answer this question.
	
	    a. **We hurried** *because* *it* *had* *started* *to rain.*
	    b. **We hurried** *after* *it* *had* *started* *to rain.*
	
	In which sentence does the adverb clause answer the question *Why?*
	
	1296

a 1482	**Tropical plants were collected by Ynes Mexia, a Spanish-American explorer.** The appositive in this sentence is the noun _____. 1483
b 1669	a. **Jim Sen received the Eagle Scout Award. The highest award in scouting.** b. **Jim Sen received the Eagle Scout Award, the highest award in scouting.** ——— 1670
aluminum, example, 1856	**Well the concert to tell the truth was disappointing. (3)** 1857
The teacher said, "Your work has improved." 2043	**The teacher said, "Your work has improved."** Like all sentences, this sentence begins with a capital letter. Does the quotation within the sentence also begin with a capital letter? (*Yes, No*) 2044
Drug Company, Saturday 2230	**When my mother was young, she liked to visit her cherokee cousins in oklahoma.** ——— 2231

a math 168	a. **Roses grow along the fence.** b. **The Nortons grow beautiful roses.** Which sentence contains a direct object? ____ The direct object is the noun _____. 169
in, through, around 356	**skated .?. park** Underline three other words that you could put between **skated** and **park** to show their relationship: **toward across tree past last** 357
came, come 544	PRESENT: **The squirrels** *come* **to our porch for food.** If you changed this sentence from present to past, you would need to change the verb *come* to _____. 545
began 732	**He _____ (*lay*) aside his paper and _____ (*run*) upstairs to see what the matter was.** 733
singular 920	In this and the following frames, underline the verb that agrees with its subject. Remember that if a verb showing present time ends in *s*, it is singular, not plural. **Your height and weight (*are, is*) perfect for football.** 921
cheapest 1108	**The new road is (*more wider, wider*) than the old one.** 1109

a
 	
1296
	An adverb clause can also answer the question *On what condition?*
	
	    a. I **went** *where my friend invited me*.
	    b. I **will go** *if my friend invites me*.
	
	In which sentence does the adverb clause answer the question *On what condition?*
	
	1297

explorer 1483	**In Laredo, a town on the Mexican border, the train stops for customs inspection.** The appositive in this sentence is the noun _____. 1484
b 1670	a. **Because they are intelligent. Elephants are easy to train.** b. **Because they are intelligent, elephants are easy to train.** ____ 1671
Well, concert, truth, 1857	**Bill Pickett I think was the greatest rodeo cowboy. (2)** 1858

Yes
 	
2044
	It is easy to see why a quotation should always start with a capital letter. It is the beginning of someone else's sentence even though it may not be the beginning of yours.
	
	    a. **A man called, "Your tire is flat."**
	    b. **A man called, "your tire is flat."**
	
	In which sentence is the capitalization correct? ____ 2045

Cherokee, Oklahoma 2231	**The Pilgrim methodist church was filled to capacity on easter.** 2232

b
roses
 	
169
	In this and the following frames, you will find a subject, action verb, and direct object in jumbled order. Put them in sensible order and write them in the proper blanks.
	
	EXAMPLE **melts ice sun milk cats drink**
	              S V DO S V DO
	        sun melts ice _____ . _____ _____
	                                                170

toward, across, past 357	A word that relates a noun or pronoun that follows it to some other word in the sentence is called a **preposition**. A preposition is a word that (*repeats, relates*). 358
came 545	**The mail** *has come* **late this morning.** If you dropped the helper *has*, you would need to change the verb *come* to _____. 546
laid, ran 733	**He found that the baby had** _____ (*throw*) **off her covers.** 734
are 921	**A doctor or a nurse** (*were, was*) **always on hand.** 922
wider 1109	**Flicka, the high-spirited colt, becomes** (*tamer, more tamer*) **at the end of the story.** 1110

b 1297	Here are some adverb clause signals. They are arranged according to the question the clause answers. WHEN? while, when, whenever, as, before, after, since, until WHERE? where, wherever These are the words that (*start*, *end*) adverb clauses. 1298
town 1484	We often write a sentence that explains *who* or *what* someone or something is in the previous sentence. a. **Mt. Everest is in Tibet.** b. **It is the world's highest mountain.** Sentence *b* explains the noun _____ in sentence *a*. 1485
b 1671	Lesson **58** Unit Review [Frames 1673-1696]
Pickett, think, 1858	**Yes our carnival on the whole was very successful. (3)** 1859
a 2045	Now let's check the several points you have just studied about punctuating quotations: a. **The nurse replied, "The patient is feeling better."** b. **The nurse replied "that the patient is feeling better."** Which sentence is correct? ____ 2046
Methodist Church, Easter 2232	**You can see the river from aunt Elsa's office in the Chase building.** _____ 2233

S V DO cats drink milk 170	puzzles enjoy children S V DO _____ _____ _____ 171
relates 358	You can already spell the word *position*. To spell the word *preposition*, you merely write the letters _____ before *position*. 359
came 546	a. **My cousin . . . to visit me.** b. **My cousin** *has* **. . . to visit me.** In which sentence would *come* be correct? ____ 547
thrown 734	**Grandfather covered the baby snugly and _____ (***sing***) her to sleep.** 735
was 922	**The teacher or a pupil (***read, reads***) the notices.** 923
tamer 1110	**The new model has a (***powerfuller, more powerful***) engine.** 1111

start 1298	Here are more clause signals: HOW? **as if, as though** WHY? **because, since, as, so that** ON WHAT CONDITION? **if, unless, although, though** Do some of these clause signals consist of more than one word? (*Yes, No*) 1299
Mt. Everest 1485	A sentence that identifies a word in the previous sentence can often be changed to an appositive word group. a. **Mt. Everest is in Tibet.** b. **It is the world's highest mountain.** **Mt. Everest,** *the world's highest mountain*, **is in Tibet.** Which sentence became an appositive word group? ____ 1486
	In this review lesson you will find the story of an unusual experience. In each frame are two word groups. If the two word groups should be written as a single sentence, put down your answer like this: EXAMPLE: **The little girl was shy and clung to her mother.** *shy and* (*Turn to the next frame.*) 1673
Yes, carnival, whole, 1859	**Bobby after all is only eight years old. (2)** 1860
a 2046	a. **"The patient is feeling better" replied the nurse.** b. **"The patient is feeling better," replied the nurse.** Which sentence is correct? ____ 2047
Aunt, Building 2233	**When it is summer in the united states, it is winter in south america.** _____ 2234

S V children enjoy DO puzzles 171	stamps Henry saves S V DO _____ _____ _____ 172
pre 359	**bee** *on* **table** The preposition *on* relates the noun **table** to the word **bee,** which is also a _____. 360
b 547	PRESENT SIMPLE PAST PAST WITH HELPER **run** **ran** **(have) run** The simple past form of **run** is _____. 548
sang 735	**Some time later, when the baby was crying loudly again,** **he** _____ (*bring*) **her downstairs in her basket,** **which he** _____ (*lay*) **on a chair.** 736
reads 923	**Snow and ice** (*cover, covers*) **the Antarctic regions.** 924
more powerful 1111	**It was so dark that we couldn't take** (*no, any*) **pictures.** 1112

Yes 1299	Every adverb clause starts with a clause signal. After this clause signal you will always find a subject and a _____. 1300
b 1486	An identifying sentence usually begins with words such as **It is, He was,** or **They are.** To change such a sentence to an appositive word group, you merely drop these words. ~~It is~~ **the world's highest mountain.** This sentence can become an appositive word group if we drop the words _____. 1487

	If the two word groups should be written as two separate sentences, put down your answer like this:
	
	    EXAMPLE: **I enjoyed the book it was full of surprises.**
	
	          book. It
	
	               (*Turn to the next frame.*)
	
	1674

Bobby, all, 1860	**Why I was delighted of course with the letter from Shirley Chisholm. (3)** 1861
˙b 2047	a. **"The patient is feeling better," replied the nurse.** b. **"The patient is feeling better", replied the nurse.** Which sentence is correct? ___ 2048
United States, South America 2234	**Both christians and jews celebrate thanksgiving day.** _____ 2235

S V Henry saves DO stamps 172	people lawns water S V DO _____ _____ _____ 173
noun 360	**skated** *through* **park** The preposition *through* relates the noun **park** to the word **skated,** which is a _____. 361
ran 548	Write the simple past form of **run:** **The truck _____ off the road.** 549
brought, laid 736	However, nothing that he _____ (*do*) would stop the baby from crying. 737
cover 924	My father or my mother (*wake, wakes*) me for school. 925
any 1112	Jerry wouldn't let (*anybody, nobody*) ride his bicycle. 1113

verb 1300	Underline one clause signal that could start an adverb clause that answers the question *When?* while so that because 1301
It is 1487	After we change a sentence to an appositive word group, we put it in the sentence *after* the word it explains. a. **Mt. Everest,** *the world's highest mountain,* **is in Tibet.** b. **Mt. Everest is in Tibet,** *the world's highest mountain.* Which sentence is correct? ____ 1488
	Dad and I like to fish therefore we accepted Uncle John's invitation to use his cabin. ———————————————— (In checking your answers, do not count comma errors. Commas will be studied in the next unit.) 1675
Why, delighted, course, 1861	**The other team it seems was out of practice. (2)** 1862
a 2048	a. **The nurse replied, "The patient is feeling better."** b. **The nurse replied, "the patient is feeling better."** Which sentence is correct? ____ 2049
Christians, Jews, Thanksgiving Day 2235	**We saw "mutiny on the bounty" at the Mercury theater.** ———————————————— 2236

S V people water DO lawns 173	Find the subject, verb, and direct object in each sentence and write them in the proper blanks: **The heavy rain flooded the street.** S V DO _____ _____ _____ 174
verb 361	a. **came** *from* **Alaska** b. **boy** *from* **Alaska** In which sentence does the preposition *from* relate the noun **Alaska** to a verb? ____ 362
ran 549	PRESENT: **The children** *run* **to the window.** If you changed this sentence from present to past, you would need to change the verb *run* to _____. 550
did 737	**In desperation, he decided to go next door to get advice from another young mother, whom the Dotys had _____ (**know**) for several years.** 738
wakes 925	**One of his front teeth (***were, was***) missing.** 926
anybody 1113	I (*can, can't*) **hardly remember when I last saw Gail.** *page 347* 1114

while 1301	Underline one clause signal that could start an adverb clause that answers the question *Where?* **when after wherever** 1302
a 1488	Here are two more sentences to be combined: a. **The Fongs took care of our dog.** b. **They are our neighbors.** Sentence *b* identifies the _____ in sentence *a*. 1489
fish. Therefore 1675	**It was a small cabin in the upper part of the state.** _____ 1676
team, seems, 1862	**However I shall let you know by Monday if possible. (2)** 1863
a 2049	In this and the following frames, supply the missing commas, periods, and quotation marks: **The waiter said We bake our own pies** 2050
"Mutiny ... Bounty," Theater 2236	**My dad generally uses dyno gasoline in his pontiac car** _____ 2237

<table>
<tr>
<td>

S   V
rain flooded

DO
street

174

</td>
<td>

The story started a good discussion.

S   V   DO

_____ _____ _____.

175

</td>
</tr>
<tr>
<td>

a

362

</td>
<td>

    a. **disappeared** *between* **the houses**
    b. **the fence** *between* **the houses**

In which sentence does the preposition *between* relate the noun **houses** to a verb? ____

363

</td>
</tr>
<tr>
<td>

ran

550

</td>
<td>

PRESENT   SIMPLE PAST   PAST WITH HELPER
run   **ran**   **(have) run**

Write the two different past forms of **run:**

    I _____ to see where our dog *had* _____.

551

</td>
</tr>
<tr>
<td>

known

738

</td>
<td>

"You should have _____ (*come*) **over earlier," she said. "Just bring the little dear over, and I'll take care of her until Lois and Jim get home."**

739

</td>
</tr>
<tr>
<td>

was

926

</td>
<td>

The leaves of the tree (*are, is*) **turning yellow.**

927

</td>
</tr>
<tr>
<td>

can

1114

</td>
<td>

After riding on the roller coaster, we were so dizzy that we (*could, couldn't*) **scarcely stand up.**

Note to student:
You are now ready for Unit Test 5.

1115

</td>
</tr>
</table>

wherever 1302	Underline one clause signal that could start an adverb clause that answers the question *Why?* **although because until** 1303
Fongs 1489	**They are our neighbors.** To change this sentence to an appositive word group, drop the two words _____. 1490
cabin in 1676	**My uncle John was working he couldn't go with us.** _____ 1677
However, Monday, 1863	**No our second game as a matter of fact was even worse than the first. (3)** 1864
The waiter said, "We bake our own pies." 2050	**We bake our own pies said the waiter** 2051
Dyno, Pontiac 2237	**The Madison club heard a talk by professor Katy Rivera on puerto rican music.** _____ 2238

S V story started DO discussion 175	The people of Athens governed themselves. S V DO _____ _____ _____ 176

a
 	
363
	There are dozens of prepositions. Here is a list of the nine we most frequently use:
	
	       in **at** **to**
	       for **on** **from**
	       of **with** **by**
	
	How many of these have only two letters? _____ 364

ran, run 551	a. **The club ... out of money.** b. **The club** *has* **... out of money.** In which sentence would *run* be correct? ____ 552
come 739	**After Grandfather Brooks had _____ (***take***) the baby to the neighbors' house, he went back to the Dotys' home.** 740
are 927	**The traffic on our streets (***increase, increases***) every year.** 928
could 1115	UNIT 6: **CHOOSING THE RIGHT PRONOUN** Lesson **38** **Recognizing Subject and Object Forms** [Frames 1117-1140]

because 1303	Underline one clause signal that could start an adverb clause that answers the question *On what condition?* where as though if 1304
They are 1490	**The Fongs,** *our neighbors,* **took care of our dog.** We have now put the appositive word group next to the noun _____, which it explains. 1491
working. He 1677	He would join us on Saturday the first day of his vacation. _____ 1678
No, game, fact, 1864	Lesson **65** **Commas** **in Addresses and Dates** [Frames 1866-1891]
"We bake our own pies," said the waiter. 2051	The dentist said Don't eat so many sweets 2052
Club, Professor, Puerto Rican 2238	At the time of this incident, general Burke was only a sergeant. _____ 2239

S V people governed DO themselves	**A little paint would improve this house.** S V DO _____ _____ _____ (two words)

176   177

---

six

We always rode .?. school.

Circle two of these prepositions that would fit into the above sentence:

in	at	to
for	on	from
of	with	by

364   365

---

b

PRESENT	SIMPLE PAST	PAST WITH HELPER
give	gave	(have) given

Is the simple past form the same as the present form? (*Yes, No*)

552   553

---

taken

It was now eleven o'clock, and he had _____ (*grow*) quite sleepy.

740   741

---

increases

One of your tires (*are, is*) flat.

928   929

---

a. *Fred* **likes** *dogs.*
b. *Dogs* **like** *Fred.*

In sentence *a*, the noun *Fred* is the subject, and the noun *dogs* is the direct object.

In sentence *b*, the noun _____ is the subject, and the

noun _____ is the direct object.

1117

1304

if	Now let's look at a one-word adverb again: **The car started** *suddenly.* *Suddenly* **the car started.** Can an adverb sometimes be moved from one position to another in a sentence? (*Yes, No*)

1304 · 1305

Fongs	Notice the difference between an appositive and an adjective clause. An adjective clause always has a subject and a verb. An appositive does not. a. **The Fongs,** *who are our neighbors,* **took care of our dog.** b. **The Fongs,** *our neighbors,* **took care of our dog.** Which sentence contains an appositive? ___

1491 · 1492

Saturday, the	**Since we had never been there before Uncle John gave us directions.** _____

1678 · 1679

An address can have one or more parts:

a. **We moved to** *86 Bay Avenue* **last fall.**
b. **We moved to** *86 Bay Avenue, Atlanta,* **last fall.**

In which sentence does the address have more than one

part? ___

1866

The dentist said, "Don't eat so many sweets."	**Today is my birthday announced Jerry**

2052 · 2053

General	**The Merritt library probably has more than one copy of Willa Cather's** *shadows on the rock.* _____

2239 · 2240

S paint V would improve DO house 177	**A thick fog covered the entire city.** S V DO _____ _____ _____ 178

Any two:
to, from, at, by
 	
365
	I worked .?. my dad.
	
	Circle two of these prepositions that would fit into the above sentence:
	
	    in at to
	    for on from
	    of with by
	
	366

No 553	The simple past form of *give* is not *give* but _____. 554
grown 741	**He _____ (*lie*) down on the sofa and soon fell asleep.** 742
is 929	**One of the dogs (*looks, look*) like Friskie.** 930
Dogs, Fred 1117	a. *Fred* **likes** *dogs.* b. *Dogs* **like** *Fred.* Is the form of a noun the same whether it is in the subject or direct object position? (*Yes, No*) 1118

Yes 1305	My dog comes *when I call it.* *When I call it,* **my dog comes.** Can an adverb clause be moved from the end to the beginning of a sentence? (*Yes, No*) 1306
b 1492	In this and the following frames, change each italicized sentence to an appositive word group. Then put it after the word it explains in the other sentence. Remember that an appositive word group does not have a subject and a verb. **I read the life of Edison.** *He was the great inventor.* _____ 1493
before, Uncle 1679	**The cabin would be easy to find it was the fourth cabin beyond a certain road.** _____ 1680
b 1866	a. **We moved to** *86 Bay Avenue* **last fall.** b. **We moved to** *86 Bay Avenue, Atlanta,* **last fall.** In *a*, the address consists of one part, the street address. In *b*, the address consists of two parts, the *street address* and the _____. 1867
"Today is my birthday," announced Jerry. 2053	**You didn't leave any cake for me complained Don** 2054
Library, Shadows . . . Rock 2240	**The Panama canal was begun by the french and completed by the americans.** _____ 2241

S V fog covered DO city 178	A direct object _____ the action of the verb or shows the _____ of this action. 179
Any two: for, with, by, on 366	**We stayed .?. a motel.** Circle two of these prepositions that would fit into the above sentence: in at to for on from of with by 367
gave 554	Write the correct past form of **give:** **My uncle _____ me his old typewriter.** 555
lay 742	**Around midnight, the Dotys _____ (*come*) home from the movie.** 743
looks 930	**The design of the cars (*has, have*) been improved.** 931

Yes
 	
1118
	Let's use pronouns instead of nouns in the sentences:
	    a. *He* **likes** *them.*
	    b. *They* **like** *him.*
	When sentence *a* is turned around, the pronoun *He* changes to _____, and the pronoun *them* changes to
	
	_____.
	
	1119

1306 — Yes

As I entered the door,   the tardy bell rang.

Each of these two word groups has a subject and a verb, but the adverb clause does not make sense by itself. The adverb clause is the (*first, second*) word group.

1307

I read the life of Edison, the great inventor.

1493

Potatoes were a failure that year. *They are our main crop.*

_____

_____

1494

---

find. It

1680

Diana Nyad started her marathon swim early in the morning   finishing late in the afternoon.

_____

1681

---

city (town)

1867

a. **We moved to** *86 Bay Avenue* **last fall.**
b. **We moved to** *86 Bay Avenue, Atlanta,* **last fall.**

We use commas when the address has (*one, more than one*) part.

1868

"You didn't leave any cake for me," complained Don.

2054

The little boy explained the broken window to the police by saying   I was cleaning my slingshot, and it went off

2055

Canal, French, Americans

2241

There are a catholic church and a hospital close to the Franklin high school.

_____

2242

receives, result 179	Must every action verb be followed by a direct object? (*Yes, No*) 180
Any two: in, at, by 367	**It rained .?. the game.** All the following words can be used as prepositions. Underline three that would fit in the above sentence: **before below during with after about** 368
gave 555	PRESENT: **Joe's parents** *give* **him too much help.** If you changed this sentence from present to past, you would need to change the verb *give* to _____. 556
came 743	**Lois immediately _____ (*run*) upstairs to check on the baby.** 744
has 931	**The causes of this disease (*are, is*) not known.** 932
him, They 1119	a. *He* **likes** *them.* b. *They* **like** *him.* Are the forms of these pronouns the same whether they are in the subject or direct object position? (*Yes, No*) 1120

first 1307	**As I** <u>entered</u> **the door, the tardy** <u>bell rang.</u> The adverb clause starts with the clause signal _____ and ends with the word _____. 1308
Potatoes, our main crop, were a failure that year. 1494	**My uncle brought me a gift.** *It was a leather wallet.* _____ _____ 1495
morning, finishing 1681	**When we entered the cabin we found it in very bad condition.** _____ 1682
more than one 1868	**We moved to** *86 Bay Avenue, Atlanta,* **last fall.** We put commas both *before* and *after* the (*first, second*) part of the address. 1869
The little boy . . . saying, "I was cleaning my slingshot, and it went off." 2055	Lesson **72** More Hints on Quotations [Frames 2057-2084]
Catholic, High School 2242	**The committee consists of major Patton, judge Ryan, and a doctor.** _____ 2243

Lesson 7 Unit Review

---

before, during,
after

368

Underline the preposition:

I bought a pound of butter.

369

---

gave

556

PRESENT   SIMPLE PAST   PAST WITH HELPER

give   gave   (have) given

Write the correct past forms of **give:**

Bill _____ **me the ticket that Dave** *had* _____
to him.

557

---

ran

744

When she _____ (*see*) **that both the baby and the basket**
were gone, she let out a scream.

745

---

are

932

Fred (*doesn't, don't*) **live there any more.**

933

No

1120

a. *Paul* **admired** *Jane.*
b. *He* **admired** *her.*

In which sentence would you need to change the italicized words if you turned the sentence around? ____

1121

When you remove an adverb clause from a sentence, a complete sentence should remain.

(*When she received the warning,*) **the pilot changed her course.**

Read this sentence without the clause. Are the remaining words a sentence? (*Yes, No*)

1309

My uncle brought me a gift, a leather wallet.

1495

Decker hit a home run. *He is our catcher.*

_____

_____.

1496

---

cabin, we

1682

The roof had been leaking   the walls were peeling.

_____

1683

---

second

1869

We moved to *86 Bay Avenue, Atlanta, Georgia 30311,* **last fall.**

Now the address consists of three parts: the *street address*, the *city*, and the _____, with the Zip Code.

1870

"The dog has been fed," said Mother.

Between the quotation and the **he said** expression, we use a (*comma, period*).

2057

Major, Judge

2243

The Fairfax hotel overlooks lake Arrowhead.

_____

2244

In this unit, we have studied three different kinds of words: nouns, pronouns, and verbs.

A noun is a word used to _____ a person, place, thing, or idea.

182

---

of

369

Underline the preposition:

Everyone looked at her paintings.

370

---

gave, given

557

My friend *gave* me his promise.

If you added the helper *has* to the verb, you would need to change *gave* to _____.

558

---

saw

745

She _____ (*fly*) downstairs and awoke Grandfather Brooks.

746

---

doesn't

933

(*Doesn't, Don't*) your ears feel frozen?

934

---

b

1121

.?. admired Jane.

Underline the pronoun in each pair that would fit in the subject position in the above sentence:

I—me, he—him, she—her, we—us, they—them

1122

Yes 1309	The weather is chilly although this is June. The adverb clause starts with the clause signal _____ and ends with the word _____. 1310
Decker, our catcher, hit a home run. 1496	**The stories were judged by Mrs. Dix.** *She is a newspaper writer.* _____. 1497
leaking. The 1683	**Several windows were broken and rain had come in.** _____ 1684
state 1870	Note that the state and Zip Code are *not* separated by a comma, as are other parts of the address. Punctuate this sentence: **Please mail the package to me at 110 State Street Detroit Michigan 48223.** 1871
comma 2057	Now let's change the quotation to a question, omitting the punctuation: **Has the dog been fed asked Mother** The entire sentence is not a question. Only the quotation is a question. Therefore, the question mark should be put after the word (*fed, Mother*). 2058
Hotel, Lake 2244	**My aunt took care of my grandfather after he returned home from the Oakhurst hospital.** _____ 2245

name 182	To avoid repeating a noun, we often use a _____ in its place. 183
at 370	Underline the preposition: **The bridge across the river was closed.** 371
given 558	a. **come run give** b. **came ran gave** Which forms of these verbs show simple past time? ____ 559
flew 746	**"The baby—the baby!" she screamed. "Someone has _____ (*take*) her away!"** 747
Don't 934	**A cactus** (*doesn't, don't*) **need much water.** 935
I, he, she, we, they 1122	a. **I, he, she, we, they** b. **me, him, her, us, them** In which group are the pronouns that fit in the subject position? ____ 1123

although ... June 1310	We put up our tent where the ground was dry. The adverb clause starts with the clause signal _____ and ends with the word _____. 1311
The stories were judged by Mrs. Dix, a newspaper writer. 1497	The fire was discovered by Mr. Pak. *He is a security guard.* _____ _____. 1498
broken, and 1684	We decided to surprise Uncle John by fixing up the cabin for him. _____ 1685
Street, Detroit, 1871	Punctuate this sentence: You can reach us at 2206 Parkside Boulevard Phoenix Arizona 85005 after next Monday. 1872
fed 2058	a. "Has the dog been fed?" asked Mother. b. "Has the dog been fed," asked Mother? In which sentence is the question mark correctly placed? ____ 2059
Hospital 2245	The Hudson river follows the Catskill mountains for many miles. _____ 2246

pronoun 183	Which is usually more definite in meaning, a noun or a pronoun? A _____. 184
across 371	Underline the preposition: **Jimmy agreed with his friends.** 372
b 559	Write the correct past forms of **come:** **My little brother _____ downstairs to see who** *had* _____ **to our house.** 560
taken 747	**Grandfather _____ (***sit***) up, still dazed with sleep.** 748
doesn't 935	**My teeth (***was, were***) chattering from the cold.** 936
a 1123	**Paul admired .?. .** Underline the pronoun in each pair that would fit in the direct object position in the above sentence: **I—me, he—him, she—her, we—us, they—them** 1124

where ... dry 1311	**When Skippy got the ball, he ran toward the wrong goal.** The adverb clause starts with the clause signal _____ and ends with the word _____. 1312
The fire was discovered by Mr. Pak, the security guard. 1498	**Two boys didn't finish the race.** *They were Pete and Alvin.* _____ _____. 1499
John by 1685	**We went to the village store where we bought paint, glass, and tar paper.** _____ 1686
Boulevard, Phoenix, Arizona 85005, 1872	**Mrs. R. V. Sanchez of** *461 Archdale Avenue* **won the car.** How many parts does this address have? _____ 1873
a 2059	**"The dog has been fed," said Mother.** **"Has the dog been fed?" asked Mother.** When we change the quotation to a question, we change the comma to a _____ mark. 2060
River, Mountains 2246	**Our club is planning a party for the last friday in april.** _____ 2247

noun 184	a. trees, desk, lamp, Ralph, potatoes b. they, some, each, you, these, several In which group can the words be used as pronouns? ____ 185
with 372	Underline the preposition: **Mr. Fritz usually travels by plane.** 373
came, come 560	Write the correct past forms of **come**: **This package must** *have* _____ **before my parents** _____ **home.** 561
sat 748	**"Oh, yes," he said, "I guess I'm not a very good baby-sitter.** **The baby wouldn't stop crying; so I** _____ *(take)* **her** **over to Mrs. Graham's house."** 749
were 936	**You** *(was, were)* **out when I telephoned.** 937
me, him, her, us, them 1124	a. **I, he, she, we, they** b. **me, him, her, us, them** In which group are the pronouns that fit in the direct object position? ____ 1125

| When ... ball

1312 | **Ralph jumped   as though he had received an electric shock.** The adverb clause starts with the clause signal (two words) _____ and ends with the word _____.

1313 |
| Two boys, Pete and Alvin, didn't finish the race.

1499 | **We spent a week in Boston.** *It is a very historical city.*

_____

_____.

1500 |
| store, where

1686 | **We repaired the windows   then we patched the roof.**

_____

1687 |
| one

1873 | **Mrs. R. V. Sanchez of** *461 Archdale Avenue* **won the car.** What preposition ties in the address with the name that it follows? _____

1874 |
| question

2060 | **"The dog has been fed," said Mother.** **"Has the dog been fed?" asked Mother.** When the quotation is a question, do we use a comma in addition to the question mark? (*Yes, No*)

2061 |
| Friday, April

2247 | **Follow Elson avenue until you reach Magnolia park.**

_____

2248 |

b	In this and the next three frames, each sentence contains two italicized nouns and one italicized pronoun.
	Underline the one pronoun:
	They **filled the** *box* **with** *ice*.
185	186
by	Underline the preposition:
	The rain came into the room.
373	374
come, came	Write the correct past forms of **run:**
	Mia _____ for the same office for which her brother *had*
	_____.
561	562
took	**Lois _____** (*give*) **a sigh of relief and started out the door.**
749	750
were	(*Here are, Here's*) **the eggs for the cake.**
937	938
b	Here the subject and object forms of the pronouns are mixed up. Underline the *five* pronouns that could come before the verb as its subject:
	they us him I he them me we she her
1125	1126

as though ... shock 1313	**Because Mother loves birds,** we gave her a parakeet for her birthday. The adverb clause starts with the clause signal _____ and ends with the word _____. 1314
We spent a week in Boston, a very historical city. 1500	Lesson **52** Unit Review [Frames 1502-1525]
windows. Then 1687	**After we painted the walls** we scrubbed the floors. _____ 1688
of 1874	a. **Mrs. R. V. Sanchez of** *461 Archdale Avenue* **won the car.** b. **Mrs. R. V. Sanchez,** *461 Archdale Avenue,* **won the car.** In which sentence is the address put right after the name with no preposition to tie it in? ____ 1875
No 2061	a. **"Has the dog been fed?," asked Mother.** b. **"Has the dog been fed?" asked Mother.** Which sentence is correct? ____ 2062
Avenue, Park 2248	**In february, my grandmother and one of my uncles plan to visit aunt Carol.** _____ Note to student: You are now ready for Unit Test 11, to be followed by the Final Test. *page 372* 2249

They	Underline the one pronoun: *Lyle* **gave** *it* **to a** *friend.*
186	187
into	Underline the preposition: **The book about ants was interesting.**
374	375
ran, run	Write the correct past forms of **run:** **The car** _____ **better than it ever** *had* _____ **before.**
562	563
gave	Lesson **25** Unit Review
750	[Frames 752-773]
Here are	**There** (*are, is*) **thirteen countries in South America.**
938	939
they, I, he, we, she	This time, underline the five pronouns that could come *after* the verb as its direct object: **he** **them** **her** **I** **us** **they** **me** **we** **she** **him**
1126	1127

Because ... birds 1314	**If I don't study this afternoon, I must stay home tonight.** The adverb clause starts with the clause signal _____ and ends with the word _____. 1315
	Do both a sentence and a clause have a subject and a verb? (*Yes, No*) 1502
walls, we 1688	**You could hardly recognize the cabin Uncle John would be surprised.** _____ 1689
b 1875	a. **Mrs. R. V. Sanchez of** *461 Archdale Avenue* **won the car.** b. **Mrs. R. V. Sanchez,** *461 Archdale Avenue,* **won the car.** When there is no preposition to tie in the address with the name, do we surround it with commas? (*Yes, No*) 1876
b 2062	Now punctuate this sentence yourself: **Has the dog been fed asked Mother** 2063
February, Aunt 2249	

it 187	Underline the one pronoun: The *boy* put *some* in the *bank*. 188
about 375	A preposition is a word that shows _____ *ship*. 376
ran, run 563	Write the correct past forms of **give:** **Mr. Otaki** *has* _____ **me a higher grade than he** _____ **me last semester.** 564
	In this and the following frames, underline the correct verb in each pair. After any form of **have** or **be,** be sure to select the helper form of the verb. **We had** (*taken, took*) **the wrong road and had** (*ran, run*) **out of gas.** 752
are 939	(*There are, There's*) **no ink in this pen.** 940

them, her, us,
me, him
 	
1127
	The pronouns *you* and *it* are different from the other pronouns.
	
	      a. *You* **followed** *it*.
	      b. *It* **followed** *you*.
	
	Do the pronouns *you* and *it* change in form when they are shifted from subject to direct object? (*Yes, No*)
	
	1128

WRITING APPLICATIONS

Contents

The Writing Process

In the first part of this textbook, you followed a step-by-step program, or process, to study grammar and usage. You were first given a bit of information in a frame; then you tried to apply it. If you did not get the correct answer the first time, you were given another opportunity to get the correct answer in another frame. You completed entire sections of this book using this process. When you write, you can also use a process that will give you additional opportunities to improve your writing. This process is called the **writing process.**[1] In this section of your textbook, you will be introduced to the six basic stages of the writing process. Once you have mastered these stages, you should be able to apply them in any writing task.

WHY STUDY THE WRITING PROCESS?

Knowing how to use this process will enable you to compose more quickly and accurately. Since an important part of the writing process is evaluating and revising, you always have several opportunities to analyze and improve your writing before you prepare the final version.

Following this introduction (pages 379–386), you will find writing applications that correspond to each of the units in the first part of this book. The applications are designed to give you practice in applying the principles of grammar and usage that you studied in the first part of this textbook. They will also enable you to practice the writing process and to improve your writing skills. In addition, you may find that they help you organize your thoughts and give you practice in analyzing information.

HOW TO USE THIS SECTION OF THE BOOK

After you read this section, refer to it to help you complete the writing applications. Use the basic models presented here whenever you need help composing. In this section, you will learn about and practice the six stages of the writing process. These six stages are (1) prewriting, (2) writing the first draft, (3) evaluating, (4) revising, (5) proofreading, and (6) writing the final version.

Prewriting

The prewriting stage enables you to formulate ideas before you write. During this thinking and planning stage, you will answer five important questions: Why am I writing? For whom am I writing? What will I write about? What will I say? How will I say it? More specifically, you will determine your purpose; identify your audience; choose and limit your topic; establish your tone; and gather, classify, and arrange information.

[1] Adapted from pp. 3–42 in *English Composition and Grammar*, Benchmark Edition, Second Course, by John E. Warriner. Copyright © 1988 by Harcourt Brace Jovanovich, Inc. Reprinted by permission of Harcourt Brace Jovanovich, Inc.

IDENTIFYING A PURPOSE

Before you begin writing, you should have in mind a clear purpose. Your purpose will guide your writing and help determine the content and language you use. There are four basic purposes for writing: to tell a story or relate a series of events; to inform or explain; to describe a person, place, or thing; or to persuade or convince. Writing to tell a story is called **narrative** writing. Writing to inform or explain is called **expository** writing. Writing to describe a person, place, or thing is called **descriptive** writing. Finally, writing that attempts to persuade or convince is called **persuasive** writing.

KNOWING YOUR AUDIENCE

You will always write for an audience, but audiences may vary widely in age, background, and opinion. Like purpose, your audience will help guide your writing since you do not write the same way for all people. Determine carefully who your reading audience will be. Then decide whether they will need background information and whether your subject will interest them. Also, decide how simple or difficult the language you use should be.

CHOOSING AND LIMITING A SUBJECT

Before you write, choose a subject that is interesting to you and your audience and draws on your experiences. Then limit your subject so that you can write about it adequately in the time and space you have. To limit your subject, consider your purpose and the form of writing you have chosen. A broad, general subject that has been limited is called a **topic.**

ESTABLISHING TONE

Determine your attitude, or feeling, toward your topic to help you establish your tone. Tone is the expression of your attitude; for example, happiness, anger, or seriousness. You express your tone through the words you choose to use in your writing.

GATHERING INFORMATION

Gather information to include in your writing that is appropriate to your purpose. For example, if your purpose is to describe someone famous, you may want to gather facts about that person's life, appearance, and mannerisms. You can use many different methods in gathering information. A few that are described here include brainstorming, clustering, asking the 5 W-How? questions, and asking point-of-view questions.

Brainstorming.   In brainstorming, you gather information by writing down ideas that come freely to mind. One way to begin brainstorming is to write your topic at the top of a sheet of paper. Then, think about your topic, listing any ideas that you associate with your topic. Do not worry if some of the ideas seem silly or incomplete. You will be able to eliminate or expand these ideas later.

EXAMPLE   *Topic:* My stamp collection

      Ideas: Have stamps from around the world
            —Philippines, Japan, Australia, Spain, France, Germany
          Also have many state stamps
          Interesting to look at—
            Different prices
            Different sizes
            Colorful designs
          Favorite stamp is of Jack London
          London is my favorite author
          London stamp is a green drawing on a white background
          First stamp was from Japan

Clustering.   Clustering is like brainstorming in that you write down ideas as they come to mind. In clustering, however, you arrange the ideas in groups, or clusters. To begin clustering ideas, write your topic in the center of your paper and circle it. Then begin thinking about ideas that relate to the topic. Write down and circle these ideas also. Draw lines to connect ideas to the topic.

Asking the 5 W-How? Questions.   Another technique for gathering information is asking the *5 W-How?* questions. The *5 W-How?* questions are *Who? What? When? Where? Why?* and *How?* Ask yourself these questions to find out specific details about your topic. You may not be able to use every question with every topic, but you will always be able to use at least several of the questions.

The Writing Process   **381**

EXAMPLE   *Topic:* My stamp collection

Who collected it? (I did.)

What makes up the collection? (stamps from around the world, including the Philippines, Japan, Australia, Spain, France, Germany, and various states in the U.S.)

When did I start the collection? (about two years ago)

Where do I keep my collection? (in an album at home)

Why did I start the collection? (liked the first stamp I received from Japan; decided to collect more)

How is the collection useful? (Stamps are interesting to look at— the changes in price over the years, the different sizes and colors. Also, I enjoy this hobby. I am pleased to have a stamp of my favorite author, Jack London.)

Asking Point-of-View Questions. Still another technique that can be used to gather information is to look at a topic from three different points of view. To determine the point of view, ask these three questions: (1) What is it? (2) How does it change or vary? (3) What are its relationships?

EXAMPLE   *Topic:* My stamp collection

1. What is a stamp collection? (stamps gathered from various places, of different sizes and shapes and various colors and designs)
2. How did I start my collection? (with a stamp from Japan)
   How did the collection grow? (I continued buying and saving stamps. Soon I had stamps from around the world, including the Philippines, Japan, Australia, Spain, France, Germany, and states in the U.S.)
   How has the collection turned out? (It is a good collection. I even have a stamp of my favorite author—Jack London.)
3. What satisfaction and rewards does a stamp collection bring? (It is interesting to look at; e.g., the differences in price, the various colors, designs, and shapes.)

ORGANIZING INFORMATION

The next step in the writing process is to classify, or sort, your ideas and information into related groups. Classifying helps you organize your information for writing. One of the simplest ways to classify information is to look for similarities and differences. Another way is to determine which ideas are more important than others. The more important ideas may become the main ideas of your paragraphs. The less important ideas will become supporting details.

EXAMPLE   *Topic:* My stamp collection

Purposes	Places Represented	Favorite Stamp(s)
Hobby	Philippines	Jack London,
Interesting to look at—	Japan	my favorite author
different colors, designs,	Australia	
sizes, and prices	Spain	
	France	
	Germany	
	Many states in U.S.	

Next, you need to arrange the ideas you have classified into some logical order or sequence. Often your purpose will determine your order. For example, if you are writing a paragraph to tell a story, you will write your paragraph in chronological order—or the order that the events occurred. If you are writing a paragraph to persuade, you might write your topic sentence first and follow it with supporting sentences that give reasons. Sometimes, however, your purpose will not dictate an exact order. In these cases, you should present your information in any way that will be interesting and clear to your audience.

EXAMPLE   *Topic:* My stamp collection
Purpose: Descriptive

1. Collection represents many countries and states in U.S.
2. Countries represented include Philippines, Japan, Australia, Spain, France, Germany.
3. My hobby is interesting; I enjoy looking at stamps' different colors, designs, sizes, and prices.
4. My favorite stamp is of Jack London, who is also my favorite author.

Writing a First Draft

The next stage of the writing process is to write a first draft, or first version. Your first draft is based on the information you prepared in the prewriting stage. In this stage, you put your ideas into sentences and paragraphs. Remember that this draft will not be your final one. Therefore, you should evaluate and revise your writing as many times as you need. Keep your prewriting notes in front of you as you write, and write freely.

EXAMPLE   I have a wonderful stamp collection that includes stamps from around the world. I also have stamps from many states in the U.S. Some of the countries represented are the Philippines, Japan, Australia, Spain, France, and Germany. My hobby is very interesting. The stamps come in many different colors, designs, sizes, and prices. They are all very interesting to look at. My favorite stamp is my Jack London stamp. Jack London was my favorite author.

Evaluating

Evaluating is the third stage of the writing process. In this stage, you review your first draft for content, organization, and style. *Content* refers to what you have said. *Organization* concerns the way you have arranged your ideas. *Style* refers to your choice of words and sentences. When you evaluate your writing, you determine your weaknesses and decide what works and what does not. Use the following checklist to help you evaluate your writing.

1. Do the ideas help to achieve a main purpose: to explain or inform, to tell a story, to describe, or to persuade?
2. Is the topic suitably limited for the form of writing?
3. Are the topic and details suitable and interesting for the audience?

4. Are enough details provided so that the topic can be easily understood? Is any information unnecessary?
5. Does the order of the information fit your purpose?
6. Are your ideas clearly connected with words such as *also, first, however,* and *therefore?*
7. Are exact and vivid words used?
8. Does the vocabulary fit your audience and purpose?
9. Do sentences vary in length and how they begin?

Revising

Once you have evaluated your writing and have determined its weaknesses, you are ready to revise it. Revising your writing means making changes to it to improve it. Four basic techniques are used when revising: adding, cutting, reordering, and replacing. Adding means putting in additional information such as words, sentences, or paragraphs to make your writing clearer. Cutting means removing unnecessary words, sentences, or paragraphs. Replacing means substituting information that will improve your writing. Reordering means moving information around so that your writing will make better sense to your readers. Note how this paragraph has been revised using these techniques.

EXAMPLE   I have a ~~wonderful~~ *I enjoy very much.* stamp collection that *My collection* includes stamps from around the world. ~~I also have stamps~~ from many states in the U.S. *and* ~~Some of the~~ *For example, I have stamps from* ~~countries represented are~~ the Philippines, Japan, Australia, Spain, France, and Germany. ~~My hobby is very interesting.~~ The stamps come in many *are interesting to look at; they* different colors, designs, sizes, *and* ~~and prices.~~ ~~They are all very interesting to~~ ~~look at.~~ My favorite stamp is *of my* Jack London *who is* ~~stamp. Jack London was~~ my favorite author.

Proofreading

In the proofreading stage of the writing process, you reread your revised draft one last time to find and correct errors. Proofreading means finding and correcting mistakes in grammar, usage, and mechanics (spelling, capitalization, and punctuation). You may want to use these general guidelines when proofreading:

1. Set aside your revised draft for a short period of time before proofreading it. Doing this will make it easier for you to see any mistakes.
2. If you made a lot of changes during the revising stage, recopy your draft before you proofread it.
3. Check all questionable spellings by looking them up in the dictionary.
4. To help you concentrate as you proofread, cover with blank paper all lines except the one you are reading.

Special standardized marks called revising and proofreading symbols are used to show corrections. You will find a complete list of these marks on the inside of the back cover of this textbook. However, here is a short list of some of the most frequently used symbols:

Symbol	Example	Meaning of Symbol
≡	australia	Capitalize a lowercase letter.
/	States in the U.S.	Lowercase a capital letter.
∧	My ^{stamp} collection	Insert a missing word, letter, or a punctuation mark.
ℐ	many many types	Leave out a word, a letter, or a punctuation mark.
ℐ	Germmany	Leave out and close up.
◡	in teresting	Close up space.
∽	wondreful	Change the order of letters.
¶	¶I have a	Begin a new paragraph.
⊙	My hobby is interesting⊙	Add a period.
⋏	Japan, Spain, and France	Add a comma.
#	Jack London	Add a space.
⹀	well=known author	Add a hyphen.

Writing the Final Version

Writing the final version is the last step of the writing process. This step includes preparing a clean copy of your revised and proofread paper. Although your teacher will provide you with specific directions, you can use these general guidelines when completing any of the writing applications.

1. Write on lined 8 1/2 x 11-inch composition paper. If you are typing your composition, use 8 1/2 x 11-inch white paper.
2. Write or type on only one side of each sheet of paper.
3. Write in blue or black ink, or type your composition using double-spacing.
4. Leave top, bottom, and side margins of one inch.
5. Indent the first line of each paragraph about one-half inch.
6. Follow your teacher's directions for writing your name, the class name, and the date.
7. Write or type any title for your paper by centering it. Do not enclose it in quotation marks. If you are writing the title, skip two lines between the title and the first line of your composition.
8. Number all pages after the first in the upper right-hand corner.
9. Write neatly and legibly. If you must erase, do so neatly.
10. Proofread your final version carefully to make sure you have made no mistakes recopying it.

DIVIDING WORDS

When you are preparing a final version of a composition, you will sometimes need to divide words at the ends of the lines. Here are a few basic rules to follow when dividing words:

1. Never divide a one-syllable word.
2. Divide words only between syllables. If you are unsure of a word's syllables, look up the word in a dictionary.
3. Do not divide a word so that only one letter is left on a line.

WRITING NUMBERS

Follow your teacher's guidelines for writing numbers. However, in most compositions, you can follow these general guidelines:

1. Always spell out a number that begins a sentence.
2. Spell out one- and two-digit numbers; e.g., *five, twelve, forty-one.*
3. Write as numerals any numbers having three or four digits; e.g., *100, 1968, 995.*
4. If you are using more than one number in a sentence, write them all the same way; e.g., Paul has *14* domestic stamps and *103* foreign stamps.
5. Write out numbers such as *sixth* and *forty-second*, unless they stand for a day of the month, such as May *23*.

UNIT 1 Words That Make Sentences

WRITING APPLICATION A: Using Precise Nouns

When you order a meal in a restaurant, you tell the server exactly what foods you want. By stating precisely the items you want, you save the server time in getting your meal to you. Similarly, when you write, you should try to use precise nouns to help your readers understand exactly what you are describing. Precise nouns enable your readers to form clear mental pictures quickly. Note how the second sentence in the examples below creates a clearer picture by using a precise noun.

EXAMPLES
1. Alexandra wanted a small *pet* for her birthday.
   Alexandra wanted a small *poodle* for her birthday.
2. Jim watched the silver *boat* glide over the waves.
   Jim watched the silver *hydroplane* glide over the waves.

Writing Assignment: On a separate sheet of paper, write a paragraph about something you have wanted for a long time. Describe exactly what it is that you have wanted and why you have wanted it.

Evaluation Checklist: Reread your first draft. Use these guidelines to help you judge the content and organization of your writing.

____ I have used precise nouns in my writing.
____ Each of my sentences is complete.
____ Each of my supporting sentences refers to the topic sentence.

Revising, Proofreading, and Writing the Final Version: Use your evaluation to help you revise the first draft of your paragraph. Make sure each of your nouns is as precise as you would like it to be. Then proofread your revised draft. Write your paragraph in final form.

WRITING APPLICATION B: Using Lively Action Verbs

Action was a key ingredient of the old silent movies. Because there was no sound to accompany the pictures, the actions shown on film had to tell the entire story. Similarly, good writing, which creates strong mental pictures for readers, must use lively action verbs to describe actions clearly. The more lively the action verbs you use, the better the picture of action you create for your readers. Note how the second sentence in each of the following examples creates a clearer picture of the action.

EXAMPLES
1. The snake *crawled* across the lawn.
   The snake *zigzagged* across the lawn.
2. The engines *started* just before the jet *moved* forward.
   The engines *roared* just before the jet *lurched* forward.

Writing Assignment: On a separate sheet of paper, write a paragraph about an interesting but unusual event you have witnessed. Give details that clearly describe actions.

Evaluation Checklist: Reread your first draft. Use these guidelines to help you judge the content and organization of your writing.

____ I have used lively action verbs in my writing.
____ Each of my sentences is complete.
____ My writing follows a logical order.
____ Each of my supporting sentences refers to the topic sentence.

Revising, Proofreading, and Writing the Final Version: Use the results of your evaluation to revise the first draft of your paragraph. Replace any dull action verbs with more lively ones. Then proofread your revised draft. Write your paragraph in final form.

WRITING APPLICATION C: Using Pronouns in Place of Nouns

Have you ever heard a record skip as you were listening to it play? If you have, you may have noticed that you began to concentrate on the repeating word and forgot about the song. Using a noun over and over again in your writing can have a similar effect on your readers. Your readers may begin to notice the word being repeated and miss part of your message. Use pronouns in place of some of your nouns to prevent this kind of needless repetition.

EXAMPLE   *Jorge* planned a surprise birthday party for *his* sister *Marianne. He* secretly invited twelve of Marianne's friends to the party. To make *her* birthday extra special that year, *he* also invited *her* best friend, Eleanor, who had moved to another state the year before. To both Jorge's and Marianne's surprise, Eleanor showed up at the party.

Writing Assignment: On a separate sheet of paper, write about an occasion that was made special because of someone else's efforts. Give details that tell what that person did to make the event special.

Evaluation Checklist: Reread your first draft. Use these guidelines to help you judge the content and organization of your writing.

____ I have used pronouns in place of some nouns.
____ I have used logical order in describing what happened.
____ Each of my paragraphs includes a topic sentence and supporting sentences.

Revising, Proofreading, and Writing the Final Version: Use your evaluation to help you revise your first draft. Change some of your nouns to pronouns if you find they are repeated too often in your writing. Then proofread your revised draft. Write your draft in final form.

WRITING APPLICATION A: Making Pictures with Adjectives

To paint pictures, artists use color and texture to give richness and detail to their subjects. In a similar way, writers use adjectives to provide color and give richness and detail to their topics. However, using too many adjectives can overpower good writing. Adjectives need not be used before every noun.

EXAMPLE   Sheila liked the way the *blue* water in the *small* lagoon sparkled in the *early morning* light. Suddenly, the *gentle* water became *dark* and *menacing*. A *large* shadow had penetrated the *shimmering* water. Sheila bent forward for just a moment to see what was moving so quickly through the tiny lagoon. Suddenly the *large dark* form darted out of the water, nearly nipping the tip of her nose. The *menacing* shape had only been a dolphin, playing its *usual coy* game with tourists.

Writing Assignment: On a separate sheet of paper, write about a frightening moment you once had that turned out to be only a false alarm. Using logical order, describe what happened.

Evaluation Checklist: Reread your first draft. Use these guidelines to help you judge the content and organization of your writing.

____ I have used adjectives to provide color and detail in my writing.
____ I have not used too many adjectives in my writing.
____ My writing follows a logical order.
____ Each of my paragraphs includes a topic sentence and supporting sentences.

Revising, Proofreading, and Writing the Final Version: Revise your draft according to your evaluation. Replace any dull adjectives with more lively ones. Then proofread your revised draft carefully. Write your draft in final form.

WRITING APPLICATION B: Using Adverbs in Directions

If you have ever had trouble putting something together because you could not understand the instructions, you know the importance of having good directions. Good directions tell exactly when and how to do something. In writing, adverbs are the part of speech that help writers tell when and how to do something. Therefore, adverbs are used frequently in writing directions.

EXAMPLE   *Carefully* plug one end of the lawn mower cord into the proper place on the handle. *Then* lock *securely* the safety latch for the cord. *Next,* plug the other end of the cord into a wall socket near the garage. *Slowly* press down on the black bar of the handle to start the mower. After you mow one row of grass, *gently* flip the handle over the mower. Doing this will enable you to mow your next row without turning the mower *around*.

Writing Assignment: On a separate sheet of paper, write directions for putting together or operating a piece of equipment. Give step-by-step directions that tell exactly when and how to do something.

Evaluation Checklist: Reread your first draft. Use these guidelines to help you judge the content and organization of your writing.

____ My directions are in correct order.
____ My directions are accurate and complete.
____ I have used adverbs to tell when and how to do something.

Revising, Proofreading, and Writing the Final Version: Revise your first draft based on your evaluation. Insert any adverbs that will help clarify your directions. Then proofread your revised draft. Write your draft in final form.

WRITING APPLICATION C: Using Conjunctions to Connect Ideas

When people organize their closets, they tend to put together items that are somehow alike. For example, they are likely to put a pair of shoes with other shoes, a hat with other hats, and a suit with other suits. In a similar way in writing, items that are somehow alike can be connected with conjunctions. Connecting like items with conjunctions can also help reduce the number of words used and eliminate repetition. Note how in the second example below, conjunctions were used to eliminate unnecessary words.

GOOD   Heather dreamed of visiting some of the famous horse farms in Lexington, Kentucky. Ryan, one of Heather's classmates, also dreamed of visiting some of the farms there. In particular, Heather wanted to visit the horse museum in Lexington. Ryan, on the other hand, wanted to try his hand at riding horses. Later that same year, Heather's teacher planned a field trip to the area. Ryan's teacher planned a similar trip.

BETTER   Heather *and* Ryan were classmates who dreamed of visiting some of the famous horse farms in Lexington, Kentucky. In particular, Heather wanted to visit the horse museum there, *while* Ryan preferred to do some actual riding. Later that same year, Heather's *and* Ryan's teachers planned a field trip to the area.

Writing Assignment: On a separate sheet of paper, write about you and your family's plans for a vacation. Give each person's reasons for wanting to visit a particular place.

Evaluation Checklist: Reread your first draft. Use these guidelines to help you judge the content and organization of your writing.

____ Each of my paragraphs has a topic sentence and supporting sentences.
____ My writing follows a logical order.
____ I have used conjunctions in some of my sentences to combine like items.

Revising, Proofreading, and Writing the Final Version: Revise your first draft carefully. Use conjunctions to help eliminate some repetition of ideas in your writing. Proofread your revised draft. Then write your final version.

WRITING APPLICATION A: Choosing Irregular Verb Forms

The framework of a house is made up of pieces of wood in many different sizes. Many of the wood pieces come in standard sizes and shapes, but other pieces are irregular in size and shape. Similarly, in writing, verbs such as *see, do, go, come, run,* and *give* are frequently used in the basic structure of sentences. However, the past-tense forms of these verbs are irregular. Since you will use these basic verbs often as you write, you need to memorize those verb forms you do not already know.

Present	Simple Past	Past with Helper
see	saw	have seen
do	did	have done
go	went	have gone
come	came	have come
run	ran	have run
give	gave	have given

Writing Assignment: On a separate sheet of paper, write about a picnic or other outing in which you participated. Describe who went, what you did and saw, and any special events in which you participated. Use four of the verbs above in your writing to give yourself practice with irregular verb forms.

Evaluation Checklist: Reread your first draft. Use these guidelines to help you judge the content and organization of your writing.

____ I have used the correct verb forms in my writing.
____ My writing follows a logical order.
____ Each of my paragraphs includes a topic sentence and supporting sentences.

Revising, Proofreading, and Writing the Final Version: Revise your draft based on your evaluation. Make sure you have included in your writing at least four verbs from the list. Proofread your revised draft carefully. Then write your draft in final form.

WRITING APPLICATION B: Using the Right Verb Forms

Have you ever stopped yourself in mid-sentence when speaking or writing because you did not know the correct word to use? For example, you may have been unsure whether to say *ate* or *eaten,* or *knew* or *known.* Knowing which word to use means knowing irregular verb forms. You should not use guesswork; instead, you must memorize the irregular forms of verbs to know which ones to use. Verb forms for three irregular verbs are shown on the next page.

Present	Simple Past	Past with Helper
break	broke	have broken
eat	ate	have eaten
know	knew	have known

Writing Assignment: On a separate sheet of paper, write in the past tense about one of the following topics. Use the verb in the topic at least three times.

An item that you have broken   An interesting person you have known
An unusual but flavorful food you have eaten

Evaluation Checklist: Reread your first draft. Use these guidelines to help you judge the content and organization of your writing.

_____ I have used the past tense in my writing.
_____ I have used the correct verb forms in my writing.

Revising, Proofreading, and Writing the Final Version: Revise your draft based on your evaluation. Write a title for your composition if you have not already done so. Then proofread your revised draft. Write your draft in final form.

WRITING APPLICATION C: Using *Lie* and *Lay, Sit* and *Set, Rise* and *Raise*

Introducing a good friend by the wrong name may embarrass you and confuse your friend. Similarly, in writing, using the wrong word in a sentence can embarrass you and confuse your readers. Three commonly confused sets of words are *lie* and *lay, sit* and *set,* and *rise* and *raise.* Memorize their meanings and their verb forms to prevent using the wrong words in your writing.

Present	Simple Past	Past with Helper
lie (recline)	lay	have lain
lay (put)	laid	have laid
sit (sitting position)	sat	have sat
set (put)	set	have set
rise (go up)	rose	have risen
raise (lift)	raised	have raised

Writing Assignment: On a separate sheet of paper, write in the past tense about one of the following topics. Use each of the verbs in the topic at least twice.

Setting Chairs Where People Like to Sit   Raising Questions About Rising Prices
Laying Down Rules About Lying on the Lawn

Evaluation Checklist: Reread your first draft. Use these guidelines to help you judge the content and organization of your writing.

_____ I have used the past tense in my writing.
_____ I have used correct verb forms in my writing.

Revising, Proofreading, and Writing the Final Version: Revise your draft based on your evaluation. Write your chosen topic as the title of your paper. Then proofread your revised draft. Write your draft in final form.

Subject and Verb Must Agree in Number

WRITING APPLICATION A: Using Subject-Verb Agreement

You probably would never buy gloves that had too few finger openings. Naturally, you would want the number of finger holes to match the number of fingers you have. Similarly, to prevent problems in having your message understood as you write, you need to use verbs that agree in number with your subjects. This is true no matter how many words separate each subject and verb.

EXAMPLE   Each week, four *members* of the student volunteer group *visit* the children's ward at the hospital. *Each* volunteer *wears* a clown costume and *does* something entertaining for the children. For example, *Steve* nervously *juggles* five *balls* that *change* color in midair. *Tina pulls* coins out of the children's mouths each time *one* of them *recites* a poem. *Eric operates* two little *robots* that *make* whizzing and beeping sounds and *answer* the children's questions. *Stacey draws* caricatures of the children. After *she has finished* each one, *she gives* it to the child to keep.

Writing Assignment: On a separate sheet of paper, write about your participation in a club or organization. Describe some of the things you do or have done. Also, include information about the activities of individual members. Concentrate on writing a good composition. You will be able to change later any verbs you have written incorrectly.

Evaluation Checklist: Reread your first draft. Use these guidelines to help you judge the content and organization of your writing.

____ I have used correct subject-verb agreement.
____ Each of my paragraphs includes a topic sentence and supporting sentences.
____ My writing follows a logical order.

Revising, Proofreading, and Writing the Final Version: Revise your draft based on your evaluation. Replace any verbs that do not illustrate clearly what you want to say. Proofread your draft after you have revised it. Then write your draft in final form.

WRITING APPLICATION B: Using Verbs with Compound Subjects

In mathematics, a plus sign in an equation means that two numbers are being added. In sentences, the word *and* between two subjects usually means those subjects are being combined. When two subjects are combined, or made compound, the verb that describes what the subjects are doing should be plural. Unlike *and*, the conjunction *or* is usually used to separate subjects. When *or* is used in this way, the verb that describes what either subject is doing is singular.

EXAMPLES
1. Raquel *and* Eduardo *are* exchange students.
2. Raquel *or* Eduardo *is* an exchange student.
3. Rome *and* Florence *are* the last cities she will visit.
4. Rome *or* Florence *is* the last city she will visit.

Writing Assignment: On a separate sheet of paper, write about two places you like to visit after school or on weekends. First, write about both places together. Connect your subjects with the word *and*. Then give reasons why either place is a good place to visit. In these cases, connect your subjects with the word *or*.

Evaluation Checklist: Reread your first draft. Use these guidelines to help you judge the content and organization of your writing.

____ I have used a plural verb with compound subjects connected by *and*.
____ I have used a singular verb with compound subjects connected by *or*.
____ Each of my paragraphs has a topic sentence and supporting sentences.

Revising, Proofreading, and Writing the Final Version: Revise your draft based on your evaluation. Correct any sentences that show incorrect subject-verb agreement. Proofread your draft after you have revised it. Then write your draft in final form.

WRITING APPLICATION C: Using Verbs That Come Before the Subject

Drivers sometimes need to back up and turn around. That is why automobiles can be driven in reverse as well as in forward. Similarly, in writing, writers sometimes need to back up mentally to check the verb forms they are using in their sentences. This is most often true in sentences in which the verb comes before the subject. Note how the verb in each of the following sentences precedes the subject.

EXAMPLES
1. How much *are* those black *puppies* in the window?
2. Here *is* the *batch* of whole-grain biscuits you ordered.
3. There *were* only twelve *students* in class that day.

Writing Assignment: On a separate sheet of paper, describe an item that has several parts. Do not name the item until the last sentence of your description. However, provide details so that your readers have clues about the identity of the item.

Evaluation Checklist: Reread your first draft. Use these guidelines to help you judge the content and organization of your writing.

____ I have used correct subject-verb agreement in my writing.
____ My description provides detailed clues about the item I have chosen.
____ Each of my paragraphs has a topic sentence and supporting sentences.

Revising, Proofreading, and Writing the Final Version: Revise your draft based on your evaluation. Make sure you have identified your selected item in your last sentence. Then proofread your revised draft. Write your revised draft in final form.

UNIT 5 Using the Right Modifier

WRITING APPLICATION A: Choosing Between *Good* and *Well*

How *good* is your understanding of when to use *good* and *well* in sentences? *Good* is an adjective that modifies only nouns and pronouns. *Well* is used primarily as an adverb and answers the question *How?* The word *well*, however, can also be used as an adjective when it refers to health. To determine which word you should use in a sentence, first determine whether the word is functioning as an adverb or an adjective. If it is an adjective, you know to use *well* when referring to health and *good* when referring to anything else.

EXAMPLES　1. Tony performed *well* in the spring athletic competition.
2. The assistant manager is a *good* person to contact about those kinds of problems.
3. She has not been feeling *well* all morning.
4. That music score David played was quite *good*.

Writing Assignment: On a separate sheet of paper, write a narrative about a time you left an event early because you were not feeling well. Explain what you thought of the event under those circumstances. Give yourself practice using *good* and *well* in your sentences. You will have the opportunity to revise your writing later.

Evaluation Checklist: Reread your first draft. Use these guidelines to help you judge the content and organization of your writing.

_____ I have used *good* and *well* correctly in my writing.
_____ I have written my narrative in chronological order.
_____ Each of my paragraphs includes a topic sentence and supporting sentences.

Revising, Proofreading, and Writing the Final Version: Revise your draft based on your evaluation. If you have found any instances in which you used *well* or *good* incorrectly, change the words now. Then proofread your revised draft. Write your revised draft in final form.

WRITING APPLICATION B: Making Comparisons

Almost everyone strives to be best at something. Being best means being supreme over all others. In writing, the word *best* is the highest level of comparison that can be made. The word itself is an example of a third-degree comparison. *Better*, on the other hand, is an example of a second-degree comparison, which is used when only two things are being compared. *Good*, which is an example of a first-degree comparison, is really not used in making comparisons. All adjectives and adverbs have these three degrees that can be used in making comparisons.

EXAMPLE   I always knew I was *good* at spelling, but I never thought I would be the *best* of all students in my school district. At the district spelling bee last year, I correctly spelled every word and won the district's *highest* award. Later that year, I participated in the state competition. Although I was a *better* speller than my closest competitor, I was no longer the *best*. I felt bad that I did not win for my school. However, I had tried *hard* to win and was grateful that I was not the *worst* speller in the state bee.

Writing Assignment: On a separate sheet of paper, write about someone famous you believe is best or worst at something. Compare that person's skills or talents to those of other people in the same field.

Evaluation Checklist: Reread your first draft. Use these guidelines to help you judge the content and organization of your writing.

_____ I have used second-degree comparison when I compared two people or things.

_____ I have used third-degree comparison when I compared more than two people or things.

_____ I have included a topic sentence in each of my paragraphs.

Revising, Proofreading, and Writing the Final Version: Revise your draft based on your evaluation. The proofread your revised draft. Write your revised draft in final form.

WRITING APPLICATION C: Avoiding Double Negatives

Few students would enjoy doing double the amount of homework every evening if doing only a normal amount was really necessary. Double homework for students is a little like double negatives in sentences. In sentences, one of the negative words is unnecessary and should be eliminated. You can correct sentences that have this error by removing one of the negative words or by making one of the words positive.

DOUBLE NEGATIVE   Maria does *not* have *nobody* to go with her on that trip.

SOLUTION 1   Maria does *not* have *anybody* to go with her on that trip.

SOLUTION 2   Maria has *nobody* to go with her on that trip.

Writing Assignment: On a separate sheet of paper, write about two or three things you do not have but need. Practice writing sentences that use negative words. You will have an opportunity to revise your writing later.

Evaluation Checklist: Reread your first draft. Use these guidelines to help you judge the content and organization of your writing.

_____ I have not used double negatives in my writing.

_____ My writing follows a logical order.

Revising, Proofreading, and Writing the Final Version: Revise your draft based on your evaluation. Then proofread your revised draft. Write your draft in final form.

UNIT 6 Choosing the Right Pronoun

WRITING APPLICATION A: Splitting Double Pronouns

Splitting a lunch with someone means sharing that lunch. Splitting double pronouns in a sentence means that two or more pronouns connected by a conjunction are sharing the rest of the sentence. Therefore, each pronoun can stand alone in the sentence and still make sense. Any time you are unsure of the correct pronoun forms to use in a sentence that splits pronouns, test each pronoun alone in the sentence. The pronouns that make best sense in the sentence are the correct ones.

SENTENCE (Her, She) and (me, I) planned to attend Greg's party.

TEST 1 *Her* planned to attend Greg's party. (makes poor sense)
She planned to attend Greg's party. (makes sense)

TEST 2 *Me* planned to attend Greg's party. (makes poor sense)
I planned to attend Greg's party. (makes sense)

SOLUTION *She* and *I* planned to attend Greg's party.

Writing Assignment: On a separate sheet of paper, write about an everyday activity you have shared with someone else. Suggestions include a meal, a letter, or after-school plans. Use double pronouns at least twice in your writing to gain practice using them. You will have the opportunity to revise your writing later.

Evaluation Checklist: Reread your first draft. Use these guidelines to help you judge the content and organization of your writing.

____ I have split double pronouns correctly.
____ My writing follows a logical order.

Revising, Proofreading, and Writing the Final Version: Revise your draft based on your evaluation. Include a topic sentence in each paragraph. Then proofread your revised draft. Write your revised draft in final form.

WRITING APPLICATION B: Using Pronouns with Missing Words

Nodding and shaking one's head from left to right are silent ways of saying yes and no. These gestures are easily understood without the words to accompany them. In a similar way when you write, you can leave out words in sentences and still be easily understood. However, a problem occurs when a pronoun is used that does not go with the missing word. The correct pronoun to use becomes obvious when the missing word is put in the sentence. In the example below, the missing word is shown in parentheses.

INCORRECT Don told funnier jokes than *me* (told).

CORRECT Don told funnier jokes than *I* (told).

Writing Assignment: On a separate sheet of paper, write about a competition in which you have participated. Compare generally what you did with what others did. Provide details that will enable your readers to picture clearly the competition you are describing.

Evaluation Checklist: Reread your first draft. Use these guidelines to help you judge the content and organization of your writing.

____ I have used correct pronouns in my writing.

____ I have provided details that enable my readers to picture clearly the competition I have described.

____ My writing follows a logical order.

____ Each of my paragraphs includes a topic sentence and supporting sentences.

Revising, Proofreading, and Writing the Final Version: Revise your draft based on your evaluation. Make sure your sentences are in logical order. Then proofread your revised draft. Write your revised draft in final form.

WRITING APPLICATION C: Using the Rule of Courtesy with Pronouns

One way that people show courtesy for others is by putting other people first. In a similar way in writing, courtesy for others is shown by putting nouns or pronouns that identify others before pronouns such as *I*, *we*, or *me*.

EXAMPLES   1. *He* and *I* attended a baseball game last night.
          (*not* *I* and *he* attended a baseball game last night.)
    2. Jennifer mailed an invitation to Andre and *me*.
          (*not* Jennifer mailed an invitation to *me* and Andre.)

Writing Assignment: On a separate sheet of paper, write about something you and someone else planned that had an unusual outcome. Examples of something planned might include a dance, an anniversary party, a talent show, or a class presentation.

Evaluation Checklist: Reread your first draft. Use these guidelines to help you judge the content and organization of your writing.

____ I have placed pronouns I have used in a courteous order.

____ I have used correct pronouns in my writing.

____ My writing follows a logical order.

____ Each of my paragraphs includes a topic sentence and supporting sentences.

Revising, Proofreading, and Writing the Final Version: Revise your draft based on your evaluation. Make sure you have used more than once the pronouns *I*, *me*, or *we* in your writing. Then proofread your revised draft. Write your revised draft in final form.

WRITING APPLICATION A: Using Adverb Clauses to Combine Sentences

In sailing, the words *choppy waters* mean water that is constantly clipped by short waves. In writing, the words *choppy paragraphs* mean that sentences in paragraphs are all simple in structure and thus sound clipped, or choppy, to readers. One way to make your writing read more smoothly is to use adverb clauses in some of your sentences. Adverb clauses can also be used to combine sentences that are related. Adverb clauses often begin with words such as *while, when, whenever, as, before, after, since, until, where, wherever, if,* and *because.* In each of the examples below, the adverb clause is underlined.

EXAMPLES   1. <u>Whenever I hear the word *rosebud,*</u> I think of the movie *Citizen Kane.*
           2. <u>Because Mr. Randolph has relatives in England,</u> he makes frequent telephone calls overseas.

Writing Assignment: On a separate sheet of paper, write a composition about a word or phrase that reminds you of something important each time you hear it. Use a variety of sentence structures and lengths in your writing.

Evaluation Checklist: After you write your first draft, use these guidelines to help you evaluate your writing.

____ I have used adverb clauses in some of my sentences.
____ I have punctuated each of my sentences correctly.

Revising, Proofreading, and Writing the Final Version: Using your evaluation, revise your first draft. Use adverb clauses, when possible, to combine choppy sentences. Proofread your revised draft. Write your draft in final form.

WRITING APPLICATION B: Using *Who* and *Whom* Correctly

Refusing to drive or ride in a car other than a sports car is snobbery. However, knowing when to use the word *whom* in your writing and speaking is not. Rather, knowing when to use *whom* is a sign that a writer knows a basic rule of grammar. To determine quickly which word you should use in your writing, mentally substitute the word *him* for *whom* and the word *he* for *who.* When *him* fits, *whom* is the correct word to use. In some cases, you will need to rearrange the sentence slightly to test the word.

EXAMPLE   She gave a letter of recommendation to (*who, whom*)?

TEST *WHO*   She gave a letter of recommendation to *he*? (*He* does not fit.)

TEST *WHOM*   She gave a letter of recommendation to *him*? (*Him* fits.)

SOLUTION   She gave a letter of recommendation to *whom*?

Writing Assignment: On a separate sheet of paper, write a general description of a person who would make an ideal friend. Practice using *who* and *whom* correctly in your sentences. Remember that you will be able to revise your first draft later.

Evaluation Checklist: After you write your first draft, use these guidelines to help you evaluate your writing.

____ I have used *who* and *whom* correctly in my sentences.
____ Each of my paragraphs includes a topic sentence and supporting sentences.
____ My writing follows a logical order.

Revising, Proofreading, and Writing the Final Version: Revise your draft based on your evaluation. Correct instances in which you have used *who* or *whom* incorrectly. Proofread your revised draft. Then write your final version.

WRITING APPLICATION C: Using Appositives to Explain

Have you ever seen a comment in parentheses in the middle of a sentence? The words in parentheses added interesting or useful information to the sentence. However, the words could have been deleted without changing the basic meaning of the sentence. An appositive is like a comment enclosed in parentheses within a sentence. It identifies or tells something about a noun or pronoun that it follows. An appositive adds information to a sentence but does not change its meaning.

EXAMPLES 1. Our cat, *Prince Albert,* will eat only tuna fish in the morning.
2. The book club, *a special project of the English Department,* offers used books at a discount to students.
3. Louise Chang, *my favorite singer and dancer,* will be performing in Seattle this week.

Writing Assignment: On a separate sheet of paper, write about someone you admire who has several talents or skills. Write details that explain exactly what that person does. Use appositives in your writing.

Evaluation Checklist: Reread your first draft. Use these guidelines to help you judge the content and organization of your writing.

____ I have used some appositives in my writing.
____ I have used a comma before and after each appositive.
____ Each of my paragraphs includes a topic sentence and supporting sentences.
____ My writing follows a logical order.

Revising, Proofreading, and Writing the Final Version: Revise your draft based on your evaluation. Then proofread your revised draft. Write your draft in final form.

WRITING APPLICATION A: Avoiding Sentence Fragments

A car that sputters, backfires, and jerks as it travels down a road provides an uncomfortable ride for its passengers. Similarly, in writing, sentence fragments cause discomfort to readers as they try to make sense of jerky, incomplete sentences. For a group of words to form a complete sentence, that group must (a) have both a subject and a verb and (b) express a complete thought. Always make sure you use complete sentences in all your writing.

SENTENCE FRAGMENTS   Ed said the sound. Was coming from the basement.

COMPLETE SENTENCE   Ed said the sound was coming from the basement.

Writing Assignment: On a separate sheet of paper, write about a sound or an odor you once noticed but could not identify immediately. Give details that describe your first reactions to the sound or odor. Examples of odors might include the smells of spring or the baking of bread. Examples of sounds might include the blare of a siren or the song of a bird.

Evaluation Checklist: Reread your first draft. Use these guidelines to help you judge the content and organization of your writing.

_____ Each of my sentences has a subject and a verb.
_____ Each of my sentences expresses a complete thought.
_____ My writing follows a logical order.

Revising, Proofreading, and Writing the Final Version: Revise your draft based on your evaluation. Change any fragments into complete sentences. Then proofread your revised draft. Write your draft in final form.

WRITING APPLICATION B: Stopping Run-on Sentences

Writing run-on sentences is like forcing someone to eat a whole pie at one time. Your reader is given more information than he or she can digest because your sentences lack punctuation. As you write, correct run-on sentences by punctuating them in one of four ways: (a) Add a period between sentences. (b) Add a semicolon between sentences. (c) Add a comma and a conjunction between two sentences. (d) Make one part of a sentence dependent on the other, and add a comma.

RUN-ON SENTENCE   Wayne likes to waterski, I like to garden.

COMPLETE SENTENCES
1. Wayne likes to waterski. I like to garden.
2. Wayne likes to waterski; I like to garden.
3. Wayne likes to waterski, and I like to garden.
4. While Wayne likes to waterski, I like to garden.

Writing Assignment: On a separate sheet of paper, compare your favorite summer activities with a friend's or a relative's activities. Use complete sentences in your writing.

Evaluation Checklist: Reread your first draft. Use these guidelines to help you judge the content and organization of your writing.

_____ Each of my sentences is complete and correctly punctuated.
_____ My writing follows a logical order.
_____ Each of my paragraphs includes a topic sentence and supporting sentences.

Revising, Proofreading, and Writing the Final Version: Revise your draft based on your evaluation. Change any fragments and run-on sentences in your writing to complete sentences. Then proofread your revised draft carefully. Write your draft in final form.

WRITING APPLICATION C: Using Adverbs as Transitional Words

Dancing well is a little like writing paragraphs that flow smoothly. In dancing, partners glide from one dance step into another to make their dancing look graceful. In writing, good writers use transitional words between sentences to help paragraphs flow smoothly. Adverbs such as *then* and *therefore* are examples of transitional words. Note that a period or semicolon rather than a comma should always be used before these words.

INCORRECT   Lucy asked students to volunteer, *then* she began to call names from her list, *therefore* she was able to get a group together within minutes.

CORRECT   Lucy asked students to volunteer. *Then* she began to call names from her list. *Therefore* she was able to get a group together within minutes.

Writing Assignment: On a separate sheet of paper, write about the steps you once took to solve a problem. Use the words *then* and *therefore* at least once in your writing.

Evaluation Checklist: Reread your first draft. Use these guidelines to help you judge the content and organization of your writing.

_____ I have used adverbs such as *then* and *therefore* to begin some of my sentences.
_____ I have correctly punctuated my sentences.
_____ My writing follows a logical order.
_____ Each of my paragraphs includes a topic sentence and supporting sentences.

Revising, Proofreading, and Writing the Final Version: Revise your draft based on your evaluation. Then proofread your revised draft. Write your draft in final form.

WRITING APPLICATION A: Using Punctuation in Making a Request

To order a product advertised in a magazine or newspaper, you might need to write a letter of request. To begin your letter, you might write the words *Will you please send me . . . .* Sentences that are written to make a request rather than to ask a question end with periods instead of question marks.

REQUEST   Will you please send me the Baja California poster advertised in the June issue of *Tangelo* magazine.

QUESTION   Do you have available any of the Baja California posters advertised in the June issue of *Tangelo* magazine?

Writing Assignment: On a separate sheet of paper, write the body of a letter requesting that a specific product be sent to you. Use an imaginary product and company in your letter. Practice writing sentences that make a request rather than ask a question. You will have an opportunity later to revise your writing.

Evaluation Checklist: Reread your first draft. Use these guidelines to help you judge the content and organization of your writing.

____ I have used periods to punctuate sentences that make a request.
____ I have used question marks to punctuate questions.
____ The tone of my letter is polite.

Revising, Proofreading, and Writing the Final Version: Revise your first draft carefully. Correct all sentence punctuation. Proofread your revised draft. Then write your final version.

WRITING APPLICATION B: Using Commas in Compound Sentences

Not knowing where to put commas in compound sentences is a little like playing a game of darts for the first time. You can only aim and hope your commas land in the right places. Fortunately, comma usage follows logical rules that anyone can master through practice. In compound sentences, a comma is always used before the conjunction. When a sentence is compound, it has a subject and a verb both before and after the conjunction. If a sentence does not also have a subject and a verb after the conjunction, it is not compound and should not have a comma.

COMPOUND SENTENCE   *Michael* wants to study agricultural engineering, and *he* someday wants to manage a farm. (A subject follows *and;* therefore use a comma before *and.*)

COMPOUND PREDICATE   *Michael* wants to study agricultural engineering and someday manage a farm. (No subject follows *and;* therefore do not use a comma before *and.*)

Writing Assignment: On a separate sheet of paper, write about two major goals you have set for yourself. Practice writing compound sentences. You will be able to revise your writing later.

Evaluation Checklist: Reread your first draft. Use these guidelines to help you judge the content and organization of your writing.

_____ I have correctly punctuated my compound sentences.

_____ I have written correctly punctuated sentences containing compound predicates.

_____ I have included a topic sentence in each paragraph I have written.

Revising, Proofreading, and Writing the Final Version: Revise your first draft based on your evaluation. The proofread your revised draft. Write your draft in final form.

WRITING APPLICATION C: Using Commas in Addresses

On maps and charts, boundary lines are used to separate cities, states, and other land divisions. In writing, commas are used to separate parts of addresses, such as street names, cities, and states. A comma is not used to separate a state and a ZIP Code.

EXAMPLES   1. I visited my niece in Bismarck, North Dakota, before continuing on to my brother's house in Billings, Montana.
            2. Ramona has moved to 1267 Spring Bark Avenue, Livonia, Michigan 48158.
            3. When I am in Naples, Florida, next year, I hope to visit the Ink Shop at 1000 Niceny Boulevard.
            4. Send the coupon to 12 Lambeth Street, New York, NY 10022, and include return postage.

Writing Assignment: On a separate sheet of paper, write directions for a person who will be driving to your house from another state. The person visiting may be imaginary or real. In your directions, mention major cities and states the person will drive through. Also, mention at least two specific addresses in your writing. You may make up address and highway names for this assignment.

Evaluation Checklist: Reread your first draft. Use these guidelines to help you judge the content and organization of your writing.

_____ I have used commas correctly with addresses.

_____ My directions follow a logical order.

_____ I have correctly punctuated my sentences.

Revising, Proofreading, and Writing the Final Version: Revise your first draft based on your evaluation. Then proofread your revised draft. Write your draft in final form.

WRITING APPLICATION A: Using Apostrophes to Show Ownership

In business, a purchase receipt shows ownership of merchandise and a deed shows ownership of property. In writing, an apostrophe or an apostrophe and an *s* shows ownership by a noun. If the noun that shows ownership is singular, add *'s* after it. If the noun that shows ownership is plural, add *'* after it.

EXAMPLES   1. The feathers on the *dancer's* skirt flew all over the stage as she danced. (The feathers belong to one dancer. *Dancer* is singular. Add *'s*.)

               2. The feathers on the *dancers'* skirts flew all over the stage as they danced. (The feathers belong to more than one dancer. *Dancers* is plural. Add *'* .)

Writing Assignment: On a separate sheet of paper, write about a play you once saw. Describe the different parts people played. Use both the singular and plural possessive forms of nouns in your writing.

Evaluation Checklist: Reread your first draft. Use these guidelines to help you judge the content and organization of your writing.

____ I have used *'s* with possessive nouns that are singular.

____ I have used *'* with possessive nouns that are plural.

Revising, Proofreading, and Writing the Final Version: Revise your draft based on your evaluation and on rules of grammar and composition. Then proofread your revised draft carefully. Write your draft in final form.

WRITING APPLICATION B: Writing Contractions

Taking a shortcut home from school is a little like writing contractions. A shortcut reduces the walking or driving distance from one place to another. In writing, a contraction shortens the length of two words by using only some letters from each word. A contraction always has an apostrophe to show that certain letters are missing. Be careful not to confuse contractions with possessive pronouns, which never have apostrophes.

EXAMPLES   1. *They're* unsure whether *their* final grades have been mailed. (They're means *they are*. Do not confuse it with the possessive pronoun *their*.)

               2. *Who's* going to decide *whose* method of repair is best? (*Who's* means *who is*. Do not confuse it with the possessive pronoun *whose*.)

               3. *Your* choice of foods shows that *you're* most interested in having a party with a Mexican theme. (*You're* means *you are*. Do not confuse it with the possessive pronoun *your*.)

Writing Assignment: On a separate sheet of paper, write about a party you would like to plan and give. Describe the people, costumes, decorations, and food you would like to see at this party. Use contractions in your writing.

Evaluation Checklist: Reread your first draft. Use these guidelines to help you judge the content and organization of your writing.

____ Each of my contractions has an apostrophe.
____ I have not confused contractions with possessive pronouns.
____ Each of my paragraphs includes a topic sentence and supporting sentences.

Revising, Proofreading, and Writing the Final Version: Revise your draft based on your evaluation and on other rules of grammar and composition. Then proofread your revised draft carefully. Write your draft in final form.

WRITING APPLICATION C: Using Quotations

Using a tape recorder is just one method that reporters use to record the actual words of a speaker. Another way is to take accurate notes that show the speaker's exact words. However, in published newswriting, as in every other type of writing, setting off quotes between quotation marks is still the only way to show the exact words of a speaker. When using quotation marks, insert a comma as a separator between the quotation and the rest of the sentence. If you are only reporting indirectly what someone else has said, you do not need to enclose the words in quotation marks.

DIRECT QUOTE	The woman on the second floor glanced down at me and said, "Be careful. A truck is turning the corner."
INDIRECT QUOTE	The woman on the second floor glanced down at me and said to be careful because a truck was turning the corner.

Writing Assignment: On a separate sheet of paper, write about a helpful oral warning you once received. Practice using direct and indirect quotations in your writing.

Evaluation Checklist: Reread your first draft. Use these guidelines to help you judge the content and organization of your writing.

____ I have enclosed all direct quotes in quotation marks.
____ I have used a comma as a separator in direct quotations.
____ My writing follows a logical order.

Revising, Proofreading, and Writing the Final Version: Revise your draft based on your evaluation. Then proofread your revised draft. Write your draft in final form.

WRITING APPLICATION A: Capitalizing Geographical Names

How would you feel if you received a special award that was printed with your first name capitalized and your last name in all small letters? Most likely, you would want both your first and last names capitalized. In a similar way when you write, you need to capitalize all important parts of names, including parts of geographical names. When writing geographical names, you should always capitalize words such as *ocean, lake, river, mountain, desert,* and *park,* if those words are part of the actual name.

EXAMPLES   1. Both the Rocky Mountains and the Appalachian Mountains have many beautiful vistas.
2. Several major rivers pour into the great Mississippi River, including the Red River, the Arkansas River, and the Ohio River.
3. Vancouver Island is a large island north of Victoria in British Columbia, Canada.

Writing Assignment: On a separate sheet of paper, write a comparison of two parks, lakes, or rivers. Give reasons you prefer one over the other.

Evaluation Checklist: Reread your first draft. Use these guidelines to help you judge the content and organization of your writing.

____ I have capitalized geographical names correctly.
____ My writing follows a logical order.
____ Each of my paragraphs has a topic sentence and supporting sentences.

Revising, Proofreading, and Writing the Final Version: Revise your draft based on your evaluation. Then proofread your revised draft. Write your draft in final form.

WRITING APPLICATION B: Capitalizing Organizations and Institutions

Often on large buildings, names of important organizations and institutions are displayed somewhere on the building's exterior. In writing, the names of important institutions and organizations are capitalized to help them stand out. However, words such as *the* and any short prepositions that are part of the names are not capitalized. These words are not capitalized because they are not considered important parts of the name.

EXAMPLES   1. Smithmore High School has the largest national student chapter of the National Chemistry Association.
2. She became an exchange student in Australia by being a member of the American Field Service.
3. Elisabeth wrote to the American Medical Association for current information.

Writing Assignment: On a separate sheet of paper, use persuasive writing to convince students from other schools that your school is the best school to attend. Give at least three reasons you believe your school is best. Describe interesting clubs and organizations to which students can belong.

Evaluation Checklist: Reread your first draft. Use these guidelines to help you judge the content and organization of your writing.

____ I have capitalized the names of organizations and institutions.

____ I have not capitalized the word *the* or any short preposition when it is part of a name.

____ I have stated at least three reasons that my school is the best school to attend.

Revising, Proofreading, and Writing the Final Version: Revise your draft based on your evaluation. Proofread your draft after you have revised it. Then write your draft in final form.

WRITING APPLICATION C: Using Capitals for Calendar Items

Almost every country of the world enjoys at least minor changes in season. However, not every country celebrates the same holidays and special occasions. In writing, the seasons are not capitalized. However, holidays, special occasions, weekdays, and months are capitalized to help them stand out.

EXAMPLES   1. Every Monday about 2 p.m., John starts counting the minutes until it is time to go home.
2. In October, the two accountants met to plan the next year's budget, which took effect in January.
3. Miriam invited five people to dinner on Thanksgiving Day but had no other guests that fall.

Writing Assignment: On a separate sheet of paper, compare and contrast the holidays you like most to celebrate. Mention specific names of holidays and seasons in your writing.

Evaluation Checklist: Reread your first draft. Use these guidelines to help you judge the content and organization of your writing.

____ I have capitalized all holidays, special occasions, days of the week, and months.

____ I have not capitalized any of the seasons.

____ I have included details that accurately describe the seasons and holidays about which I have chosen to write.

Revising, Proofreading, and Writing the Final Version: Revise your draft based on your evaluation. Then proofread your revised draft carefully. Write your revised draft in final form.

FRAME INDEX

Each entry is indexed by frame number, followed by the page, in parentheses, on which the frame appears. The references included in each entry direct the reader to Key frames. Additional information and related exercises may be found in the frames preceding and following those listed. Complete review exercises for major topics are listed in the table of contents.

agreement of subject and verb (*continued*)
  with subjects joined by *and*, 792–793 (79–81)
  with subjects joined by *or*, 795 (85), 797 (89)
  with *There is, There are*, 878 (251), 887 (269), 890 (275)
  with verb ending in -*s*, 789 (73)
  with *was* and *were*, 827 (149), 832 (159), 834 (163)
  See also number
and:
  in compound sentences, 454 (155), 457 (161), 462 (171)
  to connect sentence parts, 446 (139), 450–453 (147–153)
  in series, 1820 (262), 1822 (266)
apostrophe:
  in contractions, 1951–1953 (150–154), 1960–1961 (168–170), 1963–1964 (174–176), 1999 (246)
  with irregular plurals, 1930 (108), 1934–1936 (116–120)
  misused with pronouns, 1979 (206)
  of phrase as substitute for, 1916 (80)
  placement of, with nouns, 1924 (96)
  to show ownership, 1917 (82)
appear, as linking verb, 332 (287)
appositive(s):
  commas used with, 1479 (328)
  defined, 1477 (324)
  distinguished from adjective clause, 1492 (354)
  modifiers of, 1478 (326)
  position of, 1481–1482 (332–334)
appositive word group:
  formed from sentence 1486–1488 (342–346)
  as fragment, 1573–1574 (142–144)
as, in comparisons, 1172 (88)

be:
  agreement of subject with *was, were*, 827 (149), 832 (159), 834 (163)
  forms of, 121 (241)
  with helper form, 625 (121), 649 (169)
  as linking verb, 328 (279)
  as main verb or helper, 122 (243)
  sense verb as substitute for, 1007–1008 (133–135), 1013 (145)
  as test for linking verb, 1007 (133)
become, as linking verb, 332 (287)
begin, 636 (143), 638 (147)
break, 575 (21)
bring, 657 (185)
but:
  in compound sentences, 454–455 (155–157), 457 (161), 462 (171)
  to connect sentence parts, 446 (139), 451 (149)

capitalization:
  in addresses, 2128 (130)
  of brand names, 2181 (236), 2183 (240)
  of buildings, companies, theaters, etc., 2144 (162)
  of days, months, holidays, 2174–2175 (222–224)

  of family names, 2203 (280), 2206–2208 (286–290)
  of geographical names, 2122 (118), 2125 (124)
  of institutions, 2149 (172)
  of languages, 2130 (134)
  misused with seasons, 2178 (230)
  of nationalities, 2130 (134)
  of organizations, 2157–2158 (188–190)
  of particular names, 2120–2121 (114–116)
  of quotations, 2045 (338)
  of races, 2130 (134)
  of religious groups, 2130 (134)
  of titles (of books, movies, etc.), 2212 (298), 2214 (302), 2217 (308)
  of titles used with names, 2199 (272)
clause(s):
  adjective, *see* adjective clause(s)
  adverb, *see* adverb clause(s)
  compared with -*ing* word group, 1453 (276)
  defined, 1291 (326)
  distinguished from sentence, 1292 (328)
  as fragment, 1565–1566 (126–128)
  removed from sentence, 1309 (362), 1364 (98)
clause signal(s):
  in adjective clauses, 1360 (90)
  in adverb clauses, 1298–1299 (340–342)
come, 542 (331)
comma:
  in addresses, 1868–1870 (358–362), 1877 (2)
  with appositives, 1479 (328)
  in compound sentence, 462 (171), 1754 (130)
  in dates, 1880 (8)
  for interrupters, 1842 (306), 1845 (312), 1849 (320)
  after introductory word groups, 1784–1785 (190–192)
  omission of, in compound sentence, 1768 (158)
  omission of, after introductory word groups, 1794 (210)
  to prevent misreading, 1784 (190)
  before quotation marks, 2041 (330)
  with run-on sentences, 1595 (186)
  as signal to pause, 1593 (182)
  in series, 1815–1816 (252–254), 1822 (266)
comparison(s):
  using *than* or *as* in, 1172 (88), 1185 (114)
  words omitted in, 1175 (94), 1182 (108)
comparison of adjectives and adverbs:
  by adding -*er* and -*est*, 1038 (195)
  degrees in, 1035–1037 (189–193)
  duplication of, 1049 (217), 1052 (223)
  two forms of, 1047 (213)
  by using *more than* and *most*, 1045 (209)
complement, defined, 321 (265); *see also* subject complement; direct object
completer, *see* complement
compound:
  defined, 450 (147)
  parts of sentence, 450–453 (147–153)
compound sentence(s):
  comma in, 462 (171), 1754 (130)
  conjunctions in, 457 (161)
  defined, 457 (161)
  omission of comma in, 1768 (158)
  test for, 461 (169)